The Robbers Cave Experiment

Wesleyan University Press
Middletown, Connecticut

The Robbers Cave Experiment

Intergroup Conflict and Cooperation

Muzafer Sherif, O. J. Harvey,

B. Jack White, William R. Hood,

Carolyn W. Sherif

With a New Introduction by

Donald T. Campbell

Copyright © 1988 by Muzafer Sherif
Introduction copyright © 1988 by Donald T. Campbell
Preface to the Wesleyan Edition copyright © 1988 by O. J. Harvey
All rights reserved

This book was first published by the Institute of Group Relations, the
University of Oklahoma in 1961.

Library of Congress Cataloging-in-Publication Data

Intergroup conflict and cooperation: the robbers cave experiment
 Muzafer Sherif . . . [et al.].—1st Wesleyan ed.
  p.   cm.
 Reprint. Previously published: Norman, Okla.: University Book
Exchange, 1961.
 Includes index.
 ISBN 0-8195-5103-1   ISBN 0-8195-6194-0 (pbk.)
 1. Small groups—Case studies.   2. Intergroup relations—Case
studies.   3. Social interaction—Case studies.   I. Sherif, Muzafer,
1905–   . II. Title: Robbers cave experiment.
HM133.I545   1988
302.3'4—dc19   87-18349
              CIP

All inquiries and permissions requests should be addressed to the Pub-
lisher, Wesleyan University Press, 110 Mt. Vernon Street, Middletown,
Connecticut 06457

Distributed by Harper & Row Publishers, Keystone Industrial Park,
Scranton, Pennsylvania 18512

Manufactured in the United States of America
First Wesleyan Edition, 1988

Contents

Illustrations

Illustrations

Tables

Introduction to the Wesleyan Edition
by Donald T. Campbell

It is indeed an honor to provide an introduction to this full report on the very best of Muzafer Sherif's great field experiments on intergroup conflict and conflict resolution. I accept this honor as a representative of my generation of social psychologists, testifying to Sherif's influence upon us. This allows me a personalization of the evidence presented and requires me to place the Robbers Cave experiment in the context of Sherif's and my own life work. The social processes of esteem formation, which have made me eligible to be invited to do this introduction, have focused on my work on research methods for nonlaboratory social research. But it is not methodological concerns that bring one into a field, and the descriptive and theoretical interests of my career serve to illustrate both Sherif's agenda and his influence on our field.

Before me as I write are 10 of the 20 or so books Muzafer Sherif has produced so far in his long and productive life. These 10 not only bracket his career, they also bracket mine. His 1936 *Psychology of Social Norms* introduced me to my own 50-year-long career in social psychology. It was assigned in my first social psychology course at the University of California, Berkeley, in 1938 or 1939. My instructor was Robert Tryon who, in a midcareer change, was also beginning his career in social psychology. As I finished my degree at age 31, after wartime interruption, my education and orientation was given a finish by the great and compendious *Psychology of Ego-Involvements* (Sherif and Cantril 1947). Early in my own career as a teacher of introductory social psychology, I used his 1948 text, and later on its revisions.

Back to *The Psychology of Social Norms:* what a marvelous 200 pages. While there had been some experimental social psychology before this work—as on the effect of the presence of others on individual task efficiency—Sherif's norm-formation experiments with the autokinetic phenomena effectively founded the field, as well as providing what has probably been the single most widely used experimental task. The book is effectively addressed to introductory students, being full of current events and human interest illustrations. Yet it is impressively erudite, with an unprecedented range of interdisciplinary citations: a third of the references are to anthropology; another third to experiments and theory in Gestalt psychology. Also well represented are the old tradition of psychophysical judgment, Piaget, Freudian psychology, sociology, moral and value theory from philosophy and sociology, and the then new social psychological research on racial and ethnic attitudes.

It is because of this book that Gardner Murphy (1948) can say, "To those who have followed the extraordinary transformation of social psychology in recent years, it will seem a trifle absurd that I should write an introduction to Muzafer Sherif. To him more than any other single person is attributable the whole manner of approaching social psychology which characterizes the present period." This is from the Gardner Murphy who himself was clearly a cofounder of modern social psychology with his paradigmatic *Experimental Social Psychology* (Murphy and Murphy 1931; and especially, Murphy, Murphy, and Newcomb 1937) and who directed Sherif's dissertation. (Sherif also studied with Otto Klineberg, and notes his influence [Sherif and Sherif, 1969, p. viii].)

Whereas today experimental social psychology is carried out in isolation from the other social sciences, Sherif made it centrally relevant, with an all-important message that most psychologists and philosophers have yet to learn. The Robbers Cave Experiment, of course, moves beyond the isolated individual and group norm formation of 1936 into the still more powerful formation of social norms under conditions of intergroup competition, where the norms now include ingroup solidarity and outgroup hostility.

Sherif stresses (in 1936 and in the present volume) that we are experientially unaware of these social and individual sources of norm formation. Instead, we project them upon the world as intrinsic attributes of it, as though *directly* perceived. He refers to experiential "absolutism" and the "natural" and "common sense" nature of the resulting perceptions (1936, 16–17, and passim). He found that these attributes also obtained for the repeated estimates of the length of apparent movement of the dot of light in the autokinetic phenomena. He and the other authors of the present volume continue that interest, providing many examples of the *experiential absolutism* that accompanies distorted perceptions of visible performances of both outgroup members and ingroup leaders, as well as the skewed perceptions of their personalities and moral characteristics. Sherif's rich use of anthropological illustrations makes the same point, and led to the prominence given his work in Melville Herskovits's influential presentation of cultural relativism (Herskovits 1948). It is this most important aspect of cultural relativism that philosophers neglect most in their many recent analyses of the problem.

In one form or another, this theme has inspired a number of my scholarly efforts. In a major theoretical effort, I attempted to account for this experiential pseudo-objectivity by speculation as to where conscious experience was located in the neural chain of sensory input, association, and response (Campbell 1963, 1967, 1969). This led me to affirm Sherif's dictum of "the unity of experience and behavior" (e.g., Sherif and Sherif 1956, 72). Although I will not take the space here to explain the important hindsight involved, I nonetheless commend it to the attention of all who are interested in the phenomenon. "Experiential pseudo-objectivity," used here for the first time, is as good a term as I've come up with to epitomize the concept. I've tried "phenomenal absolutism" (e.g., Campbell 1969; Segall, Campbell, and Herskovits 1966, Chapter 1) augmenting the "absolutism" of Sherif's (1936) phrasing. In philosophy, "naive realism" has this connotation. On the other hand, some philosophers and the psychologist James Gibson have naively posited a "direct realism," which I in turn have parodied as "clairvoyant realism" (e.g., Paller and Campbell 1987).

My social psychology colleagues will be more surprised to learn of still another big investment of mine in "experiential pseudo-objectivity." Sherif (1936, 35–42) calls attention to the old psychophysical method of "absolute judgments," in which contrast illusions were produced by shifting the range of stimuli presented, and how a persistently changed range eventually changed the "frame of reference" or "anchors" upon which the perceptual judgments were based. Helson's (1947, 1964) great volume of work on "adaption level" phenomena acknowledged, in his very first article, inspiration from Sherif's concept of "frame of reference," and also employed the method of absolute judgment. So, too, did Sherif's later work on assimilation and contrast in social judgment (e.g., Sherif and Hovland 1961). I was sure that the contrast illusions regularly found for all types of stimulus materials (from length of lines and lifted weights to seriousness of crimes and judgments of insanity) were genuinely illusory, that is, that the perceivers were unaware that their perceptual processes had been influenced by recent stimulus context. But in the so-called method of absolute judgments, response terms such as "heavy" and "light," or "short" and "tall," "hot" or "cold," or "pleasant" and "unpleasant" were employed, often translated into a 9-point restricted rating scale. That is, response terms were being used that in standard linguistic usage were relative to context, leaving open the possibility that no illusion was involved when a shift in context was followed by a shift in terms used. Proving the "genuine illusoriness" of such effects was important enough to me that I set about replicating such studies employing a "judgmental language that was absolute, extensive, and extra-experimentally anchored," in an experimental design in which a "tracer stimulus" recurred at all stages during a gradual shift in stimulus range.

At the time that Sherif and Hovland (1961) were in the thick of their collaboration, I spent the spring of 1955 at Yale, at Hovland's invitation. There I met O. J. Harvey, coauthor and augmentor of the present book, who was spending a postdoctoral year at Yale after finishing a Ph.D. with Sherif. Harvey and I became close friends and soon initiated a study in which judgments of weights were made in *ounces*, apparently the first time this had been done in the vast psychophysical literature on lifted weights (Harvey and Campbell 1963). Similarly, judgments of pitch were made in terms of notes on a schematic five-octave piano keyboard, easily producing an illusory shift of one whole octave in judgments of the tracer stimulus (Campbell, Lewis, and Hunt 1958). Using the same experimental paradigm, line length was judged in terms of inches (Krantz and Campbell 1961), and an "externally anchored response language" was approximated for judgments of the psychopathology demonstrated by specific symptoms (Campbell, Hunt, and Lewis 1958). Using a different approach to absoluteness, context effects were reproduced in judgments of gifts, traffic violations, and behavioral eccentricity (Hicks and Campbell, 1965). In all of these cases, the same contrast illusions were demonstrated that had been found with the prior judgmental response terms, convincing me that they were genuinely illusory, that the judges were totally unaware of their shifts in judgment standards. Still, today this great effort—lost effort in the sense that these papers go uncited—seems worth it to me, so important is the point. This was also much of my motivation in my single (more cited) utilization of Sherif's autokinetic judgment task (Jacobs and Campbell 1961). I am happy to report that the many judgmental tasks in the present volume use natural, linguistically absolute response languages rather than linguistically comparative ones. For that matter, so did the original autokinetic movement judgment task, to wit, judgments in inches.

The influence of Sherif's several field studies on intergroup conflict in the boys' summer camp "laboratory" show up in a still larger commitment of my scholarly energies. The setting is Northwestern University in a period of high interdisciplinary participation, especially among anthropology, political science, sociology, and psychology. In addition to Herskovits, the principal fund raiser for such projects was the political scientist Richard C. Snyder, who also had the greatest admiration for Sherif and brought him to our campus as often as possible. (Appropriately, the Sherif and Sherif 1969 conference on "Interdisciplinary Relationships in the Social Sciences" had three participants from Northwestern University, including me.) Robert A. LeVine, anthropologist with a joint appointment in political science, and I (Campbell and LeVine 1961) decided that the "field manual method" of securing brief collaborations from anthropologists in the field that had worked so well on optical illusions (Segall, Campbell, and Herskovits 1966) should be put to work on the more important topic of intergroup conflict and attitudes. There followed 15 years of intensive effort (LeVine 1961, 1965, 1966; Campbell 1965, 1967; Campbell and LeVine 1968, 1970; Brewer 1968), culminating in two volumes (LeVine and Campbell, with Brewer, 1972; Brewer and Campbell 1976), although the project was never completed.

Needless to say, these efforts built upon Sherif's pioneering work and theoretical analyses in the great research program that culminated in the present volume. (We cite first Sherif and Sherif 1953, but I have on my shelf, obviously read, the very first presentation, Sherif 1951.) In *Ethnocentrism* (Campbell and LeVine, with Brewer, 1972), we presented propositional inventories of ten theories. Two chapters in particular represent Sherif's views: "Realistic Group Conflict Theory," and "Reference Group Theory." As to the latter, since we use his

own phrasing, there is no doubt that he would agree with the classification. I am less sure about the former, and do not remember that he
and I have ever discussed it. Another feature that we have not discussed is that *Ethnocentrism* placed both of the Sherifian theories
among the "societal" theories rather than among the "sociopsycho-
logical" ones (in other words, among the five sociological theories
rather than the five psychological ones). Explicating this may provide
background alerting readers of the present volume to important issues in the theory of intergroup relations, which they might otherwise miss.

From the 1930s through World War II and beyond, theories of Freudian inspiration dominated social-scientific thought about intergroup
hostility. Led by Dollard's (1938; Dollard, et al., 1939), frustration-
aggression-displacement theorists interpreted hostility toward outgroups as displaced projections of frustrations generated within the
ingroup, most likely within the family. While such theorizing was
sometimes accompanied by positing that ingroup coordination always
involved such frustration, as in MacCrone's (1937) psychoanalytic interpretation of race attitudes in South Africa, more frequently it was
explicit or implied that such ingroup frustration and displacement
onto outgroups characterized only pathological groups. Social science interpretations of Nazi Germany, including analyses done by
prominent political scientists furthered this position. After World War
II, the great "Authoritarian Personality" studies (Frenkel-Brunswik,
Levinson, and Sanford 1947; Adorno, Frenkel-Brunswik, Levinson,
and Sanford 1950) lent support to the notion that ethnocentrism and
xenophobia were characteristic of only some people and were to be
explained by the pathology-producing (even if traditional) rearing
they had received as children.

While Sherif has from the beginning (e.g., 1936; Sherif and Cantril
1947) made sympathetic use of Freudian theories, he has seen this
particular application as wrong. From the first, he has emphasized
that we are all much more ethnocentric than we realize, including lib-
eral, well-intentioned social scientists (perhaps particularly those
lacking deep cross-cultural experiences) (e.g., Sherif 1936, 16; Sherif
and Sherif 1969, viii). Indeed, the emphasis on unconscious processes was one of the features that made Freudian theory attractive.
According to Sherif, instead of being due to individual or group pathology, intergroup conflict and hostility are products of social struc-

tures, including the very organization of persons into discrete and potentially competing social groups. Given these circumstances, all of us (including the healthy, the well adjusted, those reared by non-punitive parents, etc.)—all of us are capable of participating in inter-group conflict accompanied by outgroup hatred. The meticulous care in selecting participants for this Robbers Cave study was taken to pre-clude pathology as explanation.

In the present volume, our authors—Sherif, Harvey, White, Hood, and Sherif—attend in detail to individual differences in degree of ex-pression of intergroup hostility, as by word, cartoon, provocative act, and judgmental bias. But here again, the explanatory emphasis is not on personality characteristics (pathological or otherwise), but rather on the locus of the person in the intergroup social structure. Those persons who find themselves marginal in ingroup status for whatever reason (including lack of skill in a group-valued sport) attempt to in-crease their centrality of membership by exacerbating and exaggerat-ing the ingroup-outgroup differentiation. Such individual behavior is due to the social structure and the person's locus in it. Any healthy, normal, well-adjusted person in that locus would presumably do the same.

These emphases led us to classify Sherif with others who vigor-ously rejected psychological displacement theories, for most of whom "realistic group conflict theory" was an appropriate label. In empha-sis on social organization factors he belongs. But the emphasis on "real" bases of competition (on "zero sum" intergroup competition, as it were), is more characteristic of the others we place in that cate-gory than it is of Sherif. Revisions of our classification and labeling are probably in order.

But Sherif's leadership points up a still greater need for a revision of the propositional inventories that make up our book, *Ethnocentrism*. As we realized at the time but lacked the energy to do, we should have searched each of the ten theories for their implications as to how to reduce intergroup conflict. It is going this last important step that so uniquely characterizes Sherif's efforts. In the present book, it is shown in the successful experiment in removing intergroup conflict after the successful experiment in creating it. The last third of *In Common Pre-dicament* (Sherif 1966) provides a rich discussion of many methods and "creative alternatives."

These pioneering experimental studies of intergroup conflict, needless to say, have inspired a host of small group experiments. Our coauthor, Marilynn Brewer, has done a number of them and has provided reviews of the literature (Brewer 1979; Brewer and Miller 1984). These studies confirm the Robbers Cave findings but do not replace them. Each new study involves many replications of one of the phenomena, and the pooling of studies shows how dependable the findings are. But—as Brewer would agree—each study involves a trivial amount of the participant's time, less than an hour as a rule, instead of the three weeks of 24-hour days in the present study. Each achieves a trivial degree of involvement and samples the effects in a very narrow spectrum of measures. There have been no subsequent studies of anywhere near the magnitude of the Robbers Cave experiment. Reading it, owning a copy for repeated referral, becomes essential for anyone specializing in the interdisciplinary and multidisciplinary areas of intergroup and international conflict.

Finally, an excellence and uniqueness of method needs noting. In the social sciences today, many are abandoning quantitative research methods for qualitative, humanistic ones. Experimental approaches get left behind as though uniquely appropriate to the quantitative. The polarity of methods has, of course, been continually with us since Dilthey and Weber at least, with most social scientists feeling it necessary to identify with one pole to the exclusion of the other. Not so Sherif. Just as, in his 1936 book, he assembled laboratory and anthropological evidence to corroborate the same principles, so in the present study, the methods of the ethnographic participant observer are combined with experimentation and quantification. We might well designate the Robbers Cave study as *experimental anthropology.*

The experimental generation of intergroup conflict plays an essential role that no passive ethnography of a naturally occurring intergroup conflict could achieve. In this arena the contenders are not only psychological and sociological theories. By far the commonest are historical-particularist explanations, in which hostilities and hostile images are explained in terms of the specific history of interaction of the groups in question. Such causal explanations dominate the work of historians and descriptive political scientists. They also dominate in the explanations of the contending groups. The passive anthropologist of an intergroup conflict cannot avoid such explanations, no matter how careful the effort to avoid casual interpretation entirely.

One of the valuable slogans of the new emphasis on qualitative, contextual methodology is "thick description" (Geertz 1973). The Robbers Cave study provides such thick description. Moreover, the many ingenious subexperiments that are introduced, with their "natural" opportunities for quantitative measurement, add greatly to the "thickness," creating opportunities for participant action and qualitative observation that would not otherwise have existed, as well as providing quantitative measures. In this study, better than anywhere else I can think of, the proper synthesis of the qualitative-versus-quantitative dialectic is achieved.

Donald T. Campbell

University Professor of Social Relations,
Psychology, and Education
Lehigh University
June 1987

Preface to the Wesleyan Edition

We planned originally to present the Robbers Cave experiment first as a research report and then, after slight revisions, as a book. New commitments and new careers stalled the revisions, however, and postponed publication of the book indefinitely. A report of the study was circulated in multilithed form in 1954 and, with an additional chapter, in 1961 as a publication of the Institute of Group Relations and the Book Exchange of the University of Oklahoma. Now, some 33 years later than planned, the study is appearing as a book due to the initiative of the editors of Wesleyan University Press.

The continued widespread citation of the study despite limited circulation of its earlier reports and its publication by a university press so long after its completion both attest to the timelessness of the issues with which the study dealt. We would like to believe, as Professor Donald Campbell implies in his Introduction to this volume, that our treatment of the issues, as well as their timelessness, helped to sustain the interest that has been shown in the study by representatives of diverse disciplines for over three decades.

Donald Campbell's characterization of the study as "experimental anthropology" is certainly apt. While the study employed the method of participant observation, until recently the main research tool of the social anthropologist, it did so for the unique purpose of recording information on group interactions and other social processes *elicited by experimentally induced* conditions. It might well be, in fact, that the most distinctive feature of the study was the unusual way in which it combined field and experimental methods. Most of the more important hypotheses were derived from earlier naturalistic observations of groups and larger organizations by sociologists and anthropologists. The experimental method was used to elicit the operation of the variables suggested by naturalistic observations, and both the participant observation and experimental methods were employed to record the outcomes. This approach reflected a deeply held epistemic assumption by Professor Sherif, that consistency of outcomes across different methods and levels of analysis is a far more stringent criterion of validity than one method or level can yield alone.

Although, as Don Campbell notes in his Introduction, Muzafer Sherif was one of the founding fathers of present-day social psychology and has made notable contributions to the understanding of groups and attitude change since the Robbers Cave study, that study is the object of his greatest professional pride. Those of us who participated in the study with him, including Bob Hood and Carolyn Sherif, both now deceased, shared that pride.

The present ill health of both Professors Sherif and White have sadly made it appropriate for me to be the person from among us to work with members of the Wesleyan University Press in the publication of this book. From the time when he first contacted me a few months ago, Peter Potter, an editor of the Wesleyan University Press, and Jan Fitter, the copy editor for this volume, have made my job unusually easy. Our common objective has been to produce a book that in no way changes the basic content and intent of the earlier reports of the Robbers Cave experiment. Thanks are extended to the editors for their major contribution to this objective and, even more, for their unsolicited decision to publish this study in the first place.

Muzafer Sherif, Jack White, and I wish to extend special thanks to Don Campbell for his profound and thoughtful Introduction to this book. Certainly no one is better qualified to evaluate the study, either in terms of its methodology or its historical and current significance. Both by his historical sketch of Muzafer Sherif's work prior to the Robbers Cave study and by his showing the connection between Sherif's work and his own, Professor Campbell has created a context that should allow the reader to understand more deeply and appreciate more fully the concerns, methodology, and procedures of the study. In doing so, he also provided social psychology the bonus of making clear the relationship between the works of two of the field's most notable figures.

With the publication of this book, students and other interested persons will be able to read a thorough and accurate account of the

Robbers Cave study, which often has not been the case because of the scarcity of full reports of the study and of errors in some of its second- and third-hand descriptions.

O. J. Harvey

Boulder, Colorado
July 1987

Preface to the Institute
of Group Relations Editions

The report of this large-scale experiment dealing with factors conducive to conflict and cooperation between groups was first released in August 1954 and was sent in multilithed form to colleagues active in small group research. Since then, it has appeared in condensed form in books and journals and has been presented in lecture form at various universities and professional associations.

In view of numerous requests from colleagues engaged in small group research and instructors in institutions of higher learning, and the interest expressed by colleagues in political science, economics, and social work in the applicability of the concept of superordinate goals to intergroup problems in their own areas, the original report is being released now with very minor editorial changes.

Two new chapters have been added in the present volume. Chapter 1 presents a theoretical background related to small group research and to leads derived from the psychological laboratory. It was written originally at the request of Professor Fred Strodtbeck of the University of Chicago, editor for the special issue on small group research of the *American Sociological Review* (December 1954). This chapter summarizes our research program since the mid-thirties, which was initiated in an attempt to integrate field and laboratory approaches to the study of social interaction. Chapter 8 was written especially for this release to serve as a convenient summary of the theoretical and methodological orientation, the plan and procedures of the experiment, and the main findings, with special emphasis on the reduction of intergroup conflict through the introduction of a series of superordinate goals.

We are especially indebted to Mrs. Betty Frensley for her alert help in typing and other tasks connected with the preparation of this volume. Thanks are due Nicholas Pollis and John Reich for proofreading several chapters.

The experiment could not have been realized without the utmost dedication and concentrated efforts, beyond the call of duty, of my associates whose names appear with mine on the title page. However, as the person responsible for the proposal prepared for the Rockefeller Foundation in 1951 and with final responsibility in the actual conduct of the experiment and material included in the report, I absolve them from any blame for omissions or commissions in this presentation.

On this occasion it is a pleasure to acknowledge the understanding support and encouragement extended by the Social Science Division of the Rockefeller Foundation to this project on intergroup relations, a research area notably lacking in systematic experimental studies in spite of its overriding import in the present scheme of human relations.

This preface is being written with a heavy heart. The research program of which this experiment was an important part lost a great friend by the death of Carl I. Hovland, of Yale University, in April 1961. It was Carl Hovland who, from the very inception of the research project on intergroup relations in 1947, gave an understanding and insightful ear and an effective hand to its implementation. The give-and-take with his searching questions, wise counsel, and steadfast friendship through thick and thin will be sorely missed in the continuation of our research program.

Muzafer Sherif
1961

The chapters to follow report the main points of a large-scale experiment on intergroup relations. It was carried out as a part of the research program of the Intergroup Relations Project at the University of Oklahoma. In this first presentation, sufficient time and facilities were not available to make use of data contained in recorded tapes and half a dozen short moving picture reels. Nor was it found feasible to include introductory chapters surveying major theories on intergroup relations and elaborating the theoretical outlines of the present approach, which determined the formulation of the hypotheses advanced and the design of the study in successive stages. These are presented more fully in our *Groups in Harmony and Tension* (Harper 1953), which constituted the initial work unit in the present intergroup relations project.

Therefore, we here present a brief statement of the cardinal considerations that shaped the conception of this approach to the study of intergroup relations. It is not unfair to say that the major existing theories fall within two broad categories in terms of the emphasis placed in formulation of the problem and methods involved.

In one broad category of theories, the problems are expressed in terms of actualities of events in group relations as they exist in everyday life. On the whole, theories advanced by many social scientists fall in this broad category. In this concern over actualities, the problem is frequently not stated and discussion not developed in a way that can be tested rigorously. In the second broad category of theories, problems are stated and analysis carried out in terms of concepts and units of analysis that appear more rigorous. Theories coming from psychologists, and social scientists heavily influenced by them, fall within this broad category. In this line of approach, theories are advanced without due regard to actualities, and consequently they are plagued with serious questions of validity.

The present approach starts with a serious concern over the rise and functioning of actual small groups in social life. The hypotheses advanced are formulated on the basis of recurrent events reported in sociological accounts of small groups. Testing these hypotheses under conditions that appear natural to the subjects has been a theoretical and methodological consideration of prime importance, Therefore, a great point was made of carrying on observations without the awareness of subjects that they were being observed and of giving priority to the uninterrupted and uncluttered flow of interaction under experimentally introduced stimulus conditions. The techniques of data collection were adapted to the flow of interaction, rather than cluttering or chopping off interaction for the convenience of the experimenter. This imposed the task of securing an experimental site isolated from outside influences, so that results could not be accounted for primarily in terms of influences other than the experimentally introduced ones and the interaction on that basis.

In such a natural, lifelike interaction situation, there are so many items that can be observed at a given time that it becomes impossible to observe and report all behavioral events. Therefore, there is the possibility of being selective in the choice of events to be observed. In testing vital hypotheses related to intergroup relations, restricting the number of subjects to just a few is not the proper remedy. Circumscribing the number of reactions of the subjects is no remedy. Asking the subjects to remain within optimal distance of a microphone and asking them please to speak one at a time will destroy the very properties of the interaction process in which we are interested. The dining hall adjacent to the kitchen is not the place conducive to getting the subjects to cooperate in preparing a meal of their own accord. By trying to eliminate selectivity through such resorts, we would have eliminated at the same time the essential properties of the very things we set out to study.

One remedy lies in unmistakable recurrences of behavioral trends so that observers could not help observing them, even if they tried to ignore them. If these trends are independently reported by the observers of two different groups, then they serve as a check against each other. We have secured such checks time and again in this study.

The danger of selectivity can be avoided (without disrupting the flow of interaction) by having outside observers in crucial problem situations and by having them make, for example, their own independent status ratings in terms of effective initiative in getting things started and done.

The most effective way of checking selectivity is the use of a combination of techniques. This consists of introducing, at a few choice points, laboratory-type experiments and sociometric questions. If the trends obtained through laboratory-type and sociometric checks are in line with trends obtained through observations, then selectivity of observation need not worry us as far as the relevant hypotheses and generalizations are concerned. The actual use of observational, experimental, and sociometric techniques in a combined way, whenever feasible without cluttering the main flow of interaction, has been a major point of emphasis in our study. In our previous work, the feasibility of using judgmental indices to tap norm formation and intra- and intergroup attitudes was established in various studies. This series of experiments, whose logic and techniques were made part and parcel of this large-scale experiment, are summarized in a paper "Toward Integrating Field Work and Laboratory in Small Group Research" (which appeared in Small Group Research Issue, *American Sociological Review,* December 1954).

The present study has for its background the invaluable experience of the 1949 and 1953 experiments, both carried out under my direction. In 1949 the design (in three stages) went as far as the end of Stage 2 of this 1954 study; namely, ingroups were formed and intergroup friction was produced experimentally. The 1949 study was jointly sponsored by the Attitude Change Project of Yale University and the Department of Scientific Research of the American Jewish Committee, to both of whom grateful acknowledgment is extended. Without the effective help of Professor Carl I. Hovland, this start could not have materialized. The second study was attempted in 1953 in four successive stages. We succeeded in completing only two stages in this attempt, which covered the experimental formation of ingroups. The experiment reported here, as well as other units during the last two years, were carried out with a grant from the Rockefeller Foundation to the University of Oklahoma, for which we are grateful.

It is a pleasure to note here the active participation of O. J. Harvey during the last four years in the development of this program of research. Especially his doctoral thesis, entitled "An Experimental Investigation of Negative and Positive Relationships Between Small Informal Groups Through Judgmental Indices," constitutes a distinct contribution in demonstrating the feasibility of using laboratory-type judgmental indices in the study of intergroup attitudes. Without the untiring and selfless participation of O. J. Harvey, Jack White, William R. Hood, and Carolyn Sherif the realization of this experiment and the writing of this report would have been impossible.

This program of research in group relations owes a special debt to the dedication of the University of Oklahoma and its administrative agencies to making development of social science one of its distinctive features. President George L. Cross's close interest in social science has been a constant source of encouragement and effective support. Professor Lloyd E. Swearingen, Director of the Research Institute, has cleared our way for smooth sailing whenever occasion arose. We have turned again and again to the encouragement and unfailing support of Professor Laurence H. Snyder, Dean of the Graduate College.

Muzafer Sherif
1954

The Robbers Cave
Experiment

1

Integrating Field Work and Laboratory in Small Group Research

The study of small groups has become one of the most flourishing areas of research. The influences responsible for the increased preoccupation with small groups in various social sciences and psychology spring both from developments within various academic disciplines and from agencies instituted for devising practical solutions for immediate application. Brief mention of influences contributing to the flourishing state of affairs in small group research will be helpful as orientation.

Theoretically and empirically, works of sociologists have historical priority in showing persistent concern with the topic of small groups (Faris 1953). Since the early 1920s sociology related to small groups has undergone definite research development, as represented by the works of men like Thrasher, Anderson, Clifford Shaw, Zorbaugh, Hiller, and Whyte. In the recurrent findings reported in this line of research, which was carried out over a period of a good many years, one cannot help finding crucial leads for a realistic approach to experimentation in this area.

Another major instigator of the extraordinary volume of small group research stems from the practical concerns of business and military agencies. A series of studies, initiated by Elton Mayo and his associates at the Harvard Business School in the late 1920s, has proliferated in various institutions, both academic and technological. Another impetus along this line came from the concern of military

This chapter was prepared for the special issue on Small Group Research of the *American Sociological Review* 19, no. 6 (December 1954). Grateful acknowledgment is made to the editors of the *Review* for permission to reproduce this paper here in substantially the same form.

agencies with establishing effective techniques for the assessment of leaders.

Yet another major influence in the development of small group studies comes from psychological research. Regardless of the theoretical treatment, the results of psychological experiments almost always showed differential effects on behavior when individuals undertook an activity in relation to other individuals or even in their presence, as can be ascertained readily by a glance at Murphy, Murphy, and Newcomb's *Experimental Social Psychology*. F. H. Allport's experiments, which started around 1915, illustrate this point. In the 1930s, it became increasingly evident that social behavior (cooperation-competition, ascendance-submission, etc.) could not be properly studied when the individual is considered in isolation. Psychological "trait" theories or personality typologies fell far short in explaining social relations. Therefore, when Moreno's sociometric technique for the study of interpersonal choices and reciprocities among individuals (i.e., role relations) appeared in the United States in the mid-thirties, it quickly found wide application. A few years later Kurt Lewin and his associates demonstrated the determination of individual behavior by the properties of group atmosphere. This line of experimentation was the basis of subsequent studies coming from the proponents of the Group Dynamics school. Some other major influences coming from psychology will be mentioned later.

Interdisciplinary Cooperation and the Concept of Levels

It becomes apparent from even a brief mention of the background that researchers from various disciplines contributed to make the study of small groups what it is today. As a consequence, there is a diversity of emphasis in formulating problems and hypotheses and diversity in the concepts used. This state of affairs has brought about considerable elbow-rubbing and interdisciplinary bickering among sociologists, psychologists, and anthropologists. This process and researchers' critical appraisal of each other's approaches have made the interdisciplinary approach a necessity for achieving a rounded picture.

Faced with the task of dealing with both psychological and socio-cultural factors in human relations problems, psychologists have too often yielded to the temptation of improvising their own "sociologies" in terms of their preferred concepts. Sociologists, on the other hand, have sometimes engaged in psychological improvisations. While sociological or psychological improvisation at times proves necessary on the frontiers of a discipline, it is difficult to justify on topics for which a substantial body of research exists in sociology or in psychology, as the case may be.

On the whole, interdisciplinary cooperation has usually turned out to mean rallying psychologists, sociologists, anthropologists, and other social scientists to toss their theories and concepts into the ring. But mere juxtaposition of utterances from these disciplines in the same room or between the covers of the same book does not bring interdisciplinary cooperation. Nor is interdisciplinary integration possible by laying down segments from each discipline along the same line—one yard of psychology, one yard of sociology, then a foot each of history and economics.

The outlines of an interdisciplinary approach appear more clearly with the realization that *psychological* and *sociological* signify different levels of analysis. People studying human relations are approaching related, similar, or even the same problems at different levels of analysis, necessitating units and concepts appropriate for dealing with events on that level. If we are working on the psychological level, our unit of analysis is the *individual;* hence our treatment must be in terms of the individual's psychological functioning—in terms of concepts such as motives, judging, perceiving, learning, remembering, imagining, and so on. If we are working on a sociological or cultural level, our concepts are in such terms as social organization, institutions, value systems, language, kinship systems, art forms, and technology.[1]

The concept of levels holds a fairly obvious but invaluable check on the validity of research findings. If it is valid, a generalization reached on a topic at one level of analysis is not contradicted and, in fact, gains support from valid generalizations reached at another level. For example, the psychologist's findings of differential behavior of an individual when participating in the activities of a group should be (and are) substantiated by findings on the sociological level, namely, that

---

1. "The human group is an organization of two or more individuals in a role structure adapted to the performance of a particular function. *As thus defined the group is the unit of sociological analysis.*" R. Freedman, A. H. Hawley, W. S. Landecker, H. M. Miner, *Principles of Sociology* (New York: Holt, 1952), 143, emphasis added.

collective action in a group has properties peculiar to that group. Checking and cross-checking findings obtained at one level against those obtained on the same topic at another level will make interdisciplinary cooperation the integrative meeting ground that it should be.

During the last century in the social sciences, and more recently in psychology, the dependence of sub-units upon the setting or superordinate system of which they are parts has gained increased attention, especially in view of unrewarding attempts to account for the functioning system in an additive way. Understanding part processes is possible only through analysis of their relations within the functioning system, as well as by analysis of unique properties of the part process itself. Unless knowledge of the superordinate or larger functioning system is gained first, before tackling the part processes, there is the likelihood of unwarranted generalizations concerning the parts and misinterpretation of the true functional significance of the processes observed.

In this connection, an illustration from Malinowski (1922) is instructive. Malinowski describes the complex exchange system of the Argonauts of the Western Pacific called the Kula. The Argonauts themselves

have no knowledge of the *total outline* of any of their social structure. . . . Not even the most intelligent native has any clear idea of the Kula as a big, organized social construction, still less of its sociological functions and implications. If you were to ask him what the Kula is, he would answer by giving a few details, most likely by giving his personal experiences and subjective views on the Kula. . . . Not even a partial coherent account could be obtained. For the integral picture does not exist in his mind; he is in it, and cannot see the whole from the outside.

This point can be illustrated in relation to small group studies. Since Lewin's experiments in the 1940s comparing lecture and group discussion methods in changing attitudes, various studies have shown that *in the American setting*, skillfully conducted group discussion in which members participate is more effective than lecture presentation of the same material. Results obtained in the American setting would suggest that the superiority of group discussion methods might be universal. That this is not the case is indicated by one of the studies in the UNESCO project in India (Murphy 1953). In an attempt to modify caste attitudes among college students in India using various methods, the greatest changes arose as a result of a lecture method using emotional appeals. The experimenter wrote, "Contrary to our original expectation and hypothesis, these young boys do not seem to be in a position to exploit fully the discussion technique, in bettering their social relationships. Does it indicate that our boys have got to be used to the democratic ways of discussion and at present prefer to be told what are the right attitudes rather than to be allowed to talk them out?" Within a social organization whose values clearly encourage dependence on authority and effectively discourage settling issues through give-and-take in small sub-units, particular dependencies may become so much a part of the individual's ego system that group discussion techniques would be less effective than methods more in harmony with the social organization in which they take place.

Such comparative results illustrate the value of starting *first* with due consideration of the sociocultural setting, with its organization and values, before making generalizations about small groups functioning as parts of that setting (Whyte, 1951; Arensberg 1951) because small groups are not closed systems, especially in highly complex and differentiated societies like the United States.

Facts obtained concerning the group setting are in terms of concepts and units at the social or cultural level of analysis. They will not give the step-by-step analysis of the particular interaction process; they will not be adequate for the task of dealing with interpersonal relations or the behavior of particular individual members. At this point, psychological concepts are needed for a detailed analysis of reciprocal relations, for handling motives, perceptions, judgments, and the like.

Experimental Steps Toward Integration

We devote the rest of the chapter to a summary of our prior attempts to pull together some relevant findings from sociology and psychology in the study of small groups. In these attempts the guiding considerations have been the following:

1. To extract some minimum generalizations from the sociological findings on small groups, on the one hand; on the other, to extract relevant principles from the work coming from the psychological laboratory.

2. To formulate problems and hypotheses suggesting relationships among the indications of the two sets of relevant findings from sociological and psychological research.

3. To test hypotheses thus derived with methods and techniques appropriate for the particular problem—experimental, observational, sociometric, questionnaire, or combinations thereof.

Let us start with the term *small group* itself. The term is coming to mean all things to all people. If the concept of small groups is considered at the outset, research on small groups will gain a great deal in the way of selection of focal problems for investigation and hence effective concentration of efforts.

Small group may mean simply a small number of individuals. If this is the criterion, any small number of individuals in a *togetherness situation* would be considered a small group. But a conception of small groups in terms of numbers alone ignores the properties of actual small groups that have made their study such a going concern today.

One of the objectives of concentrating on small group research should be to attain valid generalizations that can be applied, at least in their essentials, to any group and to the behavior of individual members. Accordingly, one of our first tasks was to extract from sociological work some minimum essential features of actual small groups. This task poses a methodological advantage in concentrating on *informally organized groups*, rather than formally organized groups in which the leader or head and other positions, with their respective responsibilities, are appointed by a higher authority, such as a commanding officer or board. In informally organized groups, group products and the particular individuals who occupy the various positions are determined to a much greater extent by the actual interaction of individuals. If care is taken at the beginning to refer to the general setting in which small groups form and function, their products and structure can be traced through *longitudinal observation* of the interaction process.

Based on an extensive survey of sociological findings, we abstracted the following minimum features in the rise and functioning of small groups:

1. Individuals share a common goal that fosters their interacting with one another.

2. The interaction process produces *differential effects* on individual behavior; that is, each individual's experience and behavior is affected in varying ways and degrees by the interaction process in the group.[2]

3. If interaction continues, a *group structure* consisting of hierarchical status and role relationships is stabilized and is clearly delineated as an *ingroup* from other group structures.

4. A set of norms regulating relations and activities within the group and with nonmembers and outgroups is standardized.[3]

Interaction is not made a separate item in these minimum features because interaction is the *sine qua non* of any kind of social relationship, whether interpersonal or group. Since human interaction takes place largely on a symbolic level, *communication* is here considered part and parcel of the interaction process.

When group structure is analyzed in terms of hierarchical status positions, the topic of *power* necessarily becomes an integral dimension of the hierarchy. Power relations are brought in as an afterthought only if this essential feature of group hierarchy is *not* made part of the conception of a group. Of course, power does in many cases stem from outside of the group, and in these cases the nature of established functional relations between groups in the larger structure has to be included in the picture.

Our fourth feature relates to the standardization of a set of norms. The term *social norm* is a sociological designation referring generically to all products of group interaction that regulate members' behavior in terms of the expected or even the ideal behavior. Therefore, *norm* does not denote average behavior.[4] The existence of norms, noted by sociologists, has been experimentally tested by psychologists in terms of convergence of judgments of different individuals (Sherif 1936), and in terms of reactions to deviation (Schachter 1952). A norm denotes not only expected behavior but a *range of acceptable behavior,* the

---

2. This feature, long noted by sociologists, has received repeated laboratory confirmation by psychologists, as mentioned earlier.

3. It is not possible here to review sociological findings on which these features are based or to discuss them more fully. They have been elaborated in our *Psychology of Ego-involvements* (with H. Cantril) (New York: Wiley, 1947), Chapter 10; *An Outline of Social Psychology* (New York: Harper, 1948); and *Groups in Harmony and Tension* (with C. W. Sherif) (New York: Harper, 1953), Chapter 8.

4. See E. T. Hiller, *Social Relations and Structure* (New York: Harper, 1947); and Freedman, Hawley, Landecker, Miner, *Principles of Sociology.*

limits of which define deviate acts. The extent of the range of acceptable behavior varies inversely with the significance or consequence of the norm for the identity, integrity, and major goals of the group.

With these minimum essential features of small informally organized groups in mind, a group is defined as a social unit that consists of a number of individuals who, at a given time, stand in more or less definite interdependent status and role relationships with one another, and that explicitly or implicitly possesses a set of norms or values regulating the behavior of the individual members, at least in matters of consequence to the group.

Common group attitudes or sentiments are not included in this definition because individuals form social attitudes in relation to group norms as the individuals become functioning parts in the group structure. At the psychological level, then, the individual becomes a group member to the extent that he or she internalizes the major norms of the group and carries on the responsibilities and meets expectations for the position occupied. As pointed out by various authors, individuals' very identity and self conception, their sense of security, become closely tied to their status and role in the group through the formation of attitudes relating to their membership and position. These attitudes may be termed *ego-attitudes*, which function as constituent parts of the individual's ego system.

On the basis of findings at a sociological level, hypotheses concerning the formation of small ingroups and relations between them were derived and tested in our 1949 camp experiment (Sherif and Sherif 1953). One of the principal concerns of that study was the feasibility of experimentally producing ingroups through controlling the conditions of interaction among individuals with no previous role and status relations.

We tested two hypotheses:

1. When individuals having no established relationships are brought together to interact in group activities with common goals, they produce a group structure with hierarchical statuses and roles.

2. If two ingroups thus formed are brought into functional relationship under conditions of competition and group frustration, attitudes and appropriate hostile actions in relation to the outgroup and its members will arise and will be standardized and shared in varying degrees by group members.

As sociologists will readily recognize, testing these hypotheses is not so much for the discovery of new facts as for getting a clearer picture of the formative process under experimentally controlled conditions. The testing aims at singling out the factors involved in the rise of group structure, group code or norms, and ingroup-outgroup delineations, which will make possible their intensive study with appropriate laboratory methods on the psychological level.

To test these hypotheses, 24 boys of about 12 years of age, from similar lower middle-class, Protestant backgrounds were brought to an isolated camp site wholly available for the experiment. The early phase (Stage 1) of the study consisted of a variety of activities permitting contact among all the boys and observation of budding friendship groupings. After being divided into two groups of 12 boys each, to split the budding friendship groupings and at the same time constitute two similar units, the two groups lived, worked, and played separately (Stage 2). All activities introduced embodied a common goal (with appeal value to all), the attainment of which necessitated cooperative participation within the group.

At the end of this stage, unmistakable group structures developed, each with a leader and hierarchical statuses, and also with names and appropriate group norms, including *sanctions* for deviate behavior. Friendship preferences were shifted and reversed *away* from previously budding relationships *toward* ingroup preferences. Thus our first hypothesis concerning ingroup formation was substantiated.

In the final phase (Stage 3) of the 1949 experiment, the two experimentally formed ingroups were brought together in situations that were competitive and led to some mutual frustration as a consequence of the behavior of the groups in relation to each other. The result of intergroup contact in these conditions was, on the one hand, enhancement of ingroup solidarity, democratic interaction within groups, and ingroup friendship. On the other hand, outgroup hostility, name calling, and even fights between the groups developed, indicating that ingroup democracy need not lead to democratic relations with outsiders when intergroup relations are fraught with conditions conducive to tension. The resistance that developed to postexperimental efforts at breaking down the ingroups and encouraging friendly interaction indicates the unmistakable effect of group products on individual members. Thus the results substantiated the second hypothesis, concerning determination of norms toward outgroups by the nature of relations between groups, and demonstrated some effects of intergroup relations upon ingroup functioning.

One of the main methodological considerations of this experiment was that subjects be kept unaware that they were participating in an experiment on group relations. The view that subjects cease to be mindful that their words and deeds are being recorded is not in harmony with what we have learned about the structuring of experience. The presence of a personage ever observing, ever recording our words and deeds in a situation in which our status and role concerns are at stake, cannot help but intrude as an important factor in the total frame of reference. Therefore, in our work, the aim is to establish definite trends as they develop in natural, lifelike situations and to introduce precision at choice points when this can be done without sacrificing the lifelike character that gives greatest hope for the validity of these trends.

The study just summarized illustrates the testing of hypotheses derived from sociological findings in experimentally designed situations. The next point relates to psychological findings, generalizations, and laboratory techniques relevant for the study of experience and behavior of individual group members. Here our task is to achieve a more refined analysis, on a psychological level through precise perceptual and judgmental indices, of individual behavior in the group setting. If such data are in line with findings concerning group relations on the sociological level, then we shall be moving toward integration of psychological and sociological approaches in the study of group relations.

Here we can state only the bare essentials of the psychological principles, from a major trend in experimental psychology, that have been used in designing the experiments to be reported.[5]

Judgments and perceptions are not merely intellectual and discrete psychological events. All judgments and perceptions take place within their appropriate frame of reference. They are jointly determined by functionally related internal and external factors operating at a given time. These interrelated factors—external and internal—constitute the frame of reference of the ensuing reaction. Observed behavior can

5. Fuller accounts of these principles from the works of psychologists and of their background can be found in Sherif, *The Psychology of Social Norms* (New York: Harper, 1936), and *Outline of Social Psychology;* Sherif and Sherif, *Groups in Harmony and Tension,* Chapter 6.

be adequately understood and evaluated only when studied within its appropriate frame of reference or system of relations. The external factors are stimulus situations outside of the individual (objects, persons, groups, events, etc.). The internal factors are motives, attitudes, emotions, general state of the organism, effects of past experience, and so on. The boundary between the two is the skin of the individual—the skin being on the side of the organism.

It is possible, therefore, to set up situations in which the appraisal or evaluation of a social situation will be reflected in the judgments and perceptions of the individual. In short, under appropriate and relevant conditions, the way the individual sizes up a situation in terms of the whole person he or she is at the time can be tapped through apparently simple perceptual and judgmental reactions.

An additional principle should be clearly stated because of certain conceptions in psychology which imply that perception is almost an altogether arbitrary, subjective affair. If external stimulus situations are well structured in definite objects, forms, persons, and groupings, perception will, on the whole, correspond closely to the stimulus structure. This is not to say that functionally related internal factors do not play a part in the perception of structured situations. That some well-structured situations are singled out by the individual as "figure" rather than others indicates that they do. Such facts are referred to under the concept of *perceptual selectivity.*

If, on the other hand, the external field is vague, unstructured—in short, allows for *alternatives*—to that extent the relative weight of internal factors (motives, attitudes) and social factors (suggestion, etc.) will increase. It is for this reason that the exhortations of the demagogue are relatively more effective in situations and circumstances of uncertainty. Since perceptions and judgments are jointly determined by external and internal factors, it is possible to vary the *relative weights* of these factors in differing combinations, giving rise to corresponding judgmental and perceptual variations. This has been done in various experiments. In a study carried out as part of our research program at the University of Oklahoma, James Thrasher varied the stimulus structure and the nature of interpersonal relations of subjects (strangers and friends) to determine the reciprocal effects of these variations on judgmental reactions. It was found that as the stimulus situation becomes more unstructured, the correspondence between stimulus values and judgment values decreases and the influence of social factors (established friendship ties in this case) increases (Thrasher 1954).

Following the implications of these observations, it is plausible to say that behavior revealing discriminations, perceptions, and evaluations of individuals participating in the interaction process as group members will be determined not *only* by whatever motivational components and unique personality characteristics each member brings in, nor solely by the properties of external stimulus conditions (social or otherwise). Rather, it will arise as influenced, modified, and even transformed by these features and by the special properties of the interaction process, in which a developing or established state of reciprocities plays no small part. Interaction processes are not voids.

The starting point in our program of research was the experimental production of group norms and their effects on perception and judgment (Sherif 1936). This stems from our concern for experimental verification of one essential feature of any group—a set of norms (feature 4 in the list of small group features above). Groups are not transitory affairs. Regulation of behavior in them is not determined by the immediate social atmosphere *alone.*

Especially suggestive in the formulation of the problem was F. Thrasher's observation on small groups that behavior of individual members is regulated in a binding way (both through inner attachment and, in cases of deviation, through correctives applied) by a code or set of norms. Equally provocative in this formulation was Emile Durkheim's *Elementary Forms of Religion,* which pointed strongly to the rise of *representations collectives* in interaction situations and their effect in regulating the experience and outlook of the individual.

After thus delineating the problem, the next step was to devise an experimental situation that lacked objective anchorages or standards (i.e., was vague or unstructured) in order to maximize the effects of the social interaction process. When individuals face such an unstructured stimulus situation they vary markedly in their reactions. However, such marked individual variations will not be found if the stimulus is a definite, structured object like a circle or a human hand. Individuals will agree, on the whole, when they face a circle or a normal hand even if they are 5,000 miles apart and members of different cultures. The fact of objective determination of perception and judgment and the ineffectiveness of social influences (suggestion, etc.) in relation to structured stimuli were clearly noted, in several contexts, in the original report of this experiment. A later publication, in order to stress cases of objective determination of psychological processes, devoted a chapter to the effects of technology and its decisive weight in determining social norms and practices, with numerous illustrations from various parts of the world. Among them, our study conducted in the early 1940s of five Turkish villages with varying degrees of exposure to modern technology dealt specifically with the compelling effects of such differential exposure on judgmental, perceptual, and other psychological processes.[6]

The experimental situation chosen for the study of norm formation was the autokinetic situation (the apparent movement of a point of light in a lightproof room lacking visible anchorages). The *dimension* chosen was the extent of movement. As this study is reported in detail in various places, we shall give only the bare essentials.

After first establishing that the judgment of the extent of movement for given brief exposures varies markedly from individual to individual, the experiment brings individuals to the situation to make their judgments together. If, during the course of their participation, their judgments converge within a certain range and toward some modal point, we can say they are converging to a common norm in their judgments of that particular situation. It is possible, however, that this convergence may be due to immediate social pressure to adjust to the judgments spoken aloud by the other participants in the situation. Therefore, going a step further, if it is shown that the individual maintains this common range and modal point in a subsequent session on a different day when alone, then we can say that the common range and modal point have become the individual's own.

The results substantiate these hunches. When individuals face the same unstable, unstructured situation for the first time together with other participants, a range of judgment and a norm within it are established that are peculiar to that group. After the group range and norm are established, an individual participant facing the same situation *alone* makes judgments preponderantly in terms of the range and norm brought from the group situation. But convergence of judgments is not as marked as this when individuals first go through individual sessions and then participate in group sessions.

6. See M. Sherif, "Contact with Modern Technology in Five Turkish Villages," in *Outline of Social Psychology*, Chapter 15, 374–385.

When the individual gives judgments repeatedly in the alone situation, the judgments are distributed within a range and around a modal point peculiar to the individual. This finding has important theoretical implications. The underlying psychological principle, in individual and group situations, is the same, namely, that there is a tendency to reach a standard in either case. Here we part company with Durkheim and other sociologists who maintained a dichotomy between individual and social psychology, restricting the appearance of emergent properties to group situations alone. In both cases, there are emergent properties. In the individual sessions they arise within the more limited frame of reference consisting of the unstructured stimulus situation and special psychological characteristics and states of the individual; whereas in togetherness situations the norm is the product of all of these features within the particular interaction situation. The norm that emerges in group situations is not an average of individual norms. It is an emergent product that cannot be simply extrapolated from individual situations; the properties of the unique interaction process have to be brought into the picture. Therefore, the fact remains that group norms are the products of an interaction process. In the last analysis, no interaction in groups means no standardized and shared norms.

In a subsequent unit, it was found that a characteristic mode of reaction in a given unstructured situation can be produced through the introduction of a prescribed range and norm (Sherif 1937). When one subject is instructed to distribute his or her judgments within a prescribed range and around a modal point, which vary for each naive subject, the preponderant number of judgments by the naive subjects come to fall within the prescribed range and around the modal point introduced for them, a tendency that continues in subsequent alone sessions. This trend is accentuated if the cooperating subject has prestige in the eyes of the naive subject. These findings have been substantiated in a number of studies. For example, it has been shown that the tendency to maintain the prescribed range persists after several weeks (Bovard 1948). In a recent experiment Rohrer, Baron, Hoffman, and Swander (1954) found that social norms established in the autokinetic situation revealed a rather high degree of stability even after a lapse of one year. This stability of an experimentally produced norm acquires particular significance in view of the facts in the study that (a) the subjects had first formed individual norms on the basis of actual movement *prior* to the establishment of divergent norms in a social situation and (b) the norms stabilized in the social situations were revealed after the lapse of one year in *alone* situations, that is, without further social influence.

The actual presence of another person who makes judgments within a range prescribed by the experimenter is not essential. Norman Walter (1952) demonstrated that a prescribed norm can be produced through introduction of norms attributed to institutions with high prestige. A prescribed distribution of judgments given by tape recording is similarly effective (Blake and Brehm 1954). A prescribed range can also be established, without social influence, through prior experience in a more structured situation with the light actually moving distances prescribed by the experimenter (Hoffman, Swander, Baron, and Rohrer 1953).

A technique such as the autokinetic device has two advantages for studying norm formation and other aspects of group relations. First, compared with gross behavioral observations, it yields shortcut precise judgmental indices along definite dimensions reflecting an individual's own appraisal of the situation. Second, the judgmental or perceptual reaction is an *indirect* measure; that is, it is obtained in relation to performance and situations that do not appear to the subjects as directly related to their group relations, their positive or negative attitudes. The feasibility of using judgmental variations in this study constituted the basis of its use in subsequent studies dealing with various aspects of group relations.

At this point, longitudinal research will bring more concreteness to the process of norm formation. As Piaget (1932) demonstrated in his studies of rules in children's groups, the formation of new rules or norms cannot take place until the child can perceive reciprocities among individuals. Until then the child abides by rules because people important in his or her eyes or in authority say to. But when the child is able to participate in activities and grasp the reciprocities involved and required of the situation, then new rules arise in the course of interaction, and these rules become the autonomous rules to which the child complies with inner acceptance. Although they contrast with some still prevalent psychological theories (e.g., Freud's), these longitudinal findings are in line with observations on norm formation and internalization in adolescent cliques and other informally organized groups. These considerations are among the ones that led us to

an intensive study of ego-involvements and to experimental units tapping ego-involvements in interpersonal relations and among members
occupying differing status positions in a group.

These experimental units represent extensions of the summarized
approach to the assessment of positive or negative interpersonal relations, status relations prevailing among the members of ingroups,
and positive or negative attitudes toward given outgroups and their
members.

The first units along these lines dealt with interpersonal relations. It
was postulated that since estimates of future performance are one special case of judgmental activity in which motivational factors are operative, the nature of relations between individuals (positive or negative)
will be a factor in determining variations in the direction of these estimates. This inference was borne out first in a study showing that estimates of future performance are significantly affected by strong
positive personal ties between subjects.[7] In a later unit, the assessment
of personal relations through judgments of future performance was
extended to include negative as well as positive interpersonal relations
(Harvey and Sherif 1951). In line with the hypothesis, it was found
that individuals tended to overestimate the performance of subjects
with whom they had close positive ties and correspondingly to underestimate the performance of those with whom they had an antagonistic relationship.

The study of status relations in small groups followed (Harvey 1953).
This study is related to feature 3 of the essential properties of groups
discussed earlier in this chapter, namely, the rise and effects of a status
structure. Observations by the sociologist William F. Whyte gave us
valuable leads in formulating the specific problem of this study. During one period, a street corner clique that Whyte observed was engaged seriously in bowling. Performance in bowling became a sign of
distinction in the group. At the initial stage, some low-status members
proved themselves on a par with high-status members, including the
leader. This ran counter to expectations built up in the group hierarchy. Hence, in time, the level of performance stabilized for each member in line with his relative status in the group.

In his experiment, Harvey first ascertained the status positions of

---

7. Study by C. W. Sherif summarized in Sherif, *Outline of Social Psychology*, 289–292.

individual members in adolescent cliques. He did so through status ratings by adults in close contact with the subjects, through sociometric ratings from clique members, and through observations of some of the cliques by the experimenter during their natural interaction. Cliques chosen for the final experiment were those in which there was high correspondence among the status ratings obtained.

The overall finding was that the higher the status of a member, the greater his tendency and that of other group members to overestimate his future performance. The lower the status of a group member, the less the tendency of other group members and of himself to overestimate his performance, even to the point of underestimating it. If these results are valid, it should prove possible to predict leaders and followers in informal groups through judgmental variations exhibited in over- and underestimations of performance.

The summer of 1953 marked our first attempt at a large-scale experiment starting with the experimental formation of ingroups themselves and embodying, as an integral part of the design, the assessment of psychological effects of various group products.[8] This assessment involved laboratory-type tasks to be used in conjunction with observational and sociometric data. The overall plan of this experiment was essentially like that of the 1949 study summarized earlier. However, it required carrying through a stage of ingroup formation, to a stage of experimentally produced intergroup tension, and finally to integration of ingroups. The scope of this experiment, embodying laboratory-type procedures at crucial points in each stage, proved too great for a single attempt. During the period of intergroup relations, the study was terminated as an experiment owing to various difficulties and unfavorable conditions, including errors of judgment in the direction of the experiment.

The work completed covered the first two stages and will be summarized here very briefly. The plan and general hypotheses for these stages are similar, on the whole, to those of the 1949 study summarized earlier.

Prior to the experiment, subjects were interviewed and given selected tests administered by a clinical psychologist. The results of these assessments were to be related to ratings along several behavioral di-

8. This experiment was carried out with a grant from the Rockefeller Foundation to the University of Oklahoma.

mensions made by the experiment staff during the experiment proper when ingroup interaction had continued for some time.

At the end of the stage of group formation, two ingroups had formed as a consequence of the experimental conditions, although the rate of group formation and the degree of structure in the two groups were somewhat different.

Our hypothesis concerning experimental formation of ingroups, substantiated in the 1949 study, was supported. As a by-product of ingroup delineation, we again found shifts and reversals of friendship choices *away* from the spontaneous choices made prior to the division into groups and *toward* other members of the ingroup.

At the end of this phase of ingroup formation, just before the first scheduled event in a tournament between the two groups, psychological assessment of group members within each status structure was made through judgments obtained in a laboratory-type situation. In line with methodological concerns mentioned earlier in the chapter, a member of the staff introduced the experimental situation to each group with the proposal that they might like to get a little practice for the softball game scheduled later that day. When this proposal was accepted, the experimenter took each group, separately and at different times, to a large recreation hall where he suggested turning the practice into a game in which everyone took turns and made estimates of each other's performance. This suggestion was accepted as a good idea. Thus each boy took a turn at throwing a ball at a target 25 times, and all members judged his performance after each trial.

It should be noted that in previous studies, judgments of future performance were used as an index. The important methodological departure here was using as the unit of measurement the difference between actual performance and judgment of that performance *after* it was executed. To do so, the stimulus situation had to be made as unstructured as possible so that the developing status relations would be the *weighty factor* in determining the direction of judgmental variations.

In line with our hypothesis in this experimental unit, the results indicated that variations in judgment of performance on the task were significantly related to status ranks in both groups (Sherif, White, and Harvey 1955). The performance of high-status members was overestimated by other group members; the performance of low-status members tended to be underestimated. The extent of over- or underestimation related positively to the status rankings. Variations in judgment of performance on this task did not significantly correlate with skill, or actual scores, of members. This finding should *not* be interpreted to mean that skill can be discarded as a factor, or that it would not be highly related to judgmental variation in a more structured task. Of the two groups, skill seemed to be of *relatively* greater importance in the group that achieved less stability and solidarity. This result is one of several indications that the relationship between judgmental variation and status rankings is closer in the group with greater solidarity and greater structural stability. This finding of a relationship between the degree of structural stability, on the one hand, and the psychological response of members as revealed in their judgments, on the other, points to the necessity for systematic concern with the degree of group structure and solidarity as a variable in small group studies. In particular, it should be brought systematically into the study of leadership and problems of conformity (Sherif 1954).

Following the experimental assessment of psychological effects of group structure in existing and in experimentally formed ingroups, the next step in our program of research was to extend the use of judgmental-variation techniques to the level of intergroup relations among already existing groups. Such an experimental unit was completed by O. J. Harvey in 1954. Harvey investigated relations between existing informally organized groups and their effects on ingroup functioning and on evaluations of the ingroup and outgroup. Organized cliques were chosen on the same basis as those in the study, already summarized, of status relations in existing informally organized groups. In the first experimental session, ingroup members judged each other's performance on a task. In the second session, two cliques with either positive or negative relationships with each other were brought to the situation together. Here a similar procedure was followed, with ingroup members judging performance both of other ingroup members and of members of the functionally related outgroup. In addition, subjects rated ingroup and outgroup members on ten adjectival descriptions presented on a graphic scale. These ratings were included to yield data relevant to our hypothesis in the 1949 study concerning the nature of group stereotypes and to the hypotheses of Avigdor's study (1952) on the rise of stereotypes among members of cooperating and rival groups.

Results obtained in this experiment bear out the hypotheses. Greater solidarity was evidenced in the ingroup when negatively related outgroups were present, as revealed by an increasing relationship between judgmental variation and status ranks and by greater overestimation of performance by ingroup members. Ingroup performance was judged significantly above that of outgroup members when the groups were antagonistic, which was not the case when the groups present were positively related to each other. Finally, results clearly show a much higher frequency of favorable attributes for ingroup members (e.g., "extremely considerate," "extremely cooperative") and a much higher frequency of unfavorable attributes for members of an antagonistic outgroup (e.g., "extremely inconsiderate," "extremely uncoopera-tive"). The difference between qualities attributed to ingroup mem-bers and members of friendly outgroups is much smaller and not so clear-cut, as would be expected.

Thus we demonstrated the feasibility of experimental study, through laboratory-type techniques, of norm formation, of status relations within groups, and of positive and negative attitudes between groups, on the one hand, and on the other, of experimental production of in-groups themselves, as evidenced in two previous studies. Our next step would be to carry through the large-scale experiment along the lines of our 1953 attempt, pulling together all of these various aspects into one design. Judgmental indices reflecting developing ingroup and intergroup relations would be obtained through laboratory-type techniques at choice points in a way that would not clutter the flow of the interaction process. These judgmental indices could be checked against data obtained through more familiar observational, rating, and sociometric methods. If indications of the findings through judg-mental processes were in line with the trends obtained by gross obser-vational and other methods, then we could say the generalizations reached are valid. If this could be established, the laboratory-type ex-periment could be offered as a more precise and refined method of assessing the effects of interaction processes in group relations.

This approach considers the behavior of individuals as an outcome of interaction processes into which factors enter both from the indi-vidual, with his or her unique characteristics and capacities, and from properties of the situation. As an approach, it affords a naturalistic be-havioral setting against which the claims of various personality tests can be evaluated.

This comprehensive experimental plan includes the following suc-cessive phases:

1. Experimental production of ingroups with a hierarchical structure and set of norms (intragroup relations). In line with our 1949 and 1953 studies, this is done not through discussion methods, but through the introduction of goals that arise in the situations, have common appeal value, and necessitate facing a common problem, leading to discussion, planning, and execution in a mutually cooperative way.

2. Bringing the two experimentally formed groups into functional relations in situations in which the groups find themselves in competition for given goals and in conditions that imply some frustration in their relation to one another (intergroup tension).

3. Introducing goals that cannot be easily ignored by members of the two antagonistic groups, but whose attainment is beyond the resources and efforts of one group alone. In short, *superordinate goals* are introduced with the aim of studying the reduction of intergroup tension to derive realistic leads for the integration of hostile groups.

This experimental plan was carried out during the summer of 1954 at Robbers Cave in Oklahoma. The remaining chapters of this book give an account of its planning, execution, and findings.

2

Approach, Hypotheses,
and General Design of the Study

The focal concern of this study is intergroup relations. As an experiment in social psychology, the study undertook to trace over a period the formation and functioning of negative and positive attitudes, as a consequence of experimentally introduced situations, of members of one group toward another group and its members. Therefore, the main hypotheses relate to attitudinal and behavioral trends predicted as a result of controlled alterations of the conditions in which experimentally formed ingroups interact.

The general trend of findings from the sociology of small ingroups and their intergroup relations and relevant findings from the work of experimental psychologists led us to use successive stages in the experimental study of the problem of intergroup relations. The study in the summer of 1954 was carried out in three successive stages.

Stage 1 consisted of experimental production of ingroups with a hierarchical structure and set of norms (intragroup relations). In line with our 1949 and 1953 studies, this was done not through discussion methods or through lecture or exhortation by resource persons or experts, but through *the introduction of goals which would arise as integral parts in the situations, would have common appeal value, and would necessitate facing a common problem and discussing, planning, and executing a solution in a mutually cooperative way.*

Stage 2 brought the two experimentally formed groups into functional relations in situations in which the groups found themselves in competition for given goals and in conditions implying some frustration in relation to one another (*intergroup tension*).

Stage 3 introduced goals that could not be easily ignored by members of the two antagonistic groups, but the attainment of which was beyond the resources and efforts of one group alone. Such goals are

24

referred to as *superordinate goals* throughout this report. Superordinate goals were introduced with the aim of studying the reduction of intergroup tension in order to derive realistic leads for the integration of hostile groups. Considerations that led to the selection of this approach rather than other possible alternatives (such as a common enemy, leadership technique, or discussion techniques) are stated briefly in the discussion of Stage 3 in the last part of this chapter.

It should be emphasized at the outset that individuals brought into an experimental situation to function as small groups are already members of actual groups in their social settings and thus have internalized values or norms (i.e., attitudes) that they necessarily bring to the situation. With this consideration in mind, and to give greater weight to experimentally introduced factors in the situation, this study made a special effort, in the formation and change of positive or negative attitudes toward respective ingroups and outgroups, not to appeal to internalized values or to prestige symbols coming from the larger setting.

Background

Rationale

The rationale that underlies the foregoing formulation of our approach to the study of intergroup relations stems from relevant findings in both sociology and psychology. They are stated more fully elsewhere.[1] Here, only a summary of these lines of development will be given.

Empirical observations by social scientists and inferences made by psychologists without direct experimental verification present a rather confusing picture. Therefore it is necessary to state precisely the sense

1. Leads derived from the field work of sociologists concerning relations of small groups are summarized in M. Sherif and H. Cantril, *The Psychology of Ego-Involvements* (New York: Wiley, 1947), Chapter 10; M. Sherif, *An Outline of Social Psychology* (New York: Harper, 1948), Chapters 5–7; M. Sherif and C. W. Sherif, *Groups in Harmony and Tension* (New York: Harper, 1953), especially Chapter 8.

Psychological principles derived from the work of experimental psychologists and used in our previous work as well as in the present undertaking are summarized in M. Sherif, "The Frame of Reference in Psychological Phenomena," *The Psychology of Social Norms* (New York: Harper, 1936), Chapter 3; Sherif, *Outline of Social Psychology*, especially Chapters 4, 7, and 9; Sherif and Sherif, *Groups in Harmony and Tension*, especially Chapter 6.

in which the concept *group* and the issue of relations between groups (intergroup relations) are used here.

A group may be defined as a social unit that consists of a number of individuals who, at a given time, stand in more or less definite interdependent status and role relationships with one another, and that explicitly or implicitly possesses a set of values or norms regulating the behavior of individual members, at least in matters of consequence to the group.

In order that this definition not be unwieldy, common attitudes, aspirations, and goals are omitted. Such shared attitudes, aspirations, and goals are related to and, in fact, are implicit in the concept of common values or norms of a group. From the point of view of the members within the group, the defined social unit may be referred to as an *ingroup*. Again from the point of view of members within the group, those social units of which they are not a part psychologically or to which they do not relate themselves may be referred to as *outgroups*. It follows that the term *intergroup relations* refers to the relations between two or more ingroups and their respective members. Whenever individuals belonging to one ingroup interact, collectively or individually, with another group or its members in terms of their group identification, we have an instance of intergroup relations.

From a survey of empirical literature, it can be stated that intergroup attitudes and behavior regulated by them arise, in the form of social distances and standardized stereotypes, as a consequence of functional relations between ingroups. Once these intergroup attitudes and stereotypes are standardized, they take their place in the cultural repertory of the group and in many cases, through the vehicle of language, outlast the very functional relations that were responsible for their formation.

These functional relations between groups, and their consequences, rather than the study of the deviate individual, constitute the central problem of intergroup relations. Of course, this focus does not imply a denial of various unique influences in the life history of the individual member (such as personal frustrations, special hardships in the family, or other situations). Such personal influences in the life history may have a great deal to do with the individual becoming a nonconformist or deviate in terms of the prevailing scale of attitudes of the group. But such unique or personal influences *do not themselves determine the scale*. Rather they come in an important way to determine the particular place the individual will occupy within the scale or, in the case of nonconformists or deviates, the acceptance of a position outside of the scale.

Considerations Determining the Approach, Plan, and Hypotheses

At present there are various and conflicting psychological approaches to the study of intergroup relations. It seems that no amount of argument on an abstract level will prove the advantage of one approach over another. Certain of the empirical considerations that led to the approach used in this study will be mentioned briefly in the pages that follow.

The consequential intergroup behavior of individuals (largely revealing friction and tension) is in terms of their membership in their respective groups. Intergroup behavior of an individual that deviates considerably from the prevailing trends is not a typical case. If the individual's intergroup behavior is too much out of line with the prevailing trend of that individual's group, it is brushed aside or dealt with as *deviate* by other members.

One approach to intergroup relations is through the study of *leadership*. Even though leadership undeniably contributes great weight in shaping intergroup relations, concentrating research on leadership alone leaves out functional ties to which leadership itself is organically related. Such an approach is contradictory to current trends in leadership studies, which increasingly point to the necessity of considering leadership in terms of the whole state of reciprocities within the group.

Another approach in intergroup problems concentrates efforts on *ingroup relations*. Empirical data seem to indicate that the nature of intergroup relations need not be in line with the prevailing character of ingroup relations. This approach, which concentrates on improving ingroup relations to improve intergroup relations, ignores the demonstrated consequences attributable only to the particular character of the interaction process *between groups*. Solidarity within the group need not be transferred to solidarity between groups, and in fact may contribute to sharpened delineations between groups with all the attendant by-products.

In short, the conception of the present study differs markedly from existing theories that posit one factor or a few factors as sole or primary determinants of the course of intergroup relations. (1) Inherent superiority or inferiority of human groups, (2) "national character" ("warlike people," "peaceful people"), (3) deep-seated innate instincts of aggression or destruction, (4) frustrations suffered individually, (5) direct economic gain, (6) the character of leadership—all have been variously advanced as sole or primary determinants of intergroup relations. Each of these theories still has its strong supporters.

This study's approach does not deny that some such factors (specifically excepting the first and third listed) may, singly or in combination, operate as factors in determining the course of intergroup relations. "National character," frustrations suffered in common and experienced as a common issue, certain economic gains that become shared goals, or the particular character of the group's leadership may variously become the more weighty determinant of intergroup relations under a given set of circumstances.[2]

But conflicting evidence leads us to assert that the weighty factor determining intergroup relations will not be the same for all circumstances. For example, in settled times when ingroups are in a state of greater stability, national character as formed at the time and the existing scale of social distance (or prejudice) will regulate, on the whole, the particular pattern of intergroup relations. But in times of greater flux or crises (due to the impact of technological, cultural, socioeconomic, and even military events) some other factor or factors take the upper hand.

One primary point of departure in our approach, then, is the principle that various factors are functionally interrelated. In this respect our approach opposes theories that make this or that factor sovereign in its own right; this approach attempts, rather, to ascertain the relative weights of all the possible factors that may be operative at the time.

The functional relatedness of various factors leads us to the cardinal psychological principle of our whole plan of study: *in the study of intra- and intergroup relations, the relative contribution of given external stimulus factors and internal factors pertaining to participating individuals (hunger, sex, status desire, complexes, etc.) have to be analyzed within the framework of the ongoing interaction process among the members in question.*

2. The present approach is elaborated more fully in Sherif and Sherif, *Groups in Harmony and Tension*, especially 13–15, 146–156, 182–190, 296–307.

The relative contribution of an external stimulus factor, or of an attitude, a drive, or other internal factors, cannot be simply extrapolated from individual situations to interaction situations. Interaction processes are not voids. Whatever drives, motives, or attitudes the individual brings into the situation operate as deflected, modified, and at times, transformed in the interaction process among the several individuals, who stand, or come to stand in time, in definite role relations toward one another.

The application of this cardinal principle to the study of group relations is derived from more basic findings in the field of judgment and perception. The judgment of a given weight is not determined solely by its absolute value, but also, within limits, by its relative position in the scale of which it is a part and by the presence or absence of other functionally related anchoring stimuli with values within and outside the scale. Likewise, placement of attitudinal items on a scale with categories specified by the experimenter or chosen by the subject is determined not only by whatever intrinsic value these items may have when considered singly, but also by their relation to one another and to the stand that the individual has taken on the issue.

Following the implications of this general psychological principle, it may be plausible to state that behavior revealing discriminations, perceptions, and evaluations of individuals participating in the interaction process as group members will be determined *not only* by whatever motivational components and personality characteristics each member brings with him and *not only* by the properties of stimulus conditions specified in an unrelated way. Rather, such behavior will take shape as influenced, modified, and even *transformed* interdependently by these factors and the special properties of the interaction process, in which a developing or established *state of reciprocities* (roles, statuses) plays no small part. The developing state of reciprocities between individual members can be measured in various differentiated dimensions (e.g., status, popularity, initiative, etc.).

In short, one cannot directly extrapolate from the knowledge of stimulus conditions alone or of motivational components of participating individuals alone. One has to study behavior in the framework of the actual interaction process, with its developing reciprocities.

Carrying this line of conceptualization to the area of intergroup relations, one should start with the recognition that *the area of interaction between groups* cannot be directly extrapolated from the nature of relations within groups or from prevailing practices within them, even though a careful analysis of intragroup relations is an essential prerequisite in any approach to intergroup relations. We could mention numerous instances of intergroup relations in which the pattern (positive or negative) is different from the pattern prevailing within the respective ingroups.

Thus, in addition to studying relations prevailing within the ingroups in question, one has to study the interaction process between groups and its consequences in their own right.

The conceptual orientation just outlined determined, first, the formulation of specific hypotheses; second, the design of the experiment through three successive stages; third, in selecting the subjects and choosing the setting, the choice of criteria that would not permit the direct intrusion of influences other than those experimentally introduced; and fourth, the special considerations related to observational and experimental techniques to be used in the collection of data, and the specific roles staff members would occupy.

Methodological Considerations

The problem of intergroup relations has not been the domain of experimentation. Literally, only a few studies have been specifically designed to experiment on intergroup relations. Therefore, the present study undertakes to define main functional relations involved in the problem and to point, on the basis of data obtained, to some unmistakable trends.

The experimental study of intergroup relations requires that various conditions *between* groups be experimentally introduced and manipulated; the nature of these conditions should be defined and the consequences of their variation predicted.

Recent research in both psychology and sociology and indications of attempts by practitioners in this area are making it increasingly evident that theoretical and practical problems of group relations have to be studied in terms of the *interaction processes* within and between appropriate group settings. This observation includes the study of attitudes and change of attitudes that regulate the behavior of individuals within their respective ingroups and in relations with outgroups.

The usual practice in attitude studies has been to study the effects of already existing attitudes or to measure attitudes that are already formed. When carried out apart from particular group settings, the study of motives (drives), frustrations, past experience, and similar factors (which certainly operate in the formation, functioning, and change of social attitudes pertaining to group relations) has given us items of information whose validity has not been proven in actual issues of group relations. The attempt in this study is to trace the formation, functioning, and change of attitudes toward one's own group, toward its various members, and toward outgroups and their members as these attitudes develop within the setting of group interaction processes and as consequences thereof.

The study's method was to experimentally produce ingroups themselves and the attitudes of members toward one another and toward the ingroup as a whole. In other words, *group attitudes (both intra- and intergroup) were to start from scratch and to be produced as a consequence of interaction processes in intra- and intergroup relations through the introduction of specified experimental conditions.* We need not elaborate on the methodological gain from experimentally producing attitudes whose effects or change are to be studied or measured.

Considerations such as those briefly mentioned above determined the approach taken, the specific hypotheses formulated, and the design of the experiment in three successive stages. Likewise, they determined the choice of particular methods and cautions to be pursued in the collection of data.

To approximate as much as possible the natural process of spontaneous group formation—of ingroup and outgroup delineation with its consequences so abundantly reported in the literature on small groups—*subjects were kept unaware that this was an experiment on intergroup relations.* (See "Subject Selection" in the next chapter for information given to teachers and parents concerning the experiment.)

Data concerning ingroup formation (Stage 1) and intergroup functioning (in Stages 2 and 3) were obtained through participant observers perceived as part and parcel of the situation by the subjects. All of the staff members directly in contact with the subjects participated in the role of usual camp personnel or some other role not out of the ordinary in a camp situation. Moreover, while recording observations, the participant observers were not to be detected by the subjects in a way contrary to the natural functions of their announced roles. As we stated in Chapter 1, the argument that subjects cease to be mindful that their words and other behavior are being observed and recorded is not in harmony with what we have learned concerning the structuring of perception. The presence of a personage ever observing, ever recording our words and deeds in a situation in which our status and role concerns are at stake, cannot help but intrude as an important anchorage in the framework of the interaction process in question. Candid recordings of conversation and moving pictures taken at choice points, without the awareness of the subjects, were to be valuable additions to other observational data.

All the goals in the ingroup stage and in the negative and positive intergroup stages were introduced through conditions inherent in immediate situations (such as eating, overnight camping, or some activity expressly desired by the subjects), and not in the form of abstract incentives distantly related to the immediate goals of ongoing activities and situations. For example, attainment of food was introduced not as a hypothetical problem or discussion situation, but through arranging conditions so that group members would be getting hungry in a place where the only food available required that members cooperate with one another to prepare available ingredients with facilities in the situation. (*After* subjects took the initiative along some plan, all necessary help and skill could be extended to carry out their plan more effectively.)

The technique of *problem solving*—that is, attainment of goals introduced in the manner just described—would not be through methods introduced by the experimenter, such as a *discussion method* or *lecture method*. One of the guiding principles in the present study was that an actual problem situation faced by group members, as a common goal to be attained or a common deprivation to be taken care of, would necessarily lead to various suggestions, countersuggestions, proposals, and their weighing—in short, to discussion by group members.

The study's approach also projected that when a group is faced with a situation involving common goals or deprivations, group activity will arise. This group activity may be in the form of suggestions from various members, leading to discussion, decisions, planning, and execution. When group activity in relation to common goals is initiated, effective ways of dealing with the situation may involve group discussion, or analysis of the situation by a member conceded to know more

about the topic than others, or (especially if the group is well structured or the situation and available means sufficiently compelling)
more direct action by higher-status members or by the whole group.
Those familiar with sociological findings on informally organized
small groups know well that such groups, facing plans to be executed
or problems to be solved, do discuss, do plan, and do execute plans. In
this interaction process involving an actual problem or goal situation
perceived as common to the group, discussion of alternatives has its
place, and at times exhortations (lectures) and verbal and nonverbal
skills of particular members have their places. The various activities
involved in the interaction process—namely, discussion, exhortation,
planning, and execution—may be carried out in sequence or in rapid
succession, or the common decision may be implicit in the action itself, if the goal and means stand out clearly. The sequence followed
and methods used will be determined in part by the nature of the
problem, in part by the particular character of group structure (in
which leadership, as part and parcel of the hierarchical structure of
the group, plays no small part), in part by the particular set of values
or norms prevailing in the group, and in part by the character and
norms of the general sociocultural setting of which the group is a part.

Emphasis on studying the interaction process in a natural setting,
while approximating experimental control and technique, did not
eliminate the possibility of checking the validity of observed trends by
precise laboratory techniques at "choice" points. If there is any validity
in the recent generalizations concerning perceptual and judgmental
variations ("distortions") as a function of attitude or motive, relevant
perceptual or judgmental tasks of the type used in the laboratory
could very well be introduced at a few choice points. The stimulus
materials used in these experimental units were of an indirect and
unstructured type not involving direct questions about developing
group attitudes. The subjects perceived the procedures as part of the
camp activities, and not as experiments that cluttered the flow of their
interaction process.

In fact, on the methodological side, the plan of the study aimed at
two additional objectives. The first involved the introduction of laboratory-type experimental procedures as supplements for obtaining
data concerning the effects of group interaction, with the aim of establishing shortcut methods for tapping behavioral trends to supplant
laborious, gross behavior observations (See the experimental units at

the ends of Stages 1, 2, and 3 later in this chapter.) The second objective was to secure personal data (e.g., intelligence and personal characteristics) through available testing procedures that could be related to various dimensions of behavior manifested in the interaction process in various stages. This aspect was not carried out in the 1954 study, owing to lack of facilities. As this line of research has developed, it has been brought to the foreground as one of the important problems.

Subjects

The subjects were 24 eleven-year-old boys from established middle-class Protestant families. All were normal (no "problem" cases), had not experienced any unusual degrees of frustration in their homes or other situations, were not school or social failures (no isolates), and had similar educational levels. (See the section on subject selection in Chapter 3.)

A nominal fee of $25 was charged. This fee gave us the privilege of asking parents not to visit their boys during the experiment. Staff members had no visitors.

Three Successive Stages and the Hypotheses

The study was carried out in three successive stages of approximately one week each. The hypotheses are listed under their corresponding stages, since the account of the stages specifies in outline the conditions under which the particular hypothesis holds true.

Our general hypothesis in regard to intergroup relations (which was the main concern of the study) is that intergroup attitudes and behavior are determined *primarily* by the nature of functional relations between groups in question (and *not primarily* by the pattern of relations and attitudes prevailing within groups themselves, *nor primarily* by the deviate or neurotic behavior of particular individual members who have suffered more than the usual degree of frustration in their personal life histories).

Both the 1949 and 1953 experiments started with a stage of spontaneous friendship choices.[3] This stage, to which the first days of the experiments were devoted, was introduced to rule out the possibility that the experimental ingroup formation arose from personal affinities that subjects developed for one another. On the basis of reversals of friendship choices away from interpersonal preferences and in the direction of the experimentally produced ingroups, our 1949 and 1953 experiments ruled out this alternative explanation. The stage of interpersonal friendship choices, therefore, was eliminated from the 1954 undertaking, and the study was designed in three stages instead of using the more complex four-stage design of the 1953 attempt.

The two previous studies assigned the subjects to two experimental groups toward the end of the first stage, that of spontaneous friendship choices. This division was intended not only to split spontaneous friendship choices but also to match the groups as much as possible in terms of observed skills, athletic ability, and so on, as well as in terms of data collected during the period of subject selection. Since dropping the period of spontaneous friendship choices eliminated the possibility of actual observation at the camp prior to assigning the subjects to two groups, we had to rely exclusively on data from observations at schools, on teacher evaluations, on school ratings, and on data from interviews in actual home situations during the subject-selection period. Staff members exhibited the utmost care in trying to obtain two groups matched in as many dimensions as possible, relevant to the activities to be introduced, especially those to be utilized in the intergroup stages.

Stage 1: Experimental Ingroup Formation

The chief aim of Stage 1 was to produce ingroups through manipulation of the conditions in which interaction would take place. This step was necessary to allow study of intergroup relations between ingroups whose formation and functioning could thus be specified.

With this aim of specifying the formation and structure of the ex-

3. A brief summary of our 1949 experiment was presented in J. Rohrer and M. Sherif, eds., *Social Psychology at the Crossroads* (New York: Harper, 1951), Chapter 17. A fuller account of that experiment is given in Sherif and Sherif, *Groups in Harmony and Tension*, Chapters 9 and 10. A short report of the completed part of the 1953 experiment is a given in M. Sherif, B. J. White, and O. J. Harvey, "Status in Experimentally Produced Groups," *American Journal of Sociology* 60 (1955): 370–379.

perimental ingroups, the two groups were kept apart and their activities separated as much as possible, especially during the first days of this stage. Otherwise any functional contacts between the two groups would certainly have had some consequence both for ingroup formation and for the later stages of intergroup relations.

Conditions conducive to bringing about ingroup formation (with hierarchical statuses and roles that would be clear-cut at the upper and bottom ends of the hierarchy) were to consist of a series of common and interdependent activities prompted by goals integral to the actual situations in which the subjects found themselves (e.g., getting a meal when hungry or water when thirsty). The attainment of the goal would necessarily require cooperation and reciprocal relations. As a result, the initial discussion and the activities that followed would be real to the subjects, unlike discussion topics introduced or hinted at by experimenters (or leaders) but not immediately inherent in the situation. (Topics used in many discussion-group studies are often conducive to individual "shining" in verbal skills or debating.)

The effects of the series of activities conducive to group formation were to be studied in terms of (a) behavioral observations—verbal and nonverbal; (b) ratings of *emerging* relationships by the participant observers (looking from outside); (c) sociometric ratings in several relevant dimensions (looking from inside); and (d) experimental indices of judgmental and perceptual variations reflecting the reciprocal role and status attitudes that emerge among group members toward each other. Before obtaining the latter indices, we could make predictions of the direction and degree of such variations.

As emphasized in the introductory theoretical and methodological considerations, the focal point was to maintain the natural flow of the interaction process within groups and, later, between groups under conditions that would appear lifelike to the subjects. Any observational procedure, or laboratory-type experiment or repetition of sociometric tapping that would clutter the flow of interaction was antithetical to the main conception of this study. Therefore, only one judgmental experiment would be used during the stage of ingroup formation. It would be perfectly feasible to design an experiment primarily to study ingroup formation and related problems and to devote the entire time to it. In that case, of course, it would be possible to introduce various experiments studying the progressive development of ingroup structure and its effects on ingroup members.

Hypothesis 1 (Stage 1)

A definite group structure consisting of differentiated status positions and reciprocal roles will be produced when a number of individuals (without previously established interpersonal relations) interact with one another under conditions that situationally embody goals that have common appeal value to the individuals, and that require interdependent activities for their attainment.

This hypothesis was formulated on the basis of empirical findings by sociologists like F. Thrasher, Clifford Shaw, and William Whyte. These and other authors stated generalizations in line with the hypothesis. Our findings in this respect would serve as experimental verification. The results of both our 1949 and 1953 experiments, cited previously, supported this hypothesis.

The hypothesis would be considered to be verified if the individuals could be placed on a pyramidal hierarchy (the leader being at the apex) on the basis of (a) observational data, (b) status ratings by participant observers of subjects in the respective groups, and (c) sociometric indices.

Observational data (a, b): The ratings of *emerging* status relations would be part of the daily observational reports of the participant observers. Thus, the ratings would serve as a day-to-day index of the trend from mere togetherness situations (in which unstable, transitory differential effects are manifested) to various degrees of stabilization of established reciprocities constituting the *group structure* at a given time. When three consecutive ratings (especially of positions at the top and bottom of the status hierarchy) by participant observers of their respective groups showed a high degree of correspondence, we could say a definite ingroup structure had formed. *At this point* the similar ratings independently made by junior counselors and other staff members who had sufficient contact with the groups could be used as further checks. At that time, *sociometric ratings* and the judgmental experiment with the target board were to be introduced (see c and d below).

Observational data were obtained consisting of the frequencies of *suggestions* for activities made by various members and the proportion of acceptance and observance of these suggestions. The latter measure might be termed the *initiative ratio*.

Other observational data along various dimensions were desirable. Observers made their ratings of group structure along these dimensions.

Frequency of suggestions (for engaging in this or that activity, etc.) addressed *to* various group members was one such dimension. It seemed a plausible hunch that the number of suggestions for group activities *received* by various members would be proportional to the status each achieved in the group. When members were placed according to the frequencies of suggestions addressed to them, we might get a pyramidal placement of members very much like the one mentioned above. It is plausible to state this tendency in the form of an auxiliary hypothesis:

Hypothesis 1a (Stage 1)

If a definite group structure develops, it will be reflected in a consistent pattern in directions of communication. The specific pattern in directions of communication will be as follows: *the higher the status of a group member the greater the frequency of suggestions (for group activities) addressed to him.*

It seems feasible to represent the pattern in directions of communication visually in the form of a chart. We should think that through the course of a study such as this, variations in such charts would be obtained. The chart of directions of communication at a given time should correspond closely to the chart of initiative ratios and pattern of judgmental variations in the way of overestimations and underestimations of performance. A suggestion for activities coming from any member might be kicked around among the group. Even if it is not initially addressed to the top position (leader) but to middle position members or lieutenants, it will be kicked around until a nod expressing approval or, at least, no disapproval from the top-position member (leader) is perceived.

Sociometric data (c):[4] Sociometric data obtained from the subjects themselves along various dimensions (popularity, initiative, degree of service for the well-being of the group, etc.) would be significant in-

4. It was thought that obtaining sociometric indices three times (once at the end of each stage), asking the same or similar questions within a three-week period, might appear repetitious (if not suspicious) to the subjects. Therefore, in line with our main concern not to clutter the natural flow of the interaction process, it was decided prior to the actual start of the experiment to restrict sociometric choices to the intergroup stages (2 and 3) and forgo them at the end of the ingroup stage (1).

dices in terms of relations perceived by the group members themselves. The sociometric indices (looking from within) should give very much the same trend as those represented in the ratings, frequencies, and charts obtained through observational data mentioned above. We shall consider this hypothesis verified only in cases where a high degree of correspondence exists between observational, sociometric, and experimental indices.

Experimental indices to be obtained through laboratory-type judgmental experiments (d): Recent findings indicating the feasibility of measuring attitudes and other motivational components through perceptual and judgmental indices had suggested that the reciprocities developing among members of a group as status and role relations would be reflected in the differential ways group members perceive and judge one another. One index of these differential judgments as a function of relative statuses or roles would be based on the tendency to expect higher or lower performance in activities by members occupying various status positions. (Differential expectations proportional to status positions occupied.) Relative over- and underestimates of performance in experimentally introduced tasks might be utilized to measure indirectly the status hierarchy of group members. If this proved to be the case, such experimental indices could be developed to check the validity of gross observational findings, and eventually to supplant them. Such an attempt was made in this study with the following hypotheses:

Hypothesis 1b (Stage 1)

If Hypothesis 1 holds, it can be predicted that
(a) The higher the status of a member in the group, the greater will be his tendency to overestimate his performance in an activity the group engages in.
(b) The higher the status of a member in the group, the greater will be the tendency of other group members to overestimate his performance.
(c) The lower the status of a member in the group, the less will be his tendency to overestimate his performance in an activity the group engages in.
(d) The lower the status of a member in the group, the less will be the tendency of other members to overestimate his performance, even to the point of underestimating it.

This psychological tendency was demonstrated in established informal cliques in an experiment at the University of Oklahoma, carried out as one unit of a research project supported by the Office of Naval

Research.[5] However, in that study, the indices used were estimates of future performance, whereas in the 1953 study mentioned above, direct judgments of performance were used.[6] Our 1954 experiment followed the procedures used in 1953 utilizing direct judgmental indices.

Hypothesis 2 (Stage 1)

When individuals interact under conditions stated in Hypothesis 1, concomitant with the formation of group structure, norms will be standardized regulating their behavior in relations with one another and in practices and activities commonly engaged in.

This hypothesis was also based on empirical findings by sociologists and on studies of adolescent cliques and was experimentally verified in this study.

The group norms that are standardized will be expressed as attitudes and conforming behavior of individual members. The production of a set of standards or norms can be verified by observing the reaction of group members to deviations from it. When there is a norm regulating the interpersonal relations of ingroup members in terms of their established statuses and roles or regulating behavior in some practice or activity, it can be predicted that behavior by a group member deviating from the norm will arouse corrective reactions from other group members. (This applies also to norms regulating behavior toward outgroups, which will become prominent in Stage 2.) The corrective measures or sanctions may range from actual punishment meted out to the deviate—through "silent treatment," scorn, ridicule, criticism, or expressions of disapproval—to amusement, varying according to the importance of the norm violated, the degree of deviation, and the status of the individual. Facts relating to reactions to deviation have been reported by sociologists and also in the experiment by Schachter and others.

Stages of Intergroup Relations (Stages 2 and 3)

As stated earlier in our definition, *intergroup relations* refers to interaction between two or more groups collectively or between their re-

5. O. J. Harvey, "An Experimental Approach to the Study of Status Relations in Informal Groups," *American Sociological Review* 18 (1953): 357–367.
6. Sherif, White, and Harvey, "Status in Experimentally Produced Groups."

spective members. In our study, *intergroup relations* refers to interaction between the two experimentally produced groups (as formed in Stage 1) and their respective members.

Stages 2 and 3 constitute the main stages of this experiment. All of the previous work in Stage 1 (ingroup formation) leads up to them. Stage 2 is the tension or friction phase of intergroup relations. Stage 3 is the integration phase of intergroup relations.

Stage 2: Intergroup Relations—Friction Phase

Relations between the experimentally produced groups started with a friction phase because the major problem of intergroup relations is the reduction of existing frictions between various groups. For this reason, the phase of friction preceded the attempt to reduce tension and to integrate groups into cooperative activities with common goals.

Friction between the two groups was brought about through the introduction of two sets of conditions. First, the two groups were brought into contact in a series of *competitive* activities in the form of a tournament of events yielding cumulative scores, with a reward for each member of the winning team. However, these individual rewards could be obtained only by being a member of the winning group and could not be won individually. In other words, to win the award individually, the members of each group had to contribute their individual bits to a team win.

The second set of conditions introduced situations that one group would perceive as *frustrating* and as caused by the other group, and not by the camp administration. We tried this method with positive results in 1949. The situations embodied goals that could be attained by one group and not by the other, in such a way that each group would perceive the other as an obstacle in its way to attaining the goal.

In line with the methodological point that the subjects should not perceive this as an experiment on intergroup relations, conditions set up in Stages 2 and 3 had to be designed in such a way that the subjects could not assign the source of these conditions to the staff. Situations had to be planned in such a way that group members could not ascertain by checking verbally with the members of the other group that someone (the staff) had been manipulating conditions.

Our general hypothesis is that subjects who did not have appreciable contact with members of the opposite group during Stage 1 would develop negative attitudes verging on enmity toward the out- group, which they perceived to be obstructing the attainment of goals shared in common within their group. Negative intergroup attitudes, such as prejudice, develop whenever any outgroup is perceived as causing frustration or as an obstacle. (In short, norms regulating be- havior toward outgroups, like social distance norms, are standardized group products.) Negative attitudes toward outgroups will be gener- ated situationally under these conditions and will tend to persist even though the individual members in question have not undergone any special degree of frustration in their life histories. Applying this gen- eral statement to the particular case of intergroup relations in this study, we can state our specific hypotheses.

Hypothesis 1 (Stage 2)

In the course of competition and frustrating relations between two groups, unfavorable stereotypes will come into use in relation to the outgroup and its members and will be standardized in time, placing the outgroup at a cer- tain social distance (proportional to the degree of negative relations between groups).

In our study, we obtained evidence for the rise of stereotypes by re- cording derogatory adjectives and phrases used to refer to the out- group. The specific competitive and frustrating situations and the activities and verbal utterances relating to outgroups were noted. If possible, the frequency of references made to outgroups (positive or negative) and of activities undertaken relating to outgroups, in both intra- and intergroup situations, were to be recorded. Such condi- tions, verbal utterances, and activities in relation to the outgroup con- stitute the foundation for stereotypes. In time, all members of the outgroup will be perceived in terms of the generalizations encom- passed in the standardized stereotypes. This aspect of our study con- stitutes a contribution to the study of the formation of norms of social distance (prejudice) that prevail in social groups. The tendency to- ward stereotype formation was noted in our 1949 study and verified in a more systematic way in R. Avigdor's doctoral thesis.[7]

---

7. R. Avigdor, "The Development of Stereotypes as a Result of Group Interaction" (Ph.D. diss. on file in the New York University Library, 1951). For a brief summary, see Sherif and Sherif, *Groups in Harmony and Tension*, 290–295.

In addition to observational data, the rise of stereotypes was tapped through two experimental units introduced at this stage. In one unit, experimental indices reflecting the reciprocal intergroup evaluations in terms of stereotype ratings were used (testing Hypothesis 1, Stage 2). This is essentially the technique used by Avigdor. In the other, experimental indices were used revealing overestimation of performance of ingroup members and underestimation of performance of outgroup members. In this unit a bean-toss contest between the two groups was introduced. The contest consisted of all members of each group rapidly gathering as many beans as possible within a brief period. After the contest, beans presumably picked up by each member were projected on a screen with the identity of the individual who presumably collected them. Actually the same number of items were projected each time but were spread in somewhat different arrangements in the same confined area. Estimates of the number of beans reflected overestimation of the performance of ingroup members and underestimation of the performance of outgroup members. This tendency can be stated in the form of specific hypotheses.

Hypothesis 1a (Stage 2)

Ingroup members will tend to overestimate the number of items purportedly obtained by ingroup members and to underestimate the number of items attributed to outgroup members.

Hypothesis 1b (Stage 2)

The degree to which subjects manifest this tendency will vary according to the status (low or high) of the ingroup or outgroup member being judged.

The feasibility of the two experimental units has already been clearly established in an experimental study carried out in our project.[8]

The data from these assessment techniques, as well as sociometric choices, would be obtained again at the end of Stage 3 and would serve as an index of the decrease in that stage in unfavorable attitudes toward the outgroup.

---

8. O. J. Harvey, "An Experimental Investigation of Negative and Positive Relationships Between Small Informal Groups Through Judgmental Indices," *Sociometry* 19 (1956): 201–209.

Hypothesis 2 (Stage 2)

The course of relations between two groups that are in a state of competition and frustration will tend to produce an increase in ingroup solidarity.

Increased group solidarity will be revealed in expressions glorifying the ingroup and the "feats" of its members, especially those of high standing. Another indication will be the increased encouragement of ingroup members' efforts in a way not manifested during the period when the ingroup was not in contact with the outgroup. Additional behavioral data in support of this hypothesis can be derived from the experimental units described above.

Hypothesis 3 (Stage 2)

Functional relations between groups that are of consequence to the groups will tend to bring about changes in the pattern of relations within the ingroups involved.

This hypothesis should hold true for both positive and negative intergroup relations of consequence. (See also the last paragraph of this chapter.) The changes in ingroup relations can be measured in terms of various aspects of popularity and status of ingroup members. The degree of consequence of intergroup relations for the group in question can be measured by the frequency of references to the outgroup, and by the amount of planning and activity engaged in within the ingroup in relation to the outgroup.

One way of testing this hypothesis is through special attention to ratings of status relations within the groups by participant observers. In our study these ratings were to be continued throughout the intergroup phases with the expectation that some important changes in the functional relations between groups would produce consequential changes in the ingroup structure as stabilized at the end of Stage 1. The participant observers' ratings were compared with independent ratings by other observers in contact with the groups, thus contributing to the reliability of the data.

The hypothesis is predicted for both parties (winning and losing groups in our study). In the case of the group suffering defeat, the impact of intergroup relations may be to the extent of *disorganization* of the ingroup pattern, which will be marked by shifts in status positions occupied by various members.

Related to the above hypothesis is a subsidiary one concerning the functioning of low-status members of the two contending groups. This hypothesis has theoretical implications in view of ongoing controversies.

Hypothesis 4 (Stage 2)

Low-status members will tend to exert greater efforts that will be revealed in more intense forms of overt aggression and verbal expressions against the outgroup as a means of improving their status within the ingroup.[9]

An empirical test of this subsidiary hypothesis consists of observation and comparison of the hostile and aggressive reactions of low-status members toward the outgroup when reacting in the presence of ingroup members high in status, and when reacting when high-status members of their ingroup are not in the immediate vicinity.

Stage 3: Intergroup Relations—Integration Phase

Stage 3 constitutes the crucial and novel aspect of this study. The deliberate attempt to bring about cooperation between groups follows a stage of friction produced between them experimentally. This should be the attempt in studies aiming at reduction of group tensions. Production of harmony between groups that are not in a state of tension does not present much of a problem in terms of intergroup events today.

There are various possibilities or alternatives for the study of reducing intergroup tensions. One alternative could be called the "common enemy" approach. Empirical evidence and our 1949 tryout of this

---

9. This hypothesis does not imply that high-status members will not initiate and actively participate in intergroup conflict. In line with one of the major tenets of Sherif and Sherif, *Groups in Harmony and Tension*, intergroup behavior in conflict or cooperation consists mainly in participation in the intergroup trends of one's group. A line of activity in positive or negative intergroup relations will be ineffective unless high-status members either take a lead or join in or assent to the developing intergroup trend. If they obstruct an unmistakable trend in intergroup relations or deviate from it markedly, the consequence will be sinking in the group hierarchy (see Hypothesis 3, Stage 2).

measure as an expedient manner of reducing postexperimental hostility indicate that it can be effectively used. But it implies conflict between larger group units.

Another alternative would be to arrange a series of events giving supremacy to the achievement of individuals. But this approach would simply cause disruption of the ingroups. In terms of actual happenings in intergroup events, the use of this measure in an experimental study would be unrealistic and would have few if any realistic implications for the reduction of intergroup tensions. As noted earlier, actual intergroup tensions take place either collectively between group units or between the ingroups' individual members reacting in terms of their group identifications.

A third alternative would be through leadership techniques. Appropriate manipulation can make this measure effective. But in actual groups, intrusion of an outside person as a leader is not a welcome one. In actual groups leaders, too, are part of the group structure, and they have to function within certain bounds in whatever initiative they take. For this reason, manipulation of conditions through leaders who are not part of the groups in question has little implication for the state of intergroup relations that actually exist.

Such considerations led us to choose the alternative used in this study. The main feature of this alternative is the introduction of *superordinate goals* that are integral to the situation and that cannot be ignored by the groups in question. In our study, the main criteria in the choice of procedures to be introduced in this integration stage were that goals of sufficient strength to the groups in question be superordinate, in the sense that the resources and energies of either single group would be inadequate for the attainment of the goal, thus creating a state of real and/or perceived interdependence. Before the experiment we planned and listed situations in which such a state of interdependence inhered, keeping a level of motivation sufficient to direct group members toward the superordinate goals, and introducing a series of stimulus conditions that would make the facing of the superordinate goals and the modes of their attainment compelling.

The superordinate goals will not be introduced abruptly right after this stage starts. Initially some contact situations were to be introduced. At these occasions the groups would have to be in close physical proximity under conditions in which expression of their hostility toward one another would not be very appropriate. Of course, mere get-togethers or contact will not materially help reduce the friction. The aim of this early period was to create the possibility of *communication* between members of the two groups. The improvised birthday party of an outsider (preferably a local personage not related to the subjects positively or negatively in an appreciable way) to which both groups are invited would be an example of such an occasion. The early phase of Stage 3 thus consisted of occasions that would give the two groups opportunity for *contact* or communication.

Hypothesis 1 (Stage 3)

It is predicted that the contact phase itself will not produce marked de-crease in the existing state of tension between groups.

The persistence of tension will be revealed in reactions showing re-sistance to cooperation with the outgroup, in spite of contact, and persistence of negative stereotypes. If this prediction holds, it will eliminate the alternative hypothesis that contact in itself will bring about a reduction of tensions.

After a series of contact situations, a series of superordinate goals were introduced—goals that could not help having appeal value to the members of both groups. The following are examples of super-ordinate goals inherent in the situation for members of both groups concerned, the attainment of which depended on collaboration on the part of both groups:

(a) A project related to some improvement of the water tank on the hill and the pump near the reservoir, since the tank provided water for members of both groups.

(b) Creating a situation of interdependence in a joint overnight camp in which members of both groups would need mutual aid for their meal and sleeping facilities. Probably the increased social sug-gestibility in new situations or situations of uncertainty might be uti-lized to enhance the effects of the conditions of interdependence.

(c) Other examples suggested by staff members were the possibili-ties of using the swimming pool or making the truck (which brings provisions) inoperable, for example, having the truck in a rut deep enough to require the combined efforts of both groups to free it.

Hypothesis 2 (Stage 3)

When groups in a state of friction are brought into contact under conditions embodying superordinate goals, the attainment of which is compelling but which cannot be achieved by the efforts of one group alone, the groups will tend to cooperate toward the common goal.

Hypothesis 2a (Stage 3)

Intergroup cooperation necessitated by a series of situations embodying superordinate goals will have a cumulative effect in the direction of reducing existing tensions between groups.

Even though the groups were brought into situations that permitted communication between them and then into situations requiring their collaboration toward a common goal, the effects of the friction produced in Stage 2 would tend to persist, along with the by-products of that friction. One of the indices important in the study of the changes in this stage, in addition to observational data giving a gross account, was to be the decrease in expressions of resistance to collaboration with the outgroup, which were strong at first.

Observational data were collected in the mess hall and other situations involving choices (of seating arrangements, etc.) to check the extent of intermingling among members of the two groups.

Another form of evidence of reduced tension would be a decrease in the actual use of derogatory terms and expressions toward the outgroup. After the series of superordinate goal situations had exerted a cumulative effect, the rating of relevant stereotypes would be repeated. The "bean toss" experiment or a similar procedure would be applied here if it could be carried out without spoiling the flow of the interaction process.

Toward the end of Stage 3 sociometric choices would be obtained again. It was predicted that in comparison to those obtained at the end of Stage 2, there would be a marked increase in choices of outgroup members.

As predicted in Hypothesis 3 (Stage 2), intergroup relations developing in interaction directed toward superordinate goals will also tend to bring about changes in ingroup relations. As in the case of the friction phase (Stage 2), there may be changes in ingroup structure, proportional to the demands for intergroup cooperation. A special note should be made here of those who are contributing more to intergroup cooperation—for example, lieutenants who exhibit strivings toward still higher position in the ingroup structure and those in marginal roles. Effective cooperation will be brought about when high-status members or members on the move to higher status through activities in the area of intergroup relations take a hand in initiating ingroup moves toward cooperation and in participating in intergroup communication related to superordinate goals.

3

Role of Staff; Subject Selection; Experimental Site

As specified in the statement of the approach, hypotheses, and general design (Chapter 2), the distinctive feature of this study is that subjects interacted with one another in activities that appeared lifelike to them in a natural setting—without being aware that they were being observed while interaction was going on. Therefore, it was essential to make explicit the special role of staff members in experimentally introduced problem situations, the criteria observed in selecting subjects so as to ensure adequate testing of the hypotheses, and the considerations that determined the choice of an experimental site.

Role of Staff Members

Prior to the experiment, staff members received detailed instructions. They are presented here in essentially the same form.

In every step of the work it will greatly help coordination of efforts if all participating staff members in the camp realize at every moment that the camp is not a camp in the usual sense, but is set up as a research project to test definite hypotheses pertaining to group relations, with emphasis upon the intergroup phase. The main features are stated in the outline giving approaches, stages, plan of study, and methodological considerations [as described in Chapter 2]. Conditions and activities are introduced with these objectives in mind.

Utmost care will be exercised in ruling out all influences in word, deed, or use of various procedures that are not specified in the methodology and specific characteristics stated for conditions introduced for each stage. No activity is to be initiated, sponsored, or encouraged that is not in line with the main criteria specified in the study plan as appropriate for the particular stage at the time. The behavioral effects are to be the outcome of the deliberately introduced conditions and not of verbal means or other camp practices.

Therefore, do not use verbal means to influence subjects, do not take initiative to introduce activities on your own accord, and do not try to counsel campers individually. Of course, this does *not* mean a "hands-off" or nondirection policy in any matter that even slightly concerns the *whereabouts, safety, health, and well-being* of the campers concerned.

No staff member is to be a leader to the boys during *any* stage of the study in any of the various activities introduced, after careful consideration, in line with the criteria and hypotheses. In the first stage, every activity is introduced because it is considered to be conducive to interaction among the campers, from which a pattern of status (role) relations, including the leader position, is expected to emerge. You may have to give advice when asked and institute controls when necessary to maintain order, but please refrain from giving direction and initiating action in relation to *problem situations.* Initiative should come from the subjects under the specifically designed problem conditions of each stage. *After they start along some line of action, give them help to carry it out, but do not put yourself in the foreground of ongoing activities.*

When a problem situation is introduced that demands planning, discussion, and execution on the part of the subjects, utmost care should be taken not to show any partiality or preference and not to assign any single camper to take the lead. If the experimentally introduced situation involves common appeal value (motivation), the lead will naturally evolve in the interaction process among the participating campers.

Be especially aware that the participating campers will at times turn to you, as adults, for approval or sanction for carrying out a plan of activity in relation to the experimentally introduced problem situations. Care should be taken to be responsive to such queries or appeals. If the proposals do not run counter to the health, safety, and well-being of the campers, and also if they do not run counter to the criteria specified for the given stage, the boys should be given opportunity to proceed in the direction they propose.

There will be times at which an ongoing course of action may not be in line with criteria set in the study outline. If such a situation occurs, it may be suggested to you by the experimenter that a change be made in the ongoing procedures. In the flow of activities it may be impossible to explain at the particular moment why this suggestion is made. It is expected that the suggestion will be followed, and the reasons for suggesting the change will be explained later at a more appropriate time.

It is fully realized that the end results implied in the hypotheses may be secured in a more shortcut way by using other activities. Activities and procedures introduced in the various stages, especially in the *first stage*, might appear drawn out and roundabout. Since these successive stages were planned after long and laborious deliberation of existing theories and findings, they constitute an interrelated sequence in the plan of study, and as such, all successive steps are dependent on each other. Therefore, utmost care should be taken not to appeal to shortcuts, but to satisfy the sequence as outlined.

In line with the consideration stated in relation to the rise of leadership among the campers, and of staff not assuming leadership in experimentally introduced conditions, it becomes necessary for staff members not to exhibit special performance skill that may be conducive to focusing popularity and leadership on staff members. This is particularly important for Stage 1. However, it should be repeated that this does *not* mean that a helping hand should be withheld from the campers after a line of activity is proposed or initiated by them. In line with this consideration, do not wear any clothing, especially shirts, that have insignia or other identifying symbols (e.g., a college or camp name). We do not wish subjects to adopt names or associations through adult leader identification. Do not introduce to the campers nicknames, catchwords, or slogans in a way that may cause them to be standardized by the subjects.

All the reports concerning verbal or behavioral observations should be written independently and not as a consequence of discussion with any other staff member. All ratings should also be done independently. Particular care should be taken to observe this procedure in order to secure reliability of results.

The ongoing activities will present the possibility of an infinite number of events that could be observed and recorded. Therefore, please have the hypotheses for the given stage focal in your mind so that observations will not be hodgepodge but will be relevant to the hypotheses in question. As long as any behavioral items are relevant to the hypotheses, either validating or invalidating them, utmost care should be taken to include them all. It may not be possible to record all relevant items of behavior, but indisputable recurrences of behavioral items should be recorded.

Subject Selection

Since the hypotheses to be tested required that the behavioral trends and products in ingroup formation and the development of positive and negative relations between the groups be outcomes of experimentally introduced conditions and interaction processes within them, certain strict criteria for subject selection were necessary. The criteria that were adopted stemmed from the basic consideration that ingroup formation (Stage 1) and the development of negative and positive relations between ingroups (Stages 2 and 3) should not hinge upon similarities or differences in sociocultural background or distinct differences in personal backgrounds and adjustment of the individuals composing the experimental groups. Therefore, homogeneity of subjects as to sociocultural and personal backgrounds was the guiding determination underlying the establishment of criteria for subject selection.

Subjects were to be normal, well-adjusted boys of the same age and educational level, from similar sociocultural backgrounds, and with no unusual features in their personal backgrounds insofar as extreme or prolonged frustrations, broken home life, and the like, were concerned. We excluded any potential subject who did not appear normal in terms of these general criteria and the more specific characteristics outlined below. These criteria meant elimination of all "problem" boys and of boys who might have suffered unusual degrees of frustration from deprived sociocultural and personal backgrounds. Equally important was that subjects should not have been acquainted before the experiment started. Otherwise it might be said that existing friendship ties influenced ingroup formation and that the resulting groups could not be attributed to the experimental conditions introduced. Thus special precautions, outlined below, were taken to ensure that subjects were not acquainted prior to the experiment.

Selection of subjects who met the criteria represented one of the prerequisites for the success of the study. Without adherence to such basic criteria in selecting subjects, many of the necessary conditions presented in Chapter 2 could not have been satisfied. Sociological, psychological, and physical specifications were also set up for subjects to ensure healthy, well-adjusted boys with athletic and other skills sufficient for full participation in the camp activities, which were to be introduced in line with experimental considerations.

More specifically, subjects were to be of established Protestant families (not new in the area) of middle socioeconomic class and were to be living with both parents (i.e., children from broken homes or foster homes were not accepted).

Psychological manifestations that precluded the selection of a given boy were any signs of severe homesickness, social isolation, enuresis, one or more failing grades in school (i.e., subjects had to be of normal educational standing in relation to chronological age), abrupt changes in school performance, temper tantrums, running away from home, or truancy.

All subjects were to be of normal physical development and were to possess no physical deformities or impairments that would limit their participation in the athletic activities to be introduced for experimental purposes.

In interviewing parents and teachers and examining school records, information was gathered on each boy about certain skills and abilities that might enter as important factors affecting status positions that would evolve in the interaction at camp. The athletic interests and proficiency of each potential subject were ascertained, as well as musical ability and skit skills, previous camp experience, popularity and number of friends, membership in youth organizations, and so on. In addition, data were secured on the attitudes of a boy's parents toward their son and his friends, the condition of the neighborhood in which the boy lived, how long the family had lived in the area, the size of their house and the condition of the home and its furnishings, and the make and model of the family's car.

Methods of Selection

As mentioned above, one of the most important criteria of subject selection was that the boys not be previously acquainted with one another. Thus the friendship patterns and intra- and intergroup relationships formed in the experimental setting could not be attributed to existing acquaintances and friendship preferences brought to the experimental situation. This consideration dictated even the city from which subjects were selected. It required a city of sufficient size to have enough schools for children of the appropriate age and grade level, so that only one boy could be selected from each school, thus reducing the likelihood of prior acquaintance. Oklahoma City has that many schools, and from there all the subjects were selected. (It was, though, necessary to eliminate six boys from the final subject list because they were acquainted with others previously chosen.)

To adhere to the criteria as effectively as possible, we followed a rather painstaking procedure in picking out potential subjects and in the final selection of experimental subjects. The city was divided into three areas, each containing roughly an equal number of appropriate schools. Each area was assigned to the one of three interviewers who knew best that particular section of the city. Schools from sections of the city that had very high and very low income families in large numbers were eliminated from consideration.

To get the best possible access to school records and to be permitted freedom in observing potential subjects at firsthand in the school situation, we contacted the principals of appropriate schools. After presentation of credentials from higher school authorities, a brief description of the purpose of the visit was given. It was explained to the principal that an experimental camp under the auspices of the University of Oklahoma was being conducted. The announced purpose of the camp was the study of interaction in group activities within teams and between teams. The statement of purpose was informally worded but uniform. It pointed out that one of the main things that would be studied was how team members assumed and carried out initiative and responsibility under adult supervision; another focus would be the attitude of the boys as they participated in activities toward common goals they wanted to attain and also the attitudes that would occur when they competed with another bunch of boys. A further area for study would be how the boys take it when they win or lose in various activities, when things are not going their way, when they feel others are being good or bad sports or unfair, when situations are felt as more or less frustrating, as well as how the boys pull together and cooperate toward common goals.

In order that school principals and teachers would have little opportunity to recommend favorite boys for the camp, the interviewer explained to the principal that he would like to go out to the school yard
where the fifth graders were playing so that from firsthand observation, he could pick out some candidates who best seemed to meet
the criteria. This also allowed observers who knew the specific criteria for selection to observe the boys firsthand in usual circumstances
of interaction.

The observer, who had extensive prior experience in observing informal groups, then went to the playground, and when he saw a boy
that seemed to meet the criteria, he asked the playground supervisor
for the boy's name. At all times the interviewer tried to be as incon-
spicuous as possible so as not to arouse too much curiosity on the
part of the boys. After getting the names of from five to ten candidates
who seemed to satisfy the criteria best, the interviewer then found
out all he could from the playground supervisor about each of these
boys. Then he went to the homeroom teacher (if he or she was not the
playground supervisor) and obtained school records and further information on each boy. From school records, information was secured
concerning I.Q., grades, adjustment in school, and social attitudes,
and from the teacher, the boy's relationship to teachers and to other
children, status, popularity, and membership in school cliques. The
five or six potential subjects who remained after this first screening
procedure were ranked by the interviewer in terms of the extent to
which they satisfied the criteria.

The next step in selecting subjects was to contact the parents of
those boys who best met the criteria up to this point. All the parents
were met by the same individual, the one who was to appear at the
camp as the camp director in the eyes of the boys. This policy was followed so that when the subjects were divided into two groups, neither
of the participant observers would have a particular personal preference for any given boy; so that the boys in neither group would go to
camp already knowing their participant observer; and so that boys in
neither group would know the participant observer of the other group
when the two groups first came into functional contact during Stage
2. (The participant observers appeared to the boys at camp as senior
counselors.)

Parents were contacted in the order in which their sons were ranked
by the authors in terms of the criteria. The interviewer gave parents

the same explanation of the purpose and aim of the study as had earlier been given school principals and teachers. He stressed to the parents that they would not be permitted to visit the boys. The explanation given was that such visits would contribute to problems of home-sickness, which would undermine both the boys' enjoyment of camp and the success of the study. They were also told that there was a nominal fee ($25 for the entire period) and that a doctor's examination and permission for the boys to participate in all camp activities would be required, in addition to their own permission. (The fee, a device for making mutual commitments, was lowered for a few boys who met the criteria but whose families felt this amount a sizable expenditure for recreation.)

Altogether roughly 200 names of potential subjects were obtained in the manner described. Of this number, school records and inter-views with homeroom teachers were completed for almost half. In the selection of the final experimental subjects, the parents of ap-proximately 50 boys were contacted and/or interviewed. The original goal was 24 subjects who met the criteria in every respect, but strict adherence to the criteria resulted in the procurement of only 22 ex-perimental subjects. Altogether, more than 300 hours were spent di-rectly in selecting subjects, in addition to the numerous hours spent in establishing criteria and setting up the procedures.

Final Experimental Subjects

The 22 subjects who were finally selected were relatively homoge-neous in terms of the major criteria outlined above. All were from established Protestant families. All were well adjusted both in school and at home, according to observations and school and home inter-views. According to school records, all the subjects were doing average or above school work (none was failing or had a history of failures). All were fifth graders, about 11 years old, who had been promoted to the sixth grade for the next school year. This age level was selected so that none of the boys would have reached puberty, which could have been an important additional factor in determining the status positions that would emerge in group interaction. All were taken from the same grade for similar reasons, namely, that no one should have a status advantage because of a more advanced grade in school.

The median income of the subjects' families was $4,900 a year. The income of eleven families was below $5,000, the lowest being $3,200, and only two were (slightly) above $7,000. However, on the basis of occupation, education, home, and neighborhood, and so on, the subjects' families can be characterized on the whole as "middle class."

The average (median and mean) age of subjects was 11 years and 1 month. Five boys would have their 11th birthdays shortly after camp, and only one would be 11 well after the school term started. One boy had reached 12; all others were 11.

Intelligence quotients were available for 18 of the 22 boys. The median I.Q. for these 18 boys was 112. Four boys had I.Q. scores between 90 and 105, and only one above 120. Thus, by and large, these boys were above average in intelligence test scores, 11 scores of the 18 available being between 110 and 120. The boy with the lowest I.Q. was doing satisfactory work in all school subjects and was rated by his teacher "at the low end of the upper one-third" of his class in school achievement.

The boys did, of course, differ within limits in size, manner, and other personal characteristics; ability in various games; hair coloring; and so on. However, these individual variations were within the range of normality for boys in the schools, grades, neighborhoods, types of families, and so on, that had been chosen in terms of the criteria. Home and school interviews and school records did not offer a critical indicator of the status that would be achieved in the camp situation. The status structures that developed during ingroup formation and the nature of relationships between the groups as they came into functional contact during the experiment cannot be accounted for on the basis of differentiation of individuals, or between clusters of individuals, based on characteristics stemming from different sociocultural backgrounds, from *atypical* personal backgrounds, or from previously existing relationships.

In dividing the 22 subjects into two groups of equal size prior to the experiment, we took great care to match subjects assigned to the two groups, so that the groups would be composed as similarly as possible. Matching was carried out in terms of certain of the boys' personal characteristics. Considered in their order of relevance for interaction in the camp situation, they were height; weight; sports ability (general); sports skill (special); popularity (in neighborhood and school groups); other skills relating to camp, such as musical and skit skills, cooking ability, and the like; swimming; and previous camp experience. After the two groups had been matched as closely as possible in terms of these characteristics, we flipped a coin to determine which group of subjects went to what participant observer. This was a final precaution to rule out possible effects of any personal preferences the participant observers might have for particular boys.

Experimental Site

Certain characteristics were necessary in the experimental site. It had to provide *isolation* from the outside world during the experiment so that extraneous influences would not enter in and the results would be mainly a function of conditions deliberately introduced. There had to be separate facilities for two groups to be kept isolated from each other during ingroup formation (Stage 1), so that group formation would result from conditions introduced and interaction within the ingroup, without contact with an outgroup. Also, the physical characteristics of the camp and surrounding area had to allow flexibility in choosing and planning ingroup and intergroup problem situations; such flexibility required numerous circumstances conducive both to the arousal of common goals of high appeal value and to a variety of activities.

The site finally chosen after inspection of a number of camps was a densely wooded area in the Sans Bois Mountains of southeastern Oklahoma, about 7 miles north from the small town of Wilburton, which is on U.S. Route 270. The site is a 200-acre Boy Scouts of America camp that is completely surrounded by Robbers Cave State Park (See Figures 3.1 and 3.2). It was available exclusively for purposes of the experiment for the three-week period. The nearest large town—McAlester, Oklahoma—is about 40 miles distant.

Since terrain and facilities were used as part of the stimulus conditions throughout the experiment, it will be helpful to specify them. For the reader's convenience, places of functional importance in ingroup and intergroup activities are indicated on the map in Figure 3.2, which gives approximate distances between some of the points mentioned.

Effectively isolating the camp were a surrounding fence with "Keep Out" and "Restricted" signs and by the heavy foliage that screened the camp area from a park road running some 100 yards outside the fence.

Figure 3.1 Looking from Robbers Cave down (south) at the camp area and beyond; the campsite (cabins, mess hall, etc.) is situated on the flat stretch of land below this ledge

Functional isolation of the groups from each other during ingroup formation was made possible by the terrain of the area and by careful timing of their coming and going. The cabin used by each group was out of sight and hearing of the other group, and duplicate facilities were available for both groups (bath houses, swimming, boating, and campfire facilities, etc.). Both groups used the mess hall, which was about equidistant from the two cabins. However, it was not visible from the cabin at the south end of the camp because of a hill, and its entrance could not be seen from the north cabin because of intervening buildings and trees.

Because of the characteristics of the experimental site itself, the surrounding park, and the mountainous areas within a 60-mile radius, it was possible to plan activities of high appeal to the subjects for both ingroup and intergroup stages. Within easy walking distance from each cabin, and in opposite directions, were swimming, boating,

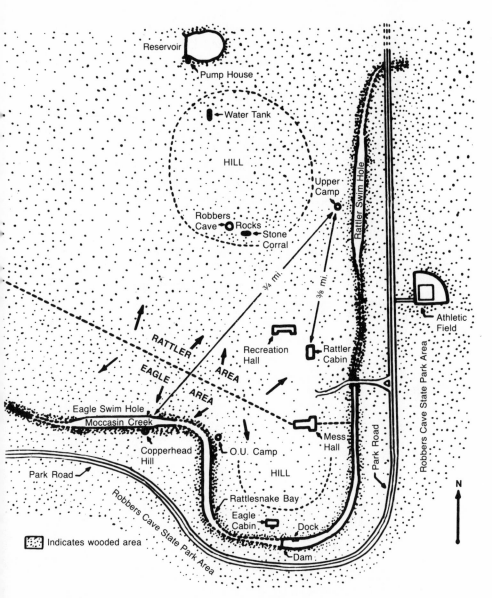

Figure 3.2 General layout of the campsite and respective areas of the two groups

and camping areas that were available for the exclusive use of each group. Campfires could be held near the cabins, at the "hideout" areas, or in a natural stone corral near Robbers Cave on the hill above camp. A very isolated reservoir in the hills above the camp supplied its water and offered facilities within hiking distance for overnight campouts. An athletic field was located across the park road, outside camp property, and nearest to the north cabin. The two groups reached the field by separate routes. Thus, when and where contact between groups would take place during competition situations could be controlled.

Lake Carlton, part of state park, was located about 3 miles from the experimental site and provided excellent swimming and picnic facilities. A number of camping areas were located on lakes and rivers within 20 to 60 miles of the camp. These could be used to advantage in increasing the interdependence of the groups (Stage 3) through cutting off their usual sources of food, housing, and so on. Of the various possibilities, Cedar Lake, about 14 miles from Heavener, Oklahoma, and 23 miles from the Arkansas state line, was used in Stage 3.

4

Experimental Formation of Ingroups

Overall Considerations Common to All Three Stages

Before summarizing Stage 1, a few considerations common to the procedures of all three stages should be emphasized. One fact that will stand out in the rest of this report is that the stimulus conditions, the activities necessitated by them, and the places in which they were carried out were numerous and varied. In such a kaleidoscope of numerous and varied events, it may be easy to lose sight of the systematic rationale on which all three stages were based.

The fundamental aim of the procedures in the experiment was to build up an interaction process that was perceived by the subjects as part and parcel of the circumstances in which they were living. The flow of interaction was followed from day to day in a longitudinal way. The interaction among subjects on a given day at a given stage of the experiment was not a discrete and unrelated event but was built up on the basis of interactions on the previous days and was functionally related to future events. A serious concern over validity, namely, a concern that events occurring in this study have some point of contact with their counterparts in real life, forced us to adopt this fundamental approach. Group behavior, in intra- and intergroup relations, is not a transitory affair. Group structure itself is anything but ahistorical. Therefore, step-by-step tracing of group structure and its norms is essential in pinpointing the factors that enter into the shaping of group behavior *now*.

Groups in actual life do not ordinarily strive toward goals furnished by the instructions of an outsider. Group goals exist or arise because group members are situated in a certain place and time, under given circumstances, and because the pattern of interaction is what it is. All of these determinants have specific implications in relation to the state of motivation of group members.

Therefore, it is decidedly unrealistic in experiments on group relations for the investigator to introduce any old task and have groups work on it at intervals in an interrupted way under certain types of "leadership," and then to draw cut-and-dried conclusions concerning group behavior on that basis. One might do well to remember abundant evidence in the sociological literature of small groups, where time and again, we find individuals in whom common motives or deprivations are generated because they are where they are and are caught in the particular set of circumstances. The result is that groups form, developing strong ingroup attitudes and strong ingroup solidarity and responsibility (at times, to the point of sacrifice of no mean proportions) without the benefit of this or that type of adult "leadership" from a personage who is not an integral part of the group. There are cases of groups formed in actual life, without the benefit of a benevolent, permissive expert, that have a strong structure and an intense sense of belongingness and solidarity. These properties may not develop in groups that are under the "leadership" of an outsider, no matter how skilled and expert. For these reasons, in each of the three stages of this experiment, a series of goals and related tasks were introduced that were derived from explicit preferences of the subjects themselves. Verbal instructions as a method of introducing goals were avoided as much as possible, the aim being instead to create situations in which the subjects would immediately perceive a problem situation or a possibility for attaining some desired end.

Similar comment applies to procedures for the study of a *group discussion* and techniques of *problem solving*. Once the group members face a problem situation of strong appeal to them, they do not have to be told to gather around and discuss their common plight or desire. You cannot stop them from being preoccupied with the problem at hand nor from making it a focal concern—and discussion does not stop there. Discussion necessarily continues, or even takes place simultaneously with active search for ways and means of doing something about the problem. The procedures in every stage of this study, therefore, involved choosing the terrain, time, stimulus conditions, equipment, and words conducive to the arousal of a problem situation implying common goals. This method, we repeat, leads to discussion, planning, searching for appropriate means and tools, and execution of planned lines of activity.

Individuals who are immersed in their plight or problems in earnest are prone to be irritated by outsiders showing cold-blooded nosiness in their affairs, not to mention having to put up with doing this or that extraneous thing for the benefit of the tape recorder or the convenience of the experimenter. Therefore, in the study of group interaction, we insisted on observation by persons who are genuinely part of the situation and who will not be caught in the act of observing by the subjects. By following the participant observer technique, in which no word was written in the presence of the subjects, we may *not* have obtained all relevant events. However, in return, we gained free and *unsuppressed* recurrence of behavioral items that will stand out in a striking way for any observer.

In short, our fundamental approach was carefully to introduce a number of problem situations appropriate to the characteristics of the stage in question and to leave the ensuing activity in word (discussion) and deed to the subjects themselves as much as possible. We did not think that reliability would be ensured by repeating the same problem situations. Doing so would have led to boredom and/or suspicion on the part of the subjects. Instead we followed the policy of introducing varied problem situations, all of which had the common property of satisfying the main conditions for the stage in question. Pitching a tent to sleep in, preparing a meal when hungry (with ingredients in bulk form), or building a rope bridge cannot be carried out by one person alone but require cooperation of all group members. Therefore, these activities satisfied the main characteristics of conditions for Stage 1, even though they require varied exertion from different groups of muscles.

We feel that this brief mention of the procedural considerations common to all three stages would be incomplete without calling attention to the very *bounds* within which the interaction was taking place and activities were being carried out. At all points of this report, it should be kept in mind that the subjects came from a given sociocultural setting that determined the overall properties of their interaction in ingroup and intergroup relations (see Chapter 2). The experimental conditions were effective within these bounds. Without keeping this in mind, it would be difficult, for example, to understand why both groups were eager to challenge each other in a competitive activity the moment they learned of the presence of another group in the camp (end of Stage 1); and why, after the groups had hurled unpleasant words at each other at the first competitive encounter, the winning team would give three cheers for the losers during the first days of Stage 2.

Even in ingroup activities, the techniques and methods in problem solving may be greatly influenced by the particular structure and norms of the group in question and by properties and values of the sociocultural setting. Certainly these methods vary from culture to culture. Therefore, this report places no special emphasis on whether a group adopted this or that method of problem solution. In certain cultures, there would probably have been a greater tendency to resort to the decision of a leader or an authority figure than found here.

The second point we must mention in this matter of the bounds for the interaction process is the role of staff members. The main function of counselors and other staff members was deliberately specified to be that of producing problem situations through setting appropriate stimulus conditions at appropriate times, in terms of the motivational state of the subjects at the time, using verbal prompting as little as possible (see Chapter 3).

An important factor in the initiation or continuation of activity is the presence, words, and deeds of staff members (junior counselors, participant observers, and other camp authorities). Even seemingly unimportant silence or prompting or negation during interaction in problem situations may greatly influence the direction activities take. We cannot say, in spite of all our efforts, that we succeeded in eliminating this factor altogether. The subjects always knew, whether they were conscious of it all the time or not, that staff members were there; that they could always appeal to them; and that they represented the ultimate authority in setting bounds. For example, at the time of exhibiting courage and bravery while engaged in group activities, the whole psychological trend might have been reversed if the subjects had been deprived of the security that the staff members afforded.

Another factor that sets bounds on the particular type of interaction among subjects is their age level. Eleven-year-old boys are certainly not to be taken as adults, nor their behavior in groups as identical with that of adult groups. Neither can the issues conducive to friction and cooperation between two groups of 11-year-old boys in an experimentally conducted camp situation be the grim and lasting problems that sometimes prevail between groups of adults. On the other hand, at this age level, ego functioning (hence group relatedness or identification) is carried on at a conceptual level. It would have been preferable to carry out the experiment with older subjects if that had been feasible. Originally, our hypotheses were derived from a survey of literature on ingroup and intergroup relations of older subjects. Validation of these hypotheses with subjects of the age level we used should have implications for future experiments with older subjects.

Notes on Data Collection

A special point was made that the participant observers always be close to their respective groups. Each participant observer spent at least 12 hours a day observing his group. Allowing for the fact that one group came to camp one day earlier, the hours participant observers alone spent observing each group (not counting observation time of other staff members) were 240 and 252 hours respectively, or a total of 492 hours for both groups. The participant observers jotted their notes in short form, out of view of the subjects, as soon as possible after an event occurred; then they expanded their notes during the afternoon rest period and after the subjects went to sleep around 9:30 P.M. At that time, the observers wrote a complete report of observations for the day and made their ratings. An additional source of data at some crucial points consisted of subjects' answers and reactions in response to naive questions by staff members who could appropriately ask about events because they had not been present when the events occurred.

In addition to the observational reports, 1,200 pictures were taken during the three-week period. To attract as little attention to the picture taking as possible, staff members, in front of the subjects as they arrived at the bus that would take them to camp, acted like shutterbugs—conspicuously taking pictures of every conceivable object in the vicinity. Conversations were recorded by a hidden tape recorder at some choice points, without the awareness of the subjects. Plans also called for portable recorders to be used in a candid way but unfortunately they did not materialize because our order for two portable recorders could not be filled at the proper time.

Stage 1: Experimental Formation of Ingroups

The focal concern of this study is intergroup relations. Extrapolations from interpersonal relations, or even from ingroup relations, have given us inadequate accounts missing crucial properties that make the topic of intergroup relations so vital today.[1] Therefore, this experiment studied intergroup relations as relations between actual ingroups and their respective members.

Rather than selecting existing groups, whose structures and norms were already formed and who had perhaps established norms toward various other groups of peers in prior intergroup contacts, the experiment started with the formation of ingroups, through controlling conditions of interaction, among individuals who were not previously acquainted. Recall that the members of each group were homogeneous in terms of sociocultural, economic, and educational backgrounds, and so on. The rest of this chapter summarizes the formation of group structures, norms, and attitudes manifested in relation to other ingroup members and toward places, persons, and objects with functional relevance to group activities.

Observation and ratings of ingroup structure and functioning did not stop at the end of Stage 1. Throughout Stage 2 (intergroup friction) and Stage 3 (intergroup integration) we continued to collect data on ingroup structure and functioning. Reciprocal effects of ingroup and intergroup relations were one of the focal points of concentration throughout.

As noted in earlier chapters, since functional relations between groups would certainly affect the formation of ingroups and their structures, the two groups of subjects were kept apart during Stage 1. Until the last days of that stage, the groups at no time had contact with one another.

One group was brought to the site on June 19, 1954, and the other on June 20, at a time when the first group was out of the immediate camp grounds on a cookout. As described in Chapter 3, because of the size and layout of the site, it was possible to center some activities of the two groups in different areas simultaneously. Separation was

---

1. See M. Sherif and C. W. Sherif, *Groups in Harmony and Tension* (New York: Harper, 1953), Chapters 1, 2, and 8.

further maintained by staggering scheduled activities (e.g., meals) for the two groups and by careful timing. Toward the end of Stage 1, in preparation for the period of intergroup relations to follow, subjects were allowed to discover definitely that there were two groups in camp.

To test our hypotheses for Stage 1, conditions consisted of activities and problem situations embodying goals with common appeal to the individuals and requiring interdependent activities for their attainment. The characteristics of conditions for this stage were set up on the basis of the period of ingroup formation in the 1949 and 1953 intergroup studies (see Chapter 2).

One activity that appealed greatly to every subject was competitive team sports, especially baseball. At one time or another, all asked about the possibility of playing baseball with another group; some even brought this up on the bus going to camp. Since competitive sport between teams composed of members of the same group could not be considered an interdependent, cooperative activity, team play was not included in the activities of Stage 1. Competitive games between teams were put off until Stage 2 (intergroup relations), with a great deal of planning, by using other activities, many of which were highly desirable to the boys—"work up" games in which group members rotated positions and exhibited their skill—and by the apparent lack of another team to play.

Following a summary running account of interaction events in each of the two groups, evidence related to the hypotheses for Stage 1 will be reported briefly.

For the sake of continuity and clarity, throughout this report the groups are called the *Rattlers* and the *Eagles*. However, it should be kept in mind that the groups did not have names when Stage 1 started and only adopted them toward the last days of the stage. For the Rattlers, who arrived first, Stage 1 lasted eight days, and for the Eagles, seven days.

Proper names used in no case correspond to real names of the subjects.

Rattler Group

Subjects were picked up in Oklahoma City at two stops. Since one boy was late at the first stop, the waiting period at the second stop (half an hour) permitted the formation of a friendship cluster of four boys that was evident on the bus in seating arrangements, a paper-wad game, and the inquiry whether "us south-siders" could stay together. Conversation on the bus concerned fathers' occupations, respective schools and ball teams, possessions, and favored activities.

Once at camp, boys were allowed to choose their bunks. The south-side boys chose neighboring bunks. At the campfire after supper, the boys selected Brown (the largest boy in the south-side clique and in the entire group) to make out a list of swimming buddies in anticipation of their most preferred activity.

At breakfast on day 2, saying grace was proposed and Brown did it. After the boys arranged church services, Simpson (who had been active on the bus) led group singing, although opposed by south-siders. On a trip to Robbers Cave, Brown and Simpson were in the lead.

After lunch, the boys "discovered" the swimming hole upstream and the campsite. They suggested improvements (such as a rock approach and diving board) and began work on them after a swim. Brown directed activity in the water and at work. Mills organized a rock-moving chain that was effective. The boys decided to stay at the "hideout" (upper camp) for supper and were furnished hamburger and other bulk ingredients, necessitating interdependent specialized efforts by all, which Simpson directed—cutting the watermelon himself. They discussed further improvements to the area, most of the suggestions being directed to Brown.

The next morning a canoe, which had simply been placed near the cabin, was transported by the boys overland to the upstream hideout, Brown directing the operation and Simpson showing the path (see Figure 4.1). The need for a latrine at the hideout was posed by staff. Brown handed the shovel to Simpson, and all helped in turn, the smallest boy finishing the task. Brown's tendency to play favorites in the use of the canoe and in work led Swift (a south-sider) to complain, in effect, "We're tired of just doing the things he leaves over."

Mills hurt his toe but did not mention it until it was discovered at bedtime. This incident marked the beginnings of a norm for being "tough" (not a sissy or cry-baby). Subsequently, injured members did not complain or cry, desiring to continue even the most strenuous activities if staff permitted. Related to this norm of toughness was group approval of cursing, which became widespread in the Rattler group. During a campfire at Stone Corral, the boys enthusiastically planned an overnight hike further upstream.

On day 4 the boys organized transportation of equipment to the reservoir and selected advance scouts. Brown carried a light load. Mills soon took over leading the party, with Simpson and Martin doing more than their share of the work. Mills's choice of a campsite was accepted even by Brown. Mills directed the securing of water and preparation of food, with various boys performing specialized tasks. Barton and Hill (low status) tried to climb the dam. Then Mills organized this activity into a game with a definite order of participation and rules for maintaining position. The boys started to pitch tents by pairs; but an approaching storm and an encounter with a rattlesnake posed the difficult problem of rapidly erecting a sturdier single tent, in which all cooperated.

The next morning the "toughness" norm was revealed on the trip home (led by Mills) over the hills and rocks, with full packs and with only one rest stop. Upon arrival, beds and personal gear were found outside the cabin. Staff explained that the cabin had been fumigated (an excuse to see how the boys would reinstall themselves). In moving back, Mills chose a bed between Brown and Newman (the two top erstwhile south-siders); the other two south-siders moved to other parts of the cabin. The subclique was clearly integrated with the rest of the group. Mills put up a "Home Sweet Home" sign.

Staff at last yielded to the boys' pleas for canteen supplies, requesting that they list only eight items on the grounds that the camp could not afford to have leftovers. Agreement on eight items was reached, and Mills was selected to announce the results.

By day 6 the route to the hideout was standard and preferred to an easier one. Boys planned the activities for the day. Swimming at Camp One (standard name for the hideout) was first. Allen, Barton, and Hill (low status) were upset to find paper cups at the hideout (probably left by the group), speculating resentfully that "outsiders" had been there. A softball workout followed, with members accepting decisions of the rest of the group on plays, except Mills, who changed a decision in his own favor. During the rest period, Mills started tossing pine cones and ended up in a tree being pelted by all the others and shouting "Where's my fellow men?" A boy replied, "Look at our leader!" (The "clown" role often kept Mills in the center of activity.)

A group treasure hunt was held by staff in which all members had to be present at the reading of each note to receive the reward of $10, to be spent as the group chose. Hardball equipment was chosen, as

Figure 4.1 Rattler group: representative activities during ingroup formation (Stage 1)

Rattlers' first exploration of Robbers Cave

Carrying their canoe to the swimming hole at their hideout

Selecting tent poles to take on their overnight hike

Practicing tent pitching

Reading a clue on the group treasure hunt

Preparing and serving a meal

Playing the spontaneously organized dam-climbing game on a campout

Skits at the Stone Corral during one of their evening campfires

suggested by Mills, who had Martin write what he called "my proposal." Mills opened nominations for baseball captain, supporting Simpson (who was selected) and choosing his own position.

Caps and T-shirts were available through the canteen for purchase at nominal cost. Mills asked if "Tom Hale" (name of the Boy Scout campsite) would be on them. The staff reply was negative. Harrison (middle status) suggested putting "Robbers Cave Robbers" on them. Later, Mills proposed stenciling "Tom Hale Rattlers" on the shirts, drew a rattler design, and requested orange and black paint, all of which was approved by the group.

The next morning the boys, with staff assistance, stenciled shirts and hats. Mills selected white material available for crafts for a flag with the same design. Staff proposed practice at tent pitching. It was undertaken in disorganized fashion. Baseball practice revealed stabilization of playing positions.

After supper, the group was allowed to wander within hearing distance of the Eagles, who were playing on the ball diamond. The immediate reaction was to "run them off" and "challenge them." After this incident, Harris (who had had to surrender the catcher's position to Hill because of a hurt hand) cried bitterly. Hill and Martin comforted him, and he stopped crying when Mills asked him to read a comic book aloud.

At baseball workout the next day, the group noted improvements they had made on the diamond and declared, "Now this is *our* diamond." The boys revealed a consciousness of the other group by frequent reference to "our baseball diamond," "our Upper Camp," "our Stone Corral." That afternoon the staff informed the group that there was another group in camp and that they wanted to challenge the Rattlers at baseball. The reaction: "They can't. We'll challenge them first. . . . They've got a nerve. . . ." Other activities in which they could be challenged were mentioned, including tent pitching. Now that tent pitching appeared a competitive activity, it was enthusiastically supported even by those formerly opposing it. The boys initiated shifts in work positions, which produced an amazing change in execution of the task. All members cheered the results.

At the hideout, Everett (a nonswimmer when camp started) began to swim a little. He was praised by all, and for the first time the others called him by his preferred nickname. Simpson yelled, "Come on, dive off the board!" All members in the water formed a large protective circle into which Everett dived after a full 2 minutes of hesitation and reassurance from the others. While he repeated the performance, little Barton, a frightened nonswimmer, plunged forward and started swimming a little too. He was called to the board and he too jumped in. Allen, a swimmer who was afraid to go off the board, then followed. Harrison, on the bank with an injured hand, was assured by the others that when his hand was healed they would all help him "so that we will *all* be able to swim." This event, which was completely spontaneous, was most effective in building group solidarity and morale. That evening the boys planned and held an enthusiastic campfire at the Stone Corral. Group skits were organized by Mills, and Brown "shone" in an individual act.

Eagle Group

The bus picking up these 11 subjects was on time at both stops so that little prior interaction was possible. Conversation on the bus started concerning Clark's bugle, which he played on request. The boys exchanged information concerning schools attended, respective standings of baseball teams, and families. Upon arrival at camp, free choice of bunks and seats at supper was allowed. At campfire, at their "hideout" camp, Myers built the fire, then disagreed with others on the proper method of roasting marshmallows. Craig stopped the argument, saying; "You're not the boss." Mason asked if they could take down a sign left by earlier campers. One boy proposed "O. U. Camp" as a name for the spot, but the boys reached no decision until the next day, when Myers suggested putting up an O. U. Camp sign as something already "decided."

On day 2, Clark was last to wake and therefore couldn't play reveille on the bugle. Later in the week, it became standard procedure for the first boy up to awaken Clark, who then woke the rest with the bugle. The boys asked to take the canoe placed near their cabin on a hike downstream after breakfast. Division of labor was complete: five boys carrying the canoe, five others supplies (including lengths of heavy rope), and one the board and paint for the O. U. Camp sign (see Figure 4.2). When Davis stopped carrying the canoe, Craig called him into line. As they prepared to swim at the hideout area, Bryan suggested a bridge across the stream. After the boys took the initiative along these lines, they were told by staff they could use the rope for

Figure 4.2 Eagle group: representative activities during ingroup formation (Stage 1)

Carrying their canoe and equipment to their hideout

Carrying rope, which was used to make a bridge, to their hideout

Putting up a sign at their swimming hole, "Moccasin Creek"

On their rope bridge over Moccasin Creek

Painting the sign for their campsite, "O.U. Camp"

Down the trail with packs and equipment for an overnight hike

Meal preparation: cutting and distributing meat

Cutting a watermelon

this purpose. During swimming, Craig took over the canoe, letting one, then another boy paddle and hitting boys who hung on the back. Mason wanted to get in the water to pull a big rope across for a bridge. All volunteered to help, and through great effort, the boys and staff completed the task.

In the afternoon when the boys returned to the hideout for a swim and supper, the rope bridge was completed, as agreed, through Mason's initiative. Craig walked the bridge about 15 feet before falling in, Mason less, and Myers about the same. When Cutler tried, someone said, "He won't make it very far," and there was amazement when he crossed it. The prediction that Cutler could not do as well as Craig and the others reveals the development of differential expectations in line with emerging status relationships within the group. The astonishment at Cutler's success indicates that some standardization of these expectations had already taken place on the second day.

When the boys were hungry, Myers ferried them to the opposite bank where they had left the food for supper. He made so many unpleasant comments to the boys that later he heard them discussing him negatively. As a result, Myers actively tried to be agreeable the next day.

A large copperhead snake was seen 8 feet away from the campsite. After the staff threw at it, the boys were permitted to help kill it. They discussed snakes at length during food preparation. All but one of the boys took over jobs in preparing the meal. After supper a snake was seen in the water, and several boys said they didn't want to swim there again. The boys dubbed this place Moccasin Creek that night. In spite of the discussion, they returned to the spot the next morning.

Because the Eagles had three possible swimming spots, discussions arose repeatedly during the next few days about where they would swim. The decision on the third morning was for Moccasin Creek. Wilson said he heard a rattler every time they passed a particular spot, which was christened Rattlesnake Bay. Davis proposed that the campfire area across the stream should be called Copperhead Hill because of the snake killed there. These names were used in all subsequent references to these places. The boys painted signs to label Moccasin Creek and Copperhead Hill.

Spontaneous discussion among the boys on the need for window screens on the cabin found opinion divided, Craig saying they were unnecessary. A later vote to request screens was favorable, and when the screens arrived three days later, Craig was among the first making immediate efforts to install them.

At workout softball near their cabin, Mason stood out as the best player. Craig and Davis bawled out Myers for clowning (playing ball was serious to these boys).

Since the boys had requested a campout, a hike to the reservoir started on day 4. The boys carried six small tents, packs, and other equipment. Myers astounded everyone by carrying tents in addition to his pack. Upon arrival, Mason said the reservoir wouldn't be good for swimming. Three boys who didn't go swimming volunteered to fix lunch. After lunch, Davis pointed out all of the features of this campsite that were inferior to Moccasin Creek. His requested vote to return there went six to five against returning. One by one, he persuaded others to switch their votes to favor leaving. Therefore, after a rest period, Craig directed transportation of supplies on the homeward trip. When Myers kept the group waiting while he returned for a forgotten bathing suit, he was pelted with pebbles, but showed no signs of being disturbed.

At Moccasin Creek, Myers swam without his suit and was christened Nudie. (This became the standard mode of swimming after Mason took it up the next day.) Several staff members were present at the group's cookout at Moccasin Creek. Craig organized its preparation and played host. The boys told the staff that Moccasin Creek was *several times better* than the reservoir for swimming and camping (which was not objectively true). A song introduced by Craig on the bus was now called "our song."

After breakfast on the fifth day, the boys were told to select eight items for the camp canteen, which they had been requesting for days. Craig and Davis took the lead in making suggestions, and Craig wrote them down. He accepted Myers's formulation for some terms to make them more general to cover more items. At softball workout Mason, the best player, accepted Craig's decision that he was "out" at second.

On the group treasure hunt, some members waited for Craig and handed him the notes to read. Suggestions by middle- and low-status members on how to spend the $10 reward were rejected in favor of Davis's proposal (hardball equipment), which was backed by Craig, who wrote down the decision and told the boys to line up to sign it. After lunch, Craig *lectured* about 10 minutes on the various baseball positions and who played them.

While screens were being put up on the sixth day, Boyd and Davis (who had shown signs of homesickness, especially at night) discussed home with Mason, who also became nostalgic as the conversation continued. Craig, Myers, McGraw, and Wilson derided homesickness. Wilson told Boyd he was homesick because he got too many letters from home.

At lunch it was mentioned that Craig had given each boy a number. During practice with the new hardball equipment, everyone ignored Myers when he refused to accept a decision and simply left him to retire from base. Craig was not ignored when he objected to an adverse ruling, but he gave in with some grumbling. During the practice, Wilson heard the other group playing at a distance and referred to "those nigger campers." Cutler asked if the Eagles could play them, and Craig instructed the staff to "ask those campers to play with us."

On the last day of Stage 1, staff decided to permit Davis and Boyd to go home, which they had requested the previous night. These boys had endured intermittent homesickness for several days. Boyd was occasionally reduced to tears even in the daytime. It was belatedly discovered that the boy had left a camp the previous summer for the same reason. Had this been known, he would not have been chosen as a subject. Davis had not been to camp before, and seemed to become homesick chiefly at night. He often went to Boyd to comfort him, and then ended up tearful too. His status was high but had been falling because he wanted to go home. Since the experiment was not set up to deal with homesickness and it would have run counter to the design to exert outside efforts to keep individuals in the group, the departure of these two boys was quietly arranged. When the group asked where they had gone, Craig said, "Things are going to be better around here now." Wilson (scornfully): "They chickened out." Mason: "They are the only boys who will." (Mason himself had not been immune to their talk of home on previous days.)

The group entered enthusiastically into tumbling, wrestling, and tent pitching. They asked when they could play the other team in baseball and decided to elect a captain. Craig, who by this time was clearly the leader, nominated Mason, and the rest voiced agreement.

Later in the day, Myers asked if the other group had a name. Staff replied they weren't sure. Myers commented that their group needed a name. Craig suggested "Eagles." Clark suggested "Rattlesnake Biters," and then said he didn't like that himself. Craig's suggestion was supported. Myers said they could make a flag to take on the field when they played. Craig asked staff to help cut a stencil of "Tom Hale Eagles" to put on T-shirts they had decided to purchase, and proposed putting an "E" on their caps. Mason said he didn't want his shirt stenciled, but Craig told him he couldn't play if he didn't do it. At ball practice, everyone criticized Lane (low status) for not playing well; but nothing was said when Mason or Craig missed a ball. Craig told staff the group had decided to sleep out in a tent that night.

Summary of Hypotheses and Results: Stage 1

The above accounts of interaction during Stage 1 in the Rattler and Eagle groups hold the pith condensed from a bulk of observational material, recordings, and pictures. The following discussion considers observational data further in relation to the hypotheses for this stage, necessarily in highly abbreviated form.

Hypothesis 1 (Stage 1)

A definite group structure consisting of differentiated status positions and reciprocal roles will be produced when a number of individuals (without previously established interpersonal relations) interact with one another under conditions that situationally embody goals that have common appeal value to the individuals, and that require interdependent activities for their attainment.

Experimental conditions with these characteristics were varied, requiring more or less equipment, occurring only once or being repeated over and over. Many of the specific conditions for the two groups were in common because they were introduced deliberately as part of the experiment. Among these common conditions were the group treasure hunts, which required joint efforts by all members in tracing the path, winning the reward, and deciding how to use it; another was the canteen problem, which staff posed by limiting the number of items for the much-desired canteen to eight.

Other conditions satisfying the characteristics of Stage 1 arose as problem situations in both groups because both groups had similar interests, and interaction in each took place in terrain common to the camp. Many activities were suggested by subjects as pastimes they especially preferred. To a great extent, subjects were allowed to engage in these activities at the times and as often as they chose (the only limitations being health considerations and the occasional necessity of temporary postponement to keep the two groups separate). Out of these pastimes preferred by both groups (like swimming, boating, hiking, camping out, baseball) a great variety of problem situations arose that required interdependent activities, and many were similar for both groups. For example, transportation of boats and equipment, planning and executing hikes, improving swimming places (with a rock approach and diving board for Rattlers and a bridge for Eagles), organizing campfires, building fires, and preparing meals in the woods with bulk ingredients (requiring division of labor in preparing hamburger, cutting chunks of meat, mixing Kool Aid, cutting watermelon, etc.) were problems common to both groups.

On the other hand, some conditions were unique to one group, because of each group's particular location in the outdoor setting, special interests, and so forth. For example, the Eagles' cabin was closer to the water than the Rattlers', and a problem arose in the Eagle group that was not at all prominent for the Rattlers. On day 3, the Eagles discussed the need for screens twice during the day, and when the screens arrived on day 6, joined to install them. Another problem situation arising from the particular situation of the Eagles was where to swim. Three spots were easily accessible (boat dock, Rattlesnake Bay, Moccasin Creek), and the proposals, counterproposals, persuasions, and decisions on this topic were frequent (e.g., two occasions on day 3, one on day 4, and one on day 6). The Rattlers swam at their hideout and there was no problem of deciding where. A number of interdependent activities embodying common goals arose that were peculiar to the Rattlers. One was the climbing game that Mills organized after two group members climbed the dam. The point of this game was to achieve the top without backsliding and to keep in the same position each time. Like most games with rules, it required reciprocal regulation along with exhibition of skill by individuals. A spontaneous activity peculiar to the Rattlers, which met experimental conditions even better, was their use of swimmer escorts and a protective circle to encourage a new swimmer to dive, and then to encourage other nonswimmers and nondivers. This activity involved almost the entire group.

As a result of repeated interaction in a variety of activities, all of which embodied both goals common to the individuals and interde-

TABLE 4.1
Status ratings by participant observers,
last two days of Stage 1

Rattlers		Eagles[a]	
Day 7	*Day 8*	*Day 6*	*Day 7*
Mills	Mills	Craig	Craig
Simpson	Simpson	[Davis]–Mason	Mason
Martin	Martin	Clark–Myers–Wilson	Myers
Brown	Brown	McGraw–Bryan–Cutler	Clark
Allen	Newman	[Boyd]	Wilson
Newman	Allen	Lane	Bryan
Swift	Harrison		McGraw
Harrison	Swift		Cutler
Barton	Barton		Lane
Hill	Everett		
Everett	Hill		

[a]Since Eagles came to camp one day later, day 7 was the last day of Stage 1 for them. (Names in brackets left camp because of homesickness.)

pendent efforts, status structures were stabilized by the end of Stage 1. One source of evidence is that the daily status ratings by participant observers of their respective groups correspond closely for the last several days. Table 4.1 shows a list of status ratings by participant observers of the Rattler and Eagle groups on the last two days of Stage 1.

On the last day of Stage 1, the participant observer of each group and another observer familiar with the group in question made *independent* status ratings of the respective groups. Table 4.2 gives rank order correlation between independent status ratings for two observers for each group.

At this point sociometric choices would have provided a further check on observational evidence and ratings, as planned in the study design (see Chapter 1). However, as noted earlier, it was decided that repetition of sociometric procedures three times (after each stage) during such a brief period might arouse the suspicion of subjects and invalidate the results. Therefore, sociometric choices were obtained only for Stages 2 and 3.

This was the crucial point at which status relations of the developing ingroups were to be tapped through judgmental indices obtained in relation to performance throwing handballs at a target (see Chapter 2). Our previous research had shown that differential judgments of

TABLE 4.2
*Rank-order correlation between independent status ratings by
two observers for each experimental group*

Group	rho	t	p
Rattlers	.919	6.90	<.001
Eagles	.984	13.01	<.001

performance on a task in an unstructured situation may serve as indices of the relative status of the person whose performance is being
judged. Attempts to carry out this unit at the end of Stage 1 met with
disappointment owing to mechanical failure of the apparatus, which
did not register the actual score attained. Since the actual scores are a
critical part of the data, the experiment could not be carried out without remedying the mechanism, which proved impossible at the time.
(The failure was due in part to loss of tension by brass and phosphor-
bronze spring contacts, but chiefly to a thin film of rust that formed
on bolt-base contacts as a result of high local humidity at night.)

On the basis of observational data and observers' ratings, it was
considered that Stage 1 had satisfied the criterion for formation of
group structure under conditions of interdependent activity toward
goals with common appeal value to individual members.

Implications for Group Structure and Leadership

Before continuing to other hypotheses for Stage 1, certain characteristics of the group structures at this time are worth considering
briefly because of their implications for theory and research in this
area, particularly that on leadership. First, the group structures at the
end of Stage 1 were not static or rigid. Fluctuations as a result of
changed conditions and status strivings of members were noted. On
the other hand, these groups had lived and interacted together for an
entire week. They were doubtless stabilized to a considerably greater
extent than many experimental groups currently employed in small
group and leadership research, which meet periodically for much
shorter periods of time and are usually set to tasks provided entirely
by the experimenter. It is possible, therefore, that our findings may be
revealing in relation to current controversies over group structure and
the stability of leadership.

It is frequently contended that a hierarchy is not necessarily a general feature of group structure and that multiple leadership frequently exists. This contention is based on the finding that in "leaderless group" situations, leadership not infrequently changes hands with the task from situation to situation, and that differentiation of other functions varies similarly. This finding is repeatedly verified and is perfectly reasonable for such situations.

However, in the present study, which is designed as a prototype of lifelike interaction in varied situations, all embodying common and valued goals, differentiation of functions within the group took place *over a period of time along hierarchical lines*. This is indeed characteristic of lasting groups whose members are highly motivated in the direction of group goals in everyday life.

The evidence for this hierarchy is not so much in the manner of treating others within the group as in the extent to which initiative (suggestions, directions, etc.) in group activities is taken, and whether or not such initiative is *effective* (viz., whether suggestions are accepted, plans tried out, etc.). The ratings by participant observers in the present study were based mainly on the extent to which each member took such initiative and the relative *effectiveness* of these efforts.

Here, concrete examples may make the theoretical point clear. Many members in each experimental group showed "leadership" in the special sense of initiating activities, making suggestions, and carrying through tasks in various situations. However, by the end of Stage 1, each group had, and recognized that they had, a "leader" (Mills in the Rattlers and Craig in the Eagles). At this time, initiative by others in the form of suggestions, plans, or action was effective *when* the leader approved it. When he did not, the matter was ordinarily dropped, perhaps after an argument. In both groups, the leaders effectively chose baseball captains by backing their choices. Baseball was extremely important to these boys, but the baseball captain *in Stage 1* was in neither case the group leader. In both groups the leader told the baseball captain which position he (the leader) would play. Two examples were given in the running accounts, and there were many more instances, of the leader taking liberties in baseball and not being censured by the captain. (The exception to this was when Craig of the Eagles wanted to umpire; the entire group—not just Mason, the captain—told him he could not, that staff should umpire, and he accepted this. In short, he was exceeding the bounds of his leadership,

and he accepted the group's judgment. Note Craig's behavior in intergroup competition in Stage 2 and its effects on his position.) On occasion, a high-status Rattler (Brown) was observed to *hold* the ball so
that Mills could get in safe. Craig told Mason, the Eagle captain, he
couldn't play if he didn't have his shirt stenciled with the group insignia.

The findings in Stage 1 of this experiment do reveal initiative displayed by various group members on different occasions. They do *not*
reveal "multiple leadership" in the sense of shifts in the *control* of
group activities with shifts from one situation or task unit to the next,
*once group structure was stabilized as a result of continuing interaction over
a time span.*

Hypothesis 1a (Stage 1)

If a definite group structure develops, it will be reflected in a consistent
pattern in directions of communication. The specific pattern in directions of
communications will be as follows: *the higher the status of a group member the
greater the frequency of suggestions (for group activities) addressed to him.*

Because of the intense and varied demands, both scientific and
practical, placed on the participant observers, the observational data
do not contain the precise quantitative evidence needed to evaluate
this hypothesis. Summaries representing the scanty evidence available are presented here as suggestive for future research.

Rattler Group

On day 1 Brown was elected to work out a buddy system. Suggestions were made to him.

On day 2, in discussion on work at the hideout, suggestions were
made directly to Brown by Mills, Swift, Simpson, and others.

On day 3, in the morning, Brown clearly ran the boat project, with
queries and suggestions coming to him and decisions made by him. In
the afternoon, during work on the diving board, lower-level members
stopped communicating with Brown. Mills organized them. Brown's
slip from leadership was noted.

On day 6 Mills started the pine cone battle, involving all boys and
centering communication toward Mills. The observer noted frequent
instances from day 1 in which Mills had made himself the center of

attention and in which he had circulated among the group communicating with both high- and low-status members. In the afternoon, during the discussion of how to spend the treasure hunt reward ($10), suggestions and remarks were counted, with the following results: to Mills—16; to others—1; at large—6. Suggestions during discussions of T-shirt and flag insignia were made to Mills, who accepted some of them but largely determined what was to be done himself and got group approval.

On day 8, at the campfire, Mills organized skits. Suggestions and requests came to him ("Let me, A. . . . !"). He included almost every boy at one time or another. He also encouraged Brown and Simpson in their individual performances.

Eagle Group

On day 5, during the group treasure hunt, Craig found only one note, but those who found five others gave them to him to read to the group. In discussion of how to spend the reward, suggestions by middle- and low-status members were ignored. Davis's suggestion (hardball equipment) was backed by Craig, who called for a vote, declared the proposal passed, wrote it down, and told others to line up to sign it. In deciding on eight items for the camp canteen, Craig and Davis made most suggestions. Other suggestions were directed toward these two, but many were ignored, and Craig put his or Davis's suggestions in their stead. Several items were decided upon by these two without consulting the group. In writing down items, Craig accepted Myers's formulations for several, which made them more general.

This evidence, presented as suggestive, is in line with the hypothesis.

Hypothesis 2 (Stage 1)

When individuals interact under conditions stated in hypothesis 1, concomitant with the formulation of group structure, norms will be standardized regulating their behavior in relations with one another and in practices and activities commonly engaged in.

As the ingroup structures of the Rattlers and Eagles became delineated, members formed attitudes toward objects and places of functional importance to them, appropriating these objects as "ours."

Rattlers

On day 2, the group explored upstream where they "found" their swimming hole and hideout. By day 6, this was "our Upper Camp" and the cabin was "home." When paper cups were found at the hideout, resentment was strong against supposed intruders.

The ball diamond was discovered on day 5, with negative reaction. Play and improvements on day 6 contributed to appropriation. On day 8 (after hearing the Eagles on it), the group called the ball diamond "ours."

The Stone Corral (behind Robbers Cave) was appropriated as "ours" and used for campfires.

Eagles

Moccasin Creek was used for swimming on day 2 and the boys decided to swim there in the future, leaving equipment there. They did so in spite of seeing snakes there, returning to it in preference to the reservoir (which was beautiful). Signs naming Moccasin Creek and Copperhead Hill (across the stream) were put up on day 4. Pictures of this area were the exclusive subject of the arts and crafts period on day 5.

The group renamed the campfire circle O. U. Camp on the first night, and put up a sign labeling it.

Attitudes toward other members of the ingroup and persons important in the group's functioning were stabilized, as is particularly evident in the case of individuals whose behavior was for some reason prominent within the group. Some of these standardizations were temporary, while others were more enduring. An example of the latter is the nickname Red for Brown (Rattlers), which typified his coloring and probably his size and "toughness." Among the Eagles, Myers, as noted briefly in the summary of interaction, engaged in considerable showing off during the first days. At one time, while preparing a fire, he spoke of himself with approval as "Smart Bob." Several boys echoed "Dumb Bob! Crazy-mixed-up Bob!" Such terms were used on occasion throughout this stage, although Myers began to make definite efforts to be accepted. A more enduring nickname for Myers was Nudie, given when he started swimming in the nude. At his suggestion the group occasionally referred to themselves with hilarity as RCNCI (Robbers Cave Nudist Colony, Inc.). Other temporary nicknames in the Eagle group were Marilyn Monroe or just Marilyn for a boy who gave a burlesque dance one night; and Screwball, senior, and Screwball, junior, for staff members.

Norms were standardized in both groups in relation to experiences and behavior that became important to the group. The "toughness" norm among Rattlers was a notable example. At various times, Mills, Martin, Simpson, and Harrison all carried on in rather strenuous activities with injuries (all minor). The staff had to remember to check Martin's bruised knee and wrist because he never mentioned them. Harrison did not cry when he injured his hand, but did cry later when he found out that it would keep him from the catcher's position, and members sympathized with him. Swift did not conform to this "toughness" norm and was completely ignored when he cried. As noted, along with the "toughness" norm went a definite approval of cursing. "Toughness" and cursing are both norms of conduct among groups in the larger social setting; they were not original to the Rattlers. However, these norms were not standardized among the Eagles. On the contrary, cursing was definitely discouraged in the Eagle group (as will be seen in Stage 2), and even Craig, the leader, indulged in crying at injuries.

In the Eagle group, Davis and Boyd were ridiculed for about the last three days for being homesick. A definite norm against being homesick was standardized, in relation to which these two were seen as deviant. Mason, who had on occasion talked longingly of home, showed no signs of wanting to go home in Stage 1 after the norm became established. Swimming in the nude was another norm that was stabilized in the Eagle group. The Rattlers never took up this practice.

In both groups, methods of rotation or *taking turns* were standardized for saying grace at meals. These activities were initially regulated verbally by high-status members but came in time to be self-regulating. In the Rattler group, Brown passed the duty around for two days; then it was rotated among low-status members. When Mills attained a stable position as leader, he designated the person to say grace. From the seventh day, the order of saying grace was predetermined by the group and was followed without prompting.

During the early part of Stage 1 in the Eagle group, Davis usually told one of the boys to give thanks after he (Davis) had figured out which one had not said grace as many times as the others. Upon losing track, Davis asked each of the boys to state how many times he had said it. When Davis became homesick, Craig took over the function for a short while, but soon quit trying to keep track of whose turn was next. Thereafter, thanks was given on a volunteer basis, the end result being the same: the boys rotated the duty among themselves.

Spontaneous games (although probably not original) were standardized in both groups: waterball among Eagles with a special "hot potato" rule; among the Rattlers, dam climbing, with definite rules governing order and maintenance of positions, as well as a paper airplane game.

One group product that clearly signifies ingroup delineation is naming the group. The name the Rattlers chose is hardly coincidental in view of the not infrequent sights of and encounters with rattlesnakes, notably during their overnight campout. Significantly enough, the only other suggestion in the Eagle group for a name was Rattlesnake Biters. Eagles adopted their name *after* becoming concerned about the other group in camp. (Myers asked if the other group had a name.)

Both groups had favored songs, the Eagles referring to one consistently as "our song."

In both groups during Stage 1, deviation from norms or from decisions by the group led to being "called down" or ignored. Myers was ignored by the Eagles when he refused to be "out" in baseball. When Swift did not live up to the "toughness" norm, other Rattlers ignored him. Members were chastised verbally by others for not doing their share of work in both groups.

Reactions to the Other Group

When the ingroup began to be clearly delineated, there was a tendency to consider all others as outgroup. Recall the Rattlers' reaction to paper cups at the Upper Camp, which they didn't remember leaving. The Rattlers didn't know another group existed in camp until they heard the Eagles on the ball diamond; but from that time on the outgroup figured prominently in their lives. Hill (Rattler) said, "They better not be in our swimming hole." The next day Simpson heard tourists on the trail just outside of camp premises and was convinced that "those guys" were down at "our diamond" again. When the definite presence of another group was announced, the Rattlers immediately wanted to challenge them, and to be the *first* to challenge.

Performance in all activities that might now become competitive (tent pitching, baseball, etc.) was entered into with more zest and also with more efficiency. Since the efforts to help "all of us" to swim occurred after this, it is possible that even this strictly ingroup activity was influenced by the presence of an outgroup and a desire to excel it in all ways.

The Eagles were informed that another group was in camp three days before the end of Stage 1, but they made no comments on the fact. On the following day, Wilson said he had seen a boy across the grounds, but no one remarked on this. When the Eagles were playing on the ball diamond and heard the Rattlers, Wilson referred to those "nigger campers." Cutler asked to play them. Craig at that time issued a challenge to the Rattlers through staff. The very fact that the Eagles decided to elect a ball captain was in anticipation of playing the Rattlers. The need for a name did not occur to the Eagles until they contemplated playing in competition.

In summary, by the end of Stage 1, as a result of repeated interaction in situations embodying goals common to all individuals and requiring interdependent activity for their attainment, clear-cut ingroup structures and by-products (norms) of the interaction process were stabilized. Discovery of another group of campers brought heightened awareness of "us" and "ours" as contrasted with "outsiders" and "intruders," an intense desire to compete with the other group in team games, and enthusiastic preparation to do so. These developments set the scene for Stage 2.

5

Intergroup Relations: Production of Negative Attitudes Toward the Outgroup

During Stage 1, the experimental conditions that were introduced at times when they had appeal value to the subjects and the interaction processes that arose produced two definite ingroup formations. In time, each group had a definite structure in terms of status for individual members. Each group had its name, symbols of identification, and places and facilities appropriated as "ours." Each group had its preferred songs, practices, and peculiar norms. In short, each group had its particular set of group products. As noted, the groups followed somewhat different rates in developing an organization and emphasized different features in their group products.

Having produced two ingroups independently of each other through control of conditions, we could proceed to the study of relations between the groups through bringing them into functional contact under specified conditions. For reasons mentioned in Chapter 2, the first task was to produce intergroup friction so that we could proceed to the main phase of the study, namely, reduction of intergroup friction.

The distinguishing characteristic of Stage 2 was the interaction of the two groups under controlled conditions that members of the respective groups perceived as competitive and reciprocally frustrating. In other words, the aim of this stage was to control conditions so that each group would see the other as a competitor and likewise as a source of frustration. In planning this stage, we had invaluable experience from our 1953 attempt, in which, at an important point during this friction phase, the source of friction was attributed to the camp administration. At that point and for that reason, the 1953 study had to be terminated.

Stage 2: Experimental Conditions and Behavioral Events

The two ingroups themselves set the stage for the friction phase of intergroup relations. During the last days of Stage 1, both the Rattlers and Eagles became insistent in their desire to challenge the other group of boys to play competitive games, especially baseball. The design of the experiment required a clear-cut stabilization of a definite structure within each group. While the staff ascertained this structure, the Rattlers and Eagles became impatient in their desire to engage in competitive games. When the staff members informed each group that there was another group in the camp area, the challenge was unanimous and enthusiastic. Delaying Stage 2 became increasingly difficult. When the Rattlers heard the other group playing on "their" ball field, they made remarks expressing that they considered others playing there to be an intrusion. Even without coming into physical contact with "those boys at the other end of the camp," the Rattlers had built up a highly competitive mood in relation to them.

The plan for a tournament of contests was made to appear to the subjects as based on their own manifest desire. The tournament plan, therefore, was not formally announced before the participant observers carried on a number of informal talks with their respective groups, explaining that the staff had to make the necessary arrangements. The formal announcement and exhibit of the trophy, prizes, and medals for the tournament were postponed until the second day of Stage 2. The first day was devoted to informal talk by staff and members of each group about the tournament, events that it was to include, and prizes. There was no physical or visual contact between groups on this day.

The Rattlers' reaction to the informal announcement was full confidence in their victory. They spent the day talking about the contests and making improvements on the ball field, which they appropriated as their own to such an extent that they spoke of putting a "Keep Off" sign there. They ended by putting their Rattler flag on the backstop. At this time, several Rattlers made threatening remarks about what they would do if anybody bothered their flag.

The Eagles did not exhibit as much enthusiasm as the Rattlers when they first learned about the tournament in this informal way, even though there were a few "Oh, boy!" expressions. They were interested to learn if the other boys were practicing. Wilson and Cutler said, "We'll beat 'em," and several other boys joined in the discussion.

Mason (best athlete in the Eagles) and Simpson (Rattler) had previously been chosen baseball captains in their respective groups. Both boys had been elected captains in consequence of their nomination by the acknowledged leaders of their groups (Craig and Mills). From the time the tournament began, Mason was to come to the foreground as leader in the Eagle group, in athletic as well as other matters, until the end of Stage 2.

Both groups spent most of the day practicing and preparing for coming events. Craig (Eagle leader) attached the Eagle flag to a pole, and another Eagle said, "Our flag shall never touch the ground." At one point during the day, Myers (E) [1] expressed the opinion that "maybe we could make friends with those guys and then somebody would not get mad and have any grudges." On the following day, just before the baseball game started, when the two groups actually set eyes on each other and came into physical contact *for the first time,* derogatory name calling began when this same Myers called one of the Rattlers "Dirty Shirt."

On the second day of Stage 2, the two groups had breakfast at different times. The members of both groups were fascinated at the sight of the tournament exhibit. When it was their turn to come to breakfast, each group saw the exhibit, consisting of a trophy, medals, and 11 four-bladed knives. After each group had breakfast, the staff made the formal announcement of the tournament to each separately, specifying the contest activities to be included in the tournament and the score for each. It was explained that the group making the highest cumulative score in the series of contests would win the trophy, and the individual members of the winning group would receive the prizes (a knife and medal for each).

The prizes had great appeal to the boys. One group had included knives as one of the eight items selected for the canteen list. (The inclusion of knives on the canteen list was to be brought up again by the losers after the tournament was over. The winners were to guard their knives scrupulously. The trophy was so valued by the winners that

---

1. From this point, (E) is used for Eagles, (R) for Rattlers.

they kissed it after they took possession and hid it in a different cabin for safety against possible seizure by the losers.)

The series of events cited in the formal announcement had to be modified, with the consent of both sides, when the tournament started, partly because some events were not very appealing to the subjects and partly because some were decided to be somewhat hazardous. The actual events were completed in four days and included the following:

A. Events whose outcomes could be checked by contestants (victors had to win two out of three contests for the asterisked activities):
  1. First baseball game (day 2)*
  2. First tug-of-war (day 2)*
  3. Second baseball game (day 3)
  4. Second tug-of-war (day 3)
  5. Touch football game (day 4)
  6. First tent pitching (day 4)*
  7. Third baseball game (day 4)
  8. Third tug-of-war (day 5)
  9. Second tent pitching (day 5)
  10. Third tent pitching (day 5)

B. Events judged by staff members separately for the two groups:
  1. First cabin inspection (day 3)
  2. Second cabin inspection (day 4)
  3. Third cabin inspection (day 5)
  4. Skits and songs (day 3)
  5. Treasure hunt (day 5)

The items under category B were included to enable the experimenters to juggle points in such a way that until the final events, both groups would be highly motivated with the hope of winning the prizes. Points had to be juggled in favor of the Eagles, who during the first day of actual competitive encounters (Stage 2, day 2) lost both the first baseball game and the first tug-of-war, the first event by a very small margin and the second in a disorganized way.

Up to the last day, with the procedure of equalizing scores through the category B events, the scores were fairly close together. The score values were indicated by rising thermometers on the official score chart. Staff increased the readings with considerable flourish at meals when all boys, from both groups, were present. This neck-and-neck race in scoring continued until the last day of the tournament, whose outcome hinged on the last event on the afternoon of day 5. This last event was the treasure hunt which, being conducted in the respective camp areas of each group, could be manipulated by the experimenters in a way to ensure the transition of two intact group structures to Stage 3, which is the crucial stage of the study. Since two boys from the Eagle group had been sent home because of homesickness at the end of Stage 1 (see Chapter 4), leaving only nine boys in that group, there was some danger of disorganization of the Eagles if they were defeated. More specifically, Mason's desire to go home might have resurfaced. He had tended somewhat in this direction during Stage 1, probably through his contact with the two boys who left the group. The fact that we could proceed two days after the end of the tournament to Stage 3 indicated that the decision to tip the scales in favor of the Eagles was sound.

Right after the treasure hunt, the two groups were brought together, each on one side of the exhibit of prizes, and the results were announced. The scores received by each group for every event were specified, making the outcome hinge on the treasure hunt. The tournament was declared to have been won by the Eagles through their completion of the treasure hunt in 8 minutes 38 seconds versus 10 minutes 15 seconds for the Rattlers. The Eagles exulted at their victory, jumping up and down, hugging each other, and making sure in loud tones that everyone present was aware of their triumph. On the other hand, the Rattlers were glum and dejected and remained silently seated on the ground.

The series of contests was the main focus of attention for both groups, as manifested in actual physical encounters and practice sessions in preparation for them. Group solidarity was evident in group discussion and in self-justifying and self-glorifying words used in relation to the ingroup. Negative intergroup relations showed in invectives and derogatory terms hurled at the outgroup in actual encounters and in reference to the outgroup in the privacy of the ingroup circle. Various contests had differential effects in producing these attitudinal and behavioral consequences. At least for these 11-year-old boys, the activities that were not too prolonged and that involved direct physical contact were most effective, with the tug-of-war heading the list. The buildup of negative attitudes was cumulative, with rapid spurts at times, as determined by the nature of the encounter. Even though the boys hurled invectives starting with the first contest of the tournament, the norms internalized from the larger social setting concerning "good sportsmanship" were clearly evident for the first two days, as revealed through the custom of giving three cheers for the losers.

After the second day of the tournament, the "good sportsmanship" stated in specific words during the initial period and exhibited after the first contests in this series (especially by the Eagles) gave way, as event followed event, to increased name calling, hurling invectives, and derogation of the outgroup. Relations reached the point that the groups became more and more reluctant to have anything to do with one another. This attitude soon intensified owing to the impact of events taking place after the tournament was over, as we shall see presently.

The first physical encounter of the two groups, their immediate "sizing up" of each other, and the explicit expressions of their rapidly developing attitudes toward each other may have significant implications for the systematic study of the rise of rather sharp ingroup and outgroup delineation and the rapid crystallization of attitudes toward an outgroup when the functional relation involved is one of rivalry. Therefore, a description of this very first contact between the two independently formed ingroups follows:

The Rattlers were first at the ball field (which they considered "ours") as befits the "home team." The Eagles approached with their flag on a pole, singing the menacing notes of the "Dragnet" theme. For a time the two groups looked each other over (see Figure 5.1). Then an Eagle used a derogatory word, a catcall from a Rattler answered him, and the razzing was on. Before the game started, Mason gave a little *lecture* to the Eagles on not getting rattled. As the game got underway, the Rattlers sang, "The first Eagle hit the deck, parley-voo . . . The second Eagle hit the deck, parley-voo . . . ," and so on. Eagles called back at them: "Our pitcher is better than yours." "Our catcher is better than yours." As the game progressed, the Rattlers referred to Wilson (E) as Fatty, Tubby, "Little Black Sambo." Myers, the Eagle of such goodwill prior to the game, was especially active in calling out at the Rattlers, although Craig tried to hush him with words about sportsmanship.

Craig's downfall from leadership of the Eagles started during this game. He wanted to pitch when Mason became tired, but Mason put in Wilson, saying later that Craig just wasn't good enough. (In spite of this, Craig rubbed Mason's arm after the game.)

As the game continued, the Rattlers called, "You're not Eagles, you're

Figure 5.1 Intergroup relations: two experimental ingroups (Rattlers and Eagles) interact in competitive and frustrating situations (Stage 2)

Initial encounter between the groups: Rattlers ("home team") watch intently as Eagles approach

Rattlers and Eagles sizing each other up prior to the first contest. Note the team captains on the field at left

Eagles in one of their huddles, praying for victory prior to a contest

Eagles' strategy in a second tug-of-war: sitting down to dig in while Rattlers (stand-ing) exhaust themselves

Rattlers adopt the Eagle strategy: both sides dig in sitting down

One incident the morning after the flag-burning episode: Eagles seizing Rattlers' other flag

Rattlers displaying blue jeans captured in the raid on Eagles and inscribed "The Last of the Eagles"

One of the tournament contests: tent pitching

Raiding Eagles entering Rattler cabin

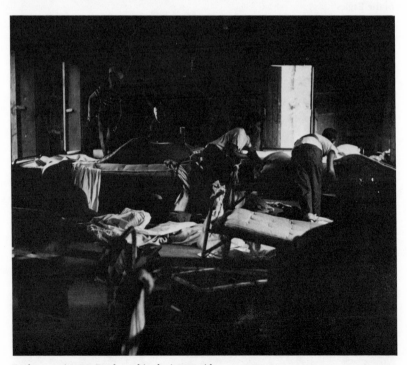

Eagles messing up Rattler cabin during a raid

pigeons!" When the game ended with a Rattler victory, the Rattlers put on a display of good sportsmanship for the losers. In the Eagle group, Mason threatened to beat up some Eagles if they didn't try harder, but he praised Lane (low status) for his improved performance. Craig, who had not made a good showing, carried a Rattler glove left at the field and dropped it in the water near the Eagle cabin.

The two competing groups were together in the mess hall *for the first time* at lunch on day 2, after the baseball game. There was considerable name calling, razzing back and forth, and singing of derogatory songs by each group in turn. Before supper that evening, some Eagles expressed a desire not to eat with the Rattlers.

In saying grace at these first meals together, the members of each group expressed their desire for victory. Myers (E) asked that God help them win the tournament and that He keep them together and not let anyone else get homesick and go home. Allen (R) prayed, "Dear Lord, we thank Thee for the food and for the cooks that cooked it, and for the ball game we won today." In the Eagle group, prayers were said at night for victory, and it became standard practice for that group to huddle in prayer before games (see Figure 5.1). Mason (E) attributed their victory in baseball on the following day to this practice.

Before continuing with the tournament events, note should be taken of the behavior of sideline participants in the various contests. Because there were 11 Rattlers and only 9 Eagles, two of the Rattlers could not participate in certain of the contests (e.g., baseball, tug-of-war, etc.). These nonplayers were chosen by the group and were always low-status members, unless injuries dictated the choice. Since these members were not actually taking part in the competition, their behavior under these circumstances is particularly significant.

At the first baseball game, on the occasion of first contact between the groups, Everett (R), who had been chosen as one nonplayer, was the loudest of the Rattlers in haranguing the Eagles, cursing them roundly and making up a song about Eagles that was supposed to be very insulting. Harrison, the other nonplayer (because of an injury), arrived after the exchange of insults between the groups had already started. Although he had not witnessed the events leading to friction between the groups, and in fact, before he had exchanged a single word with any camper, he started yelling insults at the Eagles.

Numerous other incidents of this nature at the other contests illustrate that actual physical participation is not a necessary condition for involvement and participation in some form by *good* group members.

Both groups spent the afternoon of the first day in intensive preparation for other events. The Rattlers had cabin cleanup, practiced for tug-of-war, and washed their Rattler shirts, which they had decided to wear at every game. Mason delivered a *lecture* to the Eagles on how to win, and the group practiced at tug-of-war for 45 minutes. Mason had organized a cabin-cleaning detail before lunch, insisting on full participation, although prior to the tournament he himself had shown no interest at all in such chores. Later in the tournament, Mason was to urge his group to practice other activities in which he personally had little interest, such as the skits. When he felt they were not trying hard enough, his usual procedure was to declare he was going home, even starting out the cabin door. This device was very effective, since the Eagles were aware of Mason's value as player and captain, and it therefore resulted in renewed efforts on the group's part.

The first tug-of-war was held after supper on this first day of the tournament. Simpson (R) was particularly vocal in calling taunts to the Eagles. When the referee called for captains, Mason stepped forward for the Eagles, although he had been *elected* only as baseball captain, as did Simpson for the Rattlers. The contest began and the Eagles pulled the first Rattler over the line. At this point, the Rattlers began moving the Eagles and continued doing so until all the Eagles were across the line. When Craig (E) saw the Eagles were losing, he walked away from the rope. The winning Rattlers cheered, jumped, and slapped each other on the back, then gave three cheers for the Eagles (Mills noting, "That shows *we* are good sports!"). They passed by the dejected Eagles with much yelling and razzing, particularly from Everett, who had not even taken part in the tug-of-war. Victory was on every Rattler tongue that night, and the next morning the story of how Brown, their anchor man, had shouted "Yawl come!" and they "just came," was repeated with great appreciation.

After this defeat, the downhearted Eagles stood around discussing how big the Rattlers were. Mason was crying, saying the Rattlers must be at least eighth graders, that he was going home, that he would fight a Rattler the next time they met. (Since the Eagles had lost one of their large boys through homesickness, and the Rattlers did have the largest boy in camp, there was some basis for the Rattlers looking big to the Eagles.) Craig, who was chastised for leaving the rope, said they were beaten in the tournament already. Myers, Clark, and McGraw took an optimistic view of the situation, calling for teamwork and planned tactics. (The next day, as we shall see, the Eagles actually did work out tactics before the tug-of-war, which proved highly effective.)

Finally someone suggested the Eagles go back to their cabin. Lane (low status) started off first and noticed the Rattlers' flag on the ball field backstop. He yelled that they could take it down. The Eagles all ran for the backstop, Craig trying to knock down the flag and then climbing up to take it down. Mason grabbed it and tried, with the help of others, to tear it up. Someone suggested, "Let's burn it." So Mason, Craig, and McGraw (who found matches) set the flag on fire; Mason held it while it burned. Then they decided to hang the scorched remnant back up. Craig did so, and the boys sang, "Taps." Mason said, "You can tell those guys *I* did it if they say anything. I'll fight 'em!"

As they walked to their cabin, the Eagles spoke hopefully of how they would beat the Rattlers at baseball the next day. Everyone told how they contributed to the contest, comparing rope burns and aching muscles. As they went to bed, Mason found some hope for victories over the Rattlers.

This flag-burning episode started a chain of events that made it unnecessary for the experimenters to introduce special situations of mutual frustration for the two groups. The only manipulation necessary to ensure that the actions of one group were frustrating to the other was careful timing of arrivals and departures of the groups on certain occasions. For this reason, it was arranged that the Rattlers would complete breakfast and proceed to the athletic field before the Eagles on the next morning, so that the Rattlers would discover the damage to their flag before the Eagles arrived.

At breakfast the next morning the Eagles were relatively quiet, not being elated over their progress thus far and perhaps wondering how the Rattlers would act when they found their flag. Later the Rattlers agreed that the Eagles had looked *happy* at breakfast, but this judgment was made only after they had found their flag.

As arranged, the Rattlers finished breakfast first and went to the ball field. When they arrived and discovered their burnt flag, their reaction was noisy and resentful. All sorts of suggestions for retaliation were made in a disorganized fashion. Mills climbed the backstop to bring down the burnt remnant, leaving a portion there for "evidence" at the suggestion of Barton and Harrison. Simpson, the baseball captain, suggested that he ask the Eagles if they did it. The Rattlers then made a plan of action to follow when the Eagles arrived. Simpson was to go and ask the Eagles if they burned the flag. If the Eagles said that they did (and there was little doubt in the Rattlers' minds that this would be the reply), Simpson was to start fighting and others were to come to his aid. Martin (a mild boy who had earlier espoused sportsmanship) volunteered to grab the Eagles' flag and burn it. When the Eagles arrived, this plan was put into effect. Simpson went to the Eagles and asked if they burned the flag, which they admitted. The Rattlers followed up Simpson, calling invectives; Martin worked his way close to the Eagle flag, grabbed it and ran down the road with some other Rattlers and with Mason (E) in hot pursuit.

In the meantime, on the field, the Eagles ran for the Rattlers' second flag, which they had left on the field (see Figure 5.1). The remaining Rattlers tried to get it back, but the Eagles tore it up. Swift (R) grabbed Craig and held him in a wrestling hold, asking which Eagle had burned the flag. Craig said *they all had*. Simpson (R) had gotten Cutler (E) down in a fist fight, and the physical encounters had to be stopped.

The Rattlers who burned the Eagle flag returned with Mason (E), who was crying mad. He yelled for someone "my size" to whip, and Mills, the Rattler leader, said, "Here I am!" Staff prevented further fighting and started the game, over the Rattlers' violent objections to the Eagles being "home team" that day, since the diamond was "ours" and "we built everything but the backstop." The game finally got underway, with continued razzing and name calling from both sides.

From the point of view of leadership (see Chapter 4), it is very interesting to note that the Eagles noticed that although Simpson was the baseball captain for the Rattlers, Mills was in fact the leader of the group. Myers (E) yelled, "One guy's calling all the time-outs—Mills!" Then he asked a Rattler if Mills was their captain, but the Rattler replied, "No, he's at first base" (Simpson).

A jubilant Eagle group won the game. There was cheering for the losers again, and Wilson and Myers said "Nice game" to the Rattlers. Everett (R), who had been extremely noisy in calling names at the Eagles from the beginning, said, "I think they are trying to be friendly," but none of the dejected, tired Rattlers who had played even bothered to reply.

As the Eagles walked down the road, they discussed the reasons for their victory. Mason attributed it to their prayers. Myers, agreeing heartily, said the Rattlers lost because they used cuss words all the time. Then he shouted, "Hey, you guys, let's not do any more cussing, and I'm serious, too." All the boys agreed on this line of reasoning. Mason concluded that since the Rattlers were such poor sports and such "bad cussers," the *Eagles should not even talk to them anymore.*

For the Rattlers, the immediate effect of losing the game was internal friction and mutual recriminations among ingroup members. This sort of *immediate* reaction to a loss was observed for both groups on some occasions in this study. In this case, Brown (R) criticized Newman (pitcher) and Simpson (captain), who in turn retaliated and were supported by Allen and Barton (both low status). Brown said he was going to write to go home. Later, Allen (a nonplayer in this event) was criticized by Simpson for not giving enough support from the bench. Allen, in turn, criticized Martin, who was supported vehemently by several others. Mills, the Rattler leader, saved the day by making a joke out of the whole verbal skirmish, and Brown and Allen both tore up letters asking to go home, amid general rejoicing.

The second tug-of-war was notable both because the Eagles had planned a strategy that caught the confident Rattlers off balance and because it revealed in a striking way the differential experience of two contending groups, one on the verge of victory and one on the verge of defeat. This contrast between the experiences of the two groups was so striking that observers followed it up with questions the next day. The results are reported separately later in this chapter, at the end of this running account of interaction in Stage 2.

The strategy adopted by the Eagles was to sit down, on prearranged signal, and dig in their feet. The Rattlers tugged strenuously for about 7 minutes and were almost exhausted when they finally sat down and dug in too (see Figure 5.1). The Eagles were slowly but surely pulling the fatigued Rattlers across the line when, after 40 minutes of the contest, a time limit of 15 additional minutes was announced. Later the Eagles were to talk about how short the contest seemed and the Rattlers how long it seemed. After the event, Mason (E) started to shake hands with the Rattlers. The Rattlers told him to "shut up" and called him names. Good sportsmanship was on the downgrade.

All afternoon Simpson (R) made suggestions that the Rattlers raid the Eagles' cabin. Now, as a result of the tug-of-war, in which the Rattlers believed the Eagles had used decidedly unfair tactics, the Rattlers' mood was definitely favorable to a raid. Mills, their leader, set the time for 10:30, after the event of skits, which each group put on separately that night. Enthusiasm for a raid was high, and the Rattlers decked themselves out for it in true commando style (darkening faces, arms, etc.). The Eagles had gone to bed by this time, and all were asleep but Mason, who jumped up to arouse others when the banging and noise began. Some of the Rattlers entered the cabin to turn beds over and rip screens on the windows, while others stood outside and challenged the Eagles to come out and fight. Some of the Eagles slept through the raid, but those who were awake sat on their beds as though stunned. After the Rattlers left, Mason shouted to the Eagles that they were "yellow," especially Craig, who had pretended to be asleep. Mason said the Rattlers had tried to blind them with a light (in reality a flashbulb from a staff camera). Most Eagles were aroused enough to want to retaliate that night; but staff prevented this when it was mentioned that rocks would be used.

Back in the Rattlers' cabin, many wild tales of the raid were being repeated over and over. Mills was considered especially heroic because he jumped in a window and secured comic books and a pair of blue jeans which, much to the Rattlers' delight, turned out to be Mason's (E leader). Mills painted these jeans the next day with orange paint, inscribing the legend "The Last of the Eagles" on each leg, and carried them like a flag (see Figure 5.1).

On day 4 after breakfast, the Eagles, who ate first, prepared for the retaliatory raid they had planned the previous night. After making sure that the Rattlers were in the mess hall, they started off, armed with sticks and bats and led by Cutler, who had balked at participating in a raid the previous night. The Eagles messed up the Rattlers' cabin—turning over beds, scattering dirt and possessions—and then returned to their cabin, where they entrenched and prepared weapons (socks filled with rocks) for a possible return raid by the Rattlers.

The Rattlers were furious at the Eagles for the mess created in their cabin, but their counselor stopped them from rushing to "get" the Eagles by suggesting that the raid might have been planned so that they would lose cabin inspection. The Rattlers returned to cleaning up, cursing the Eagles to a man. Simpson (baseball captain) called the Eagles "communists," which was echoed by Everett (low status).

Rain delayed the start of the touch football game. The Eagles spent this time planning what they would do if the Rattlers came to their cabin; the Rattlers went to work with a vengeance making posters and "raiding flags." At the game itself, the Rattlers were exceedingly vocal and abusive. Everett and Allen (R) repeatedly told the Eagle staff members to get off their side of the field and to "shut up" and called them derogatory names. The Rattlers victoriously waved Mason's pants, now a flag; but the Eagles ignored all this as much as possible. The high-status Eagles were telling their group not to yell at the Rattlers or brag in front of them, as doing so was thought to bring bad luck. Occasionally, Wilson (who had risen near the top in status) forgot this admonition and had to be reminded. Clark (middle status) was the most vocal Eagle, and he was reprimanded several times.

After winning the touch football game (narrowly) and the tent pitching, the Rattlers were convinced that they were "winners" not quitters. The Rattler victory in football was so narrow that the Eagles did not feel too bad at losing; but they thought they erected their tent much better (although more slowly) than the Rattlers. Craig (E) walked away immediately after this contest, and one of the Eagles said, "He's quit on us again" (as he had in the first tug-of-war). The Eagles' morale shot skyward later in the afternoon when they won their second baseball victory. True to their determination to be "good sports," they carefully refrained from bragging in the Rattlers' presence. Bragging was approved behavior *within* the confines of the Eagle group, but by this time it was frowned upon in the presence of the outgroup.

In seeking to explain their loss, which put them one point behind in the tournament, the Rattlers pointed out the weak plays various members had made but reached general agreement that their loss was due to their bats being larger and heavier than the Eagles'. Martin expressed the current mood: "It was just like having those [prize] knives in our pockets before we lost the game." Simpson and Everett talked much of a raid, but nothing came of it at the time. The Eagles discussed the possibility of being raided by the Rattlers and collected a bucket of stones just in case, even "scouting" the Rattler cabin.

At breakfast on the last day of the tournament, the Rattlers sang "The enemy's coming. . . ." as the Eagles approached. After the meal the Rattlers decided to post flags on "everything that's ours," including "home," "the swimming hole," "our Upper Camp," "our baseball diamond," and the Stone Corral. They drifted off with the idea of raiding the Eagles' cabin but met staff members and abandoned the attempt.

The Rattlers won the third tug-of-war easily but lost the second tent-pitching contest to the Eagles decisively. Before lunch, Mason (E) directed, "Take all [the food] you can get; let's don't leave much for them [Rattlers]." However, lunch was a relatively quiet meal. The Eagles were figuring out whether or not they had to win both afternoon events (tent pitching and treasure hunt) or just one. They got into a discussion of their standing in the tournament up to that time and decided they would have to win both of the remaining contests to win the tournament.

Talk of raids had been in the air in both groups all day. The Eagles had mentioned the possibility and indulged in bravado talk, but no plans were made. Simpson was pushing the raid idea in the Rattler group, and as the possibility of their winning the tournament faded during the day, it became generally accepted. Mills (leader) stipulated that it should not be a night raid, because the Eagles had told them they were cowards to raid at night while the Eagles had come in broad daylight. Martin said he would raid if the Rattlers *won*, but not if they lost because that would be bad sportsmanship. (This same Martin entered into the raid without question that same day after the Rattlers lost. He was one of few boys actually engaging in a physical clash with two Eagles and had to be forcibly restrained from fighting.)

The Eagles won the third tent pitching easily and also won the treasure hunt (through experimenters' manipulation in plotting the routes). Their elation and the dejection of the Rattlers was described earlier in this chapter. Mason (E) was so happy that he cried. After entrusting the beloved trophy to staff for safekeeping, the Eagles set off for their Moccasin Creek, some boys jumping in with their clothing on to celebrate.

The Rattlers raided while the Eagles were gone, messing up beds, piling personal gear in the middle of the cabin, setting boats at the dock loose and absconding with the prize knives and medals. When the Eagles found what had happened, they rushed to the Rattler cabin shouting invectives. Mason (E) was in the lead, furious and ready to fight. Lane and Clark were right behind him, and Wilson, Myers, and Cutler arrived within seconds. (Craig, Bryan, and McGraw returned to the Eagles' cabin.) The groups lined up, separated by an invisible line. Mason and others shouted at the Rattlers. Mason refused to fight the big Rattlers (Brown and Swift), and the smaller Rattlers refused to step out to fight him. At last, Mason turned rapidly on his heel and strode toward the Eagle cabin. The other Eagles started to retreat, but did so *facing* the jeering Rattlers, thus walking backward the entire distance. Clark and Wilson were the last to leave and closest to the pursuing Rattlers.

About 10 feet from the Eagle cabin, Mason came back with McGraw yelling to Craig and Bryan in the cabin, "Come on, you yellow bellies. Are you going to lay down and take this?" At this, Craig came out and the Eagles made a last-ditch stand before their cabin. Mason, Clark, Wilson, and Lane were in the front line; Cutler, McGraw, and Myers (who was frightened) composed the second echelon, and Craig stood in the rear. The Rattlers told the Eagles that if they would get down on their bellies and crawl, they would return the prize knives and medals they had taken. Mason (E) begged the Rattlers to take out their two big boys and fight, which the Rattlers refused to do. Martin (R) got into a fist fight with Lane (low-status E). Mills (R) was scuffling with Clark (E). At this point, staff decided to stop the interaction altogether to avoid possible injury. The Rattlers' staff started forcing their boys up the trail to their cabin, one by one. Hill was the last Rattler to be pulled away, and he struggled to go back.

As the Rattlers were being herded up the trail, the Eagles came right behind them yelling that the Rattlers were running away. Eagle staff got the boys back to the cabin, but Mason ran out, determined to "get" the Rattlers. He was returned shortly. Lights were brought to the cabin (lanterns and flashlights had been taken during the raid), and the boys began to clean up the mess. When the staff member who had the role of camp director arrived with some of the stolen prizes, the Eagles brightened up and told him about the event (since he had not been present). By the time they were through telling of their exploits, the Eagles had turned the whole affair into a magnificent victory for themselves. They related that the Rattlers would not take their two big men out of the fight and how they had chased the Rattlers "over halfway back to their cabin" (actually about 40 feet).

The end result of the series of competitive contests and reciprocally frustrating encounters between the Eagles and Rattlers was that neither group wanted to have anything whatsoever to do with the other under any circumstances. On previous days, the now familiar invectives and names had been hurled back and forth ("stinkers," "braggers," "sissies," and many considerably worse) and derogation of the outgroup had been expressed in word and deed (e.g., holding noses when in their vicinity). Now both groups objected even to eating in the same mess hall at the same time.

Clearly negative attitudes and social distance in relation to the outgroup were standardized in both groups. These products of intergroup friction could have been tapped at that time through judgments of performance and stereotype ratings. Nevertheless, it was decided to delay these crucial checks of the products of intergroup friction for one more day to avoid the possibility of obtaining merely momentary reactions to the outgroup and to ensure that the attitudes toward the outgroup had some stability; and to secure further checks through a planned encounter between the groups. Accordingly, the day after the tournament ended (that is, the day after the Rattlers raided the Eagles) was set aside as an interim period devoted entirely to ingroup activity with the exception of one planned contact between the groups.

The Eagles were taken to Lake Carlton, a public picnic ground about 2 miles south of the campground and a more civilized and comfortable place to swim and picnic than their usual venue. They spent the day in self-contained and contented ingroup activity, all pitching in to make the swim and picnic a success. There was discussion of the Rattlers—what a "bunch of cussers," "poor losers," and "bums" they were—and of the Eagles' glorious "victory" in the previous night's raid. Craig carried the Eagle flag, and the group stayed entirely apart from other people on the beach. The only exchange with outsiders occurred when Lane bumped into someone and said, "Excuse me."

The Rattlers spent most of the time at their hideout, swimming, playing, and working in a congenial and happy manner with everyone included (Mills, the leader, making special efforts to involve low-status members in games). There were occasional references to the Eagles as "sissies," "cowards," "little babies," and so on. Upon returning to camp for supper, the Rattlers made it clear that they did not want to eat with the Eagles, who as it happened were not there. Martin and Hill asked if knives were on the canteen list. Mills said he didn't want the kind of knives the Eagles had won, and others expressed interest in having knives, but not the kind the Eagles had won.

The Eagles returned after supper. As planned for the "test situation" arranged by the staff, the Rattlers were taken on a hike in the Eagle area, passing within about 20 to 30 yards of the Eagles' cabin. Mason heard the Rattlers approaching and yelled, "Come on, you guys, we're being raided!" After the boys had rushed toward the cabin, Mason stopped to listen. Bryan and McGraw had by this time taken to the bushes to hide. In the meantime, the Rattlers, with Mills, Brown, Simpson, and Everett in the lead, decided to take a look at the Eagles' hideout (Moccasin Creek). There they became quite engrossed in crossing the Eagles' rope bridge, and although the Rattlers mentioned above spoke of cutting it before they left, this was not done.

The Eagles were discussing the possibility that the Rattlers might do something to their swimming hole, Wilson, Clark, and Mason arguing that they should protect it. Wilson said he thought they must be at O. U. Camp: "That's our camp and they'll try to tear down our sign." The Rattlers returned past the Eagle cabin, yelling insults in loud voices. Mills (R) said, "They were afraid to even look at us." The Eagles inspected their swimming place the next morning and commented that there were more rocks in the water than before and that the Rattlers must have been responsible.

Thus, reaction in this test situation further confirmed the prior evidence that this friction phase of intergroup relations had by this time crystallized in negative attitudes toward the outgroup (by virtue of stereotypes of the outgroup's characteristics and considerable social distance in relation to its members). These negative attitudes persisted even after intergroup contact in competitive and reciprocally frustrating situations ceased.

How Long the Tug-of-War Lasted

Viewpoints of Groups on the Verge of Victory and Defeat

Among the factors frequently reflected in judgments of objects, persons, or events in Stage 2 were immediate and long-range trends in intergroup relations, strenuous physical efforts, victory or defeat, and so forth. A striking contrast between groups, as evidenced by differential effects along group lines, was seen in estimates of the time consumed by the second tug-of-war. As noted above, participant observers followed up reactions of the two groups to this event and found evidence for differential experience by the members of the two rival groups, both when estimates were made individually and when they were a matter of consensus within groups.

The Rattlers had won the first tug-of-war easily. When the groups met again, the Eagles had adopted a strategy of sitting down and digging in their feet. The Rattlers stood up and pulled mightily for about 7 minutes (losing ground steadily) and were almost exhausted when they finally sat down and dug in too. The Rattlers' fatigue gave the Eagles a decided advantage, and they were gradually pulling their opponents across the line when, at the 40th minute of the contest, a time limit of 15 additional minutes was announced. The event ended in a tie through a mighty effort by the Rattlers to keep their last man from crossing the line.

Later in the evening, at their own cabins, both groups talked about the event. Most of the Eagles seemed to feel that the time had literally flown by, one of them saying, "That was the shortest 10 minutes in my life" (referring to the last 15 minutes of the contest). However, remarks at the Rattler cabin revealed that they felt the event had lasted a "helluva long time."

Since these remarks indicated differential biases according to group membership, the members of both groups were asked individually by their participant observers on the morning following the event, "How long did the tug-of-war last after both groups sat down and dug in?" The objective time was 48 minutes. The estimates made are tabulated in Table 5.1.

It is significant that the Eagles all gave their estimates in minutes and the Rattlers all gave theirs in hours, even though the *same* question was asked both groups and all boys were questioned individually. The members of the two competing groups used the same dimension (elapsed time) in making estimates, but used *different units*—the shorter unit being used by those on the verge of victory and the longer by those on the verge of defeat. Also, it was found on further questioning that the Rattlers were unable to differentiate between the length of time occupied by the whole event and the time after both groups sat down.

Note that the median judgment for the Eagles represents an 18-minute *under*estimation of elapsed time; that of the Rattlers a 12-minute *over*estimation. The median judgment for Rattlers was twice

TABLE 5.1

*Estimates of how long the second tug-of-war lasted,
made individually by Eagles (who almost won)
and Rattlers (who almost lost)*

Eagles	Rank	Rattlers	Rank
22½ minutes	2.0	1 hour	12.5
22½ minutes	2.0	1 hour	12.5
22½ minutes	2.0	1 hour	12.5
25 minutes	4.0	1 hour	12.5
ª30 minutes	5.5	1 hour	12.5
30 minutes	5.5	ª 1 hour	12.5
32½ minutes	7.0	1 hour plus	16.0
45 minutes	8.5	1½ hours	17.0
45 minutes	8.5	2 hours	18.0
		3½ hours	19.5
		3½ hours plus	19.5

Note: When an interval was given as an estimate, the midpoint was tabulated, e.g., 22½ minutes for 20 to 25 minutes.
ªMedian.

that of the Eagles, giving a 30-minute difference between groups. Although judgments of the members of the two groups do not overlap at all, and the significance of the results is obvious, they can be put in the more formal language of statistics. According to the Mann-Whitney U test (1947) the probability of getting these estimates, so distributed between groups, by chance is less than .001.

After polling the group members individually, each participant observer asked his group (at a time when the group was all in one place) how long the event had lasted. After some discussion the Eagles decided the estimate should be 45 minutes (the original estimate of the group's leader). The Rattlers decided it was "over an hour." These estimates arrived at by consensus still represent under- and overestimations of the objective time.

6

Intergroup Relations: Assessment of Ingroup Functioning and Negative Attitudes Toward the Outgroup

To ensure the validity of findings and to increase their precision, the plan of this experiment on intergroup relations specified that different methods of data collection would be used and the results checked against each other (see Chapter 2). On the other hand, it was noted that excessive interruption of the interaction processes would result in destroying the main focus of study—the flow of interaction within groups and between groups under varying conditions. Therefore, it was necessary to exercise great restraint in introducing special measurement techniques and experimental units to cross-check the observational data.

At the end of Stage 2, special methods were used to check observations related to the main hypotheses for the friction phase of intergroup relations. In addition to sociometric techniques, two experimental units were introduced to tap the subject's attitudes toward their respective ingroups and the outgroup. The results of these units are presented in this chapter, along with additional observational data pertaining to the various hypotheses for Stage 2. These results are not intended to test any separate hypotheses, but to provide further evidence to be evaluated in conjunction with the observational data.

The chapter's first section summarizes the effects of intergroup friction on ingroup functioning, while the second section deals with end products of intergroup friction and conflict, and their assessment through judgmental reactions.

Intergroup Friction and Ingroup Functioning

The study of ingroup structure and functioning was not confined to the first stage of the experiment, which was devoted to experimental formation of ingroups. Several of the hypotheses for Stage 2 specifically concern the effects of intergroup relations (friction, in this case) on ingroup structure and functioning. The summary of interaction in the last chapter pointed out some effects consequential to the respective ingroups. Further data will be summarized here.

Throughout the experiment, we tried, whenever possible, to obtain data by as many methods as feasible without disrupting the ongoing interaction. Checking results obtained by several methods (e.g., observational, sociometric, ratings, judgments of the subjects) leads to confidence in the reliability and validity of the conclusions reached. In considering the hypotheses and data concerning ingroup relations in Stage 2, it was necessary to rely heavily on observational data. The more precise techniques of data collection (viz., stereotype ratings and laboratory-type judgments) were used for testing the validity of observational findings concerning negative attitudes (see the second section of this chapter).

Because of space limitations, the observational data of this experiment have been given in summary form. Piling example on example does not surmount the danger of selectivity in observation and in reporting observational data. The illustrations chosen are representative of the many available. The conclusions drawn from them are justified by available evidence. These conclusions are intended to be suggestive for future research in which observational methods are supplemented increasingly by other, more precise techniques of data collection.

At the end of Stage 2, the Rattlers and Eagles were both clearly structured, closely knit ingroups. This is revealed in observational data, in observers' ratings, and in sociometric choices obtained at this time from each member individually by the participant observer of his group (who appeared as counselor to the subjects).

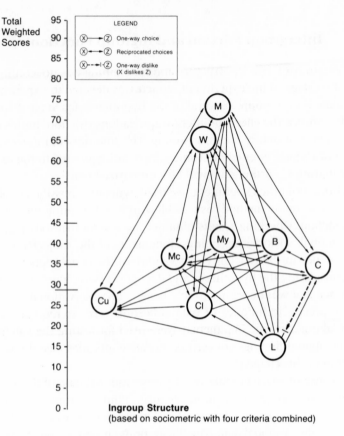

Figure 6.1 Sociogram for Rattlers (end of Stage 2)

Testing in Terms of Sociometric Indices

The most general criterion on the sociometric questionnaire specified that friendship choices should be made *from the entire camp*. Table
6.1 presents the resulting choices for this criterion by members of the
Rattler and Eagle groups. Even though choices of outgroup members
were forced somewhat by the manner in which this item was presented, the proportion of choices of ingroup members in both groups
was approximately 93 percent, and the differences between choices
of ingroup members and outgroup members are too large to be attributed to chance.

Sociograms were constructed for the Rattlers and Eagles using the

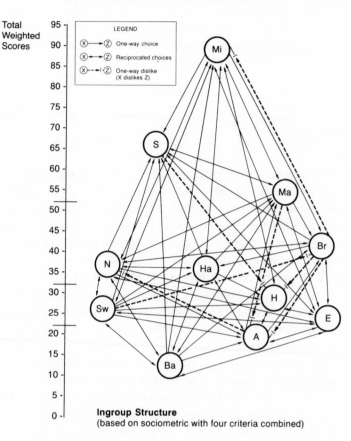

Total Weighted Scores

Figure 6.2 Sociogram for Eagles (end of Stage 2)

total score on four criteria as a basis for placement of members (see Figures 6.1 and 6.2). The score on each criterion was the total of weighted choices, first choices receiving a weight of 4, second choices of 3, third choices of 2, and those thereafter a weight of 1. The choice network was based on the most general criterion (friendship) and rejections were obtained from an item included in the interview but not used as a criterion in computing total scores. The lines on the ordinates of the sociograms represent Q_1, Q_2, and Q_3 of these ranks in ascending order, the lowest line being Q_1.

Several discrepancies in ratings of group members based on the various criteria were noted. Two of these criteria were concerned with friendship choices (one general, one more specific), and two

TABLE 6.1

Friendship choices of ingroup and outgroup members
by Rattlers and Eagles (end of Stage 2)

	Rattlers		Eagles	
Choices of	ƒ	%	ƒ	%
Ingroup members	73	93.6	62	92.5
Outgroup members	5	6.4	5	7.5

were concerned with initiative displayed by various members. It is significant that the scores obtained for these two kinds of choice were widely disparate in several cases. For example, Everett (R) ranked second on the friendship criteria but only ninth (out of 11) on the initiative criteria. Craig (E) ranked seventh on the friendship criteria, but fourth on the initiative criteria, as did Hill (R).

Since observers' ratings were made more on the basis of effective initiative than on popularity, it is interesting to compare the status ratings by observers and the ranks in total sociometric score (four criteria). As Table 6.2 indicates, the rank order correlation for these two rating measures is significant and high. Observers, in their status ratings, undoubtedly gave greater weight to effective initiative than did the combined sociometric scores. This greater weight is revealed in cases of discrepancy between sociometric ranks and observer ratings. For example, Brown (R) ranks fourth in sociometric score, but only eighth in the observer's ratings. In this case, the sociometric score as computed from choices does not reveal what the observer knew, and what was also revealed during the sociometric interviews. Although Brown received only one rejection from his group, he was mentioned by six members (more than any other member) as the member who would stand in the way of what most of the group wanted to do. To take another example, Bryan (E) ranked fourth in sociometric score and eighth in the observer's ratings. In his case, nothing in the sociometric interview revealed, or could reveal, that Bryan was frightened of physical conflict and that during the closing days of Stage 2 he withdrew from interaction altogether on several occasions (even hiding in the bushes). For this reason, he was rated near the bottom of the group by the observer at this time (in terms of effective initiative and influence in the group). On the other hand, the observer noted that since many Eagles were frightened of the Rattlers, they did not

TABLE 6.2

Comparison of ranks in sociometric scores and status ratings
by participant observers of Rattler and Eagle groups
(end of Stage 2)

	rho	t	p
Rattlers	.70	2.94	<.001
Eagles	.731	2.83	<.013

(except Mason, the leader) impose sanctions because of Bryan's behavior. He participated effectively when physical contact with the outgroup was not in the picture. Nevertheless, Bryan had very little influence in the group at the end of Stage 2. Such cases illustrate some difficulties in interpreting sociometric scores based on *choice,* and they point to serious problems of validity when sociometrics are used apart from concrete observational material.

Testing in Terms of Observational Data

Three of the hypotheses for Stage 2 are concerned with ingroup functioning. We summarize data pertinent to them here.

Hypothesis 2 (Stage 2)

The course of relations between two groups that are in a state of competition and frustration will tend to produce an increase in ingroup solidarity.

Observational data supports this hypothesis with the qualification that in several instances defeat in a contest with the rival group brought *temporarily increased* internal friction in its wake. This was noted in the Rattler group on day 3 when they lost the second baseball game. Disruptive tendencies within the group reached their peak when Brown and Allen wrote letters that afternoon saying they wanted to go home, thus threatening to leave the group. Solidarity was achieved shortly afterward through the integrative leadership of Mills, whose joking about these events led the boys to tear up their letters amid rejoicing by all members.

Similar signs of temporary disorganization followed the first tug-of-war, when the downhearted Eagles stared loss of the tournament in the face. In this case, Myers, Clark, and McGraw took the optimistic view that the group had to plan tactics that would defeat the Rattlers. After the group joined wholeheartedly in burning the Rattler flag, this view was accepted by the leader as well, and considerable hope was seen for the next day.

The Rattlers made a somewhat similar adaptation to defeat at the end of the tournament. In this important instance, group action in raiding the outgroup was agreed upon right after defeat, sanctioned and planned by the leader and lieutenants, and executed soon afterward. The aftermath was self-glorification with reference to the group and all its members. The next morning, when Mills "roughed up" several group members, not one tried to challenge his prerogatives, although any one of them could have whipped him easily. (It should be noted here that the Rattler leader, Mills, was one of the group's smallest boys.) The rest of that day was spent in highly congenial play in which Mills made special efforts to involve the low-status members and succeeded in effecting their active participation.

It should be emphasized that such temporary disruptive tendencies following defeat did *not* follow every loss of a contest. Some defeats were accepted, by both Rattlers and Eagles, with remarkably little concern or depression, either because the group in question had decided prior to the event that they probably would *not* win it or because they felt they did not have to win that particular event to win the tournament.

In instances where temporary disorganization did follow defeat, heightened solidarity within the group was achieved *through united cooperative action by the ingroup against the outgroup,* and this is in line with our hypothesis. It should be noted and emphasized that the aggressive actions toward the outgroup, which followed frustration of group efforts experienced *in common* by ingroup members, were taken *after they were sanctioned by the leaders* (Mills or Mason, the leaders of the Rattlers and Eagles respectively). These aggressive actions were sometimes suggested by high-status members (notably Simpson and Mills in the Rattlers and Mason in the Eagles), and sometimes by low-status members (e.g., Everett in the Rattlers, and Lane in the Eagles). In no instance did an ingroup engage, as a group, in aggressive action toward the outgroup if doing so had not been approved by the leader.

Other evidence supporting this hypothesis as stated is the recurring glorification of the ingroup, recounting of feats and accomplishments of individual members, support and approval given low-status members, support given the leader, and intensified claims on areas appropriated as belonging to the group.

The Eagles bragged to each other that they were "good sports" who did their best and who prayed and didn't curse. Later they refrained from bragging in the presence of the outgroup, since doing so was agreed to bring bad luck. The Rattlers were constantly telling each other, and all within hearing distance of the Eagles, that they were brave, winners, not quitters, tough, and (naturally) good sports.

After the contests and raids, stories were told over and over of the accomplishments of this person and that person, blisters acquired in the tug-of-war were compared in both winning and losing groups, and these tales of individual feats grew with each telling. (The Eagles' dramatic reversal of their role in the last raid was noted in the account of that event in Chapter 5.) Brown (R) revealed special gifts for recounting such episodes.

During Stage 2, Lane (low-status E) was praised for his playing for the first time (by Mason). Lane became more active in ingroup affairs and said the group must not swim so much, in order to save their strength for the tournament, even though he had earlier been a constant agitator to go swimming at every possible moment. Approval was also given to low-status Rattlers during games. After the big raid in which Mason (E) had accused several Eagles of being "yellow-bellied" and cowards, he "covered up" for them completely in telling staff of the events. No mention was made of any defection; all Eagles were made to appear heroic.

The leaders (Mills and Mason) were supported by group opinion consistently, especially after the first day or so, when Mason was effectively extending his elected leadership in baseball to all areas of group life. Mills was supported by the group even during games when he interfered in decisions made by Simpson (baseball captain); and on one occasion he took Simpson out as pitcher and put in another member in his place.

We mentioned the increased concern, at the end of Stage 1, of the ingroups over places appropriated as "theirs." Swift (R) even went so far as to object, when he saw fishermen near the Rattlers' swimming hole, that they had no business taking "our fish." The Rattlers talked, near the end of Stage 2, of putting signs on all of "their" places, including the ball diamond and Stone Corral (which was a part of Robbers Cave). The Eagles were extremely concerned that the Rattlers went to their hideout on the day after the big raid and claimed they could detect changes there that did not actually exist.

Hypothesis 3 (Stage 2)

Functional relations between groups that are of consequence to the groups will tend to bring about changes in the pattern of relations within the ingroups involved.

The most striking change in relationships within the ingroups arising from the particular functional relationship between them (rivalry and friction) was in the Eagle group. At the end of Stage 1, Craig was the acknowledged leader of the Eagles. Mason was elected captain of the baseball team (only) with Craig nominating and backing him. Even after this, Craig informed Mason that he could not play ball if he didn't have the Eagle insignia stenciled on his T-shirt, and Mason submitted to this requirement after some argument. From the first day of the tournament, however, Mason began to extend his leadership to all group activities, while Craig lost ground throughout Stage 2, being in the middle of the hierarchy (fifth in rank) by the end. Some of the incidents revealing this alteration in the Eagles' status structure are mentioned in the final chapter's summary of interaction.

Mason took the group goal of winning the tournament very seriously, giving talks on how to keep from getting rattled, threatening to beat up everyone if they didn't try harder, lecturing on how to win after the first loss in baseball. Although he had not shown interest in keeping the cabin clean before the tournament, he organized cabin-cleaning details and struck Lane (low status) for not helping pick up papers. He had praised Lane's playing baseball earlier, and the combined effect of Mason's attention was that Lane saw the necessity of reducing the groups' swimming time to "save our strength"—for him a sacrificial act.

When captains for the tug-of-war were called, Mason stepped forward, although he had been elected only as baseball captain, and there was no discussion on the point. When the Eagles burned the

Rattler flag, Lane first directed attention to it, but Mason took the initial action in trying to tear it up.

Rather convincing evidence of Mason's leadership followed the second tug-of-war, which ended in a tie. Estimates of the time consumed were first obtained individually for each boy, as reported in the last chapter. Subsequently, the boys were asked in a group how long they thought it lasted. Every single Eagle agreed with Mason's estimate of 45 minutes, although only one other boy had individually made an estimate that high.

Craig allowed leadership of the Eagles to slip through his fingers by submitting to Mason's decisions, perhaps in part because he recognized Mason's superiority as an athlete. (The Rattlers' Mills was not as good a ball player as a few other members; nevertheless he kept control of the group's progress even during baseball games.) However, Craig fell as far as he did in the status hierarchy because of his defection at several critical points during the tournament. When the group was losing the first tug-of-war, Craig simply walked away from the rope before the contest was over. Afterward he said the Eagles were already beaten in the tournament and tried to blame others for the tug-of-war loss. However, the Eagles blamed Craig for the loss. When he walked away after the Eagles' loss in tent pitching, the comment was, "He's quit on us *again*." Craig pretended to be asleep during the first Rattler raid and stayed in the background during the second.

Another shift in the Eagle group that accompanied Mason's rise to leadership was Wilson's increasing importance in the group. From a position in the middle of the group's hierarchy (fifth) at the end of Stage 1, Wilson rose to become Mason's lieutenant through his effective playing in sports, his concern with maintaining joint efforts to win the tournament, and his support of Mason's decisions. Mason chose Wilson as pitcher, in preference to Craig, during the first baseball game, and the two figured together in most of the group efforts and activities throughout Stage 2.

The most pronounced changes in the pattern of status relations in the Rattler group during intergroup competition were in the cases of Allen and Brown. After the second baseball game, which the Rattlers lost, Allen was accused of not contributing to the game. He, in turn, accused Martin (higher status) of bragging; but Martin was supported by the other members in the argument. The group members were ruthless in denouncing Allen, who cried, wanted to go home, and was talked out of it by Mills (leader). After this incident, Allen was ignored a good deal, was not chosen to play on the team, and fell from a middle-status level to the bottom. Mills's friendship was his chief tie with the group.

Brown, the largest Rattler, slowly slipped downward in the status structure during Stage 2, until just before the second raid on the Eagles. Because of a pronounced tendency to rough up the smaller boys, Brown was subject to group sanctions and fell to the bottom level of the group. During the raid, his size so impressed the Eagles that he became something of a hero of that event to the Rattlers and had attentive audiences of smaller boys in recounting his feats. Intergroup conflict was the medium by which Brown regained a position higher in the group at the end of Stage 2, after having slipped to the bottom level.

Thus changes in the pattern of relations within the ingroups occurred during Stage 2. These changes related to the altered contributions of the various members to group activities and efforts as the ingroup functioned in a competitive and mutually antagonistic relationship with another group.

Hypothesis 4 (Stage 2)

Low-status members will tend to exert greater efforts that will be revealed in more intense forms of overt aggression and verbal expressions against the outgroup as a means of improving their status within the ingroup.

The observations relevant to this hypothesis are inconclusive. This hypothesis was not intended to imply that high-status members will not initiate and actively participate in conflict with the outgroup. In line with one of the major tenets of *Groups in Harmony and Tension* (1953), its implication should be that intergroup behavior of members consists mainly in participation in the trends of one's group in relation to other groups. Since low-status members would be highly motivated to improve their status, it seemed a reasonable hypothesis that they might do so through active participation in the trend of group antagonism and conflict toward the outgroup. On the other hand, the establishment and responsibility for such a trend in intergroup affairs rests heavily with the high-status members, as does responsibility for sanctioning and conducting affairs strictly within the group. If an upper-status member, even the leader, stands in the way of an unmistakable trend in intergroup affairs, he is subject to loss of his standing in the group. This is precisely what happened to Craig, the erstwhile Eagle leader, in the present study. He did not enter into the tournament with sufficiently wholehearted identification with the group's efforts to win; he even walked out on them at critical points when they were losing and "played possum" (during a raid) to avoid conflict with the outgroup.

In view of the necessity to clarify the intent and implications of this hypothesis, it should probably be reformulated along the following lines: aggressive behavior and verbal expression against the outgroup, in line with the trend of intergroup conflict sanctioned by high-status members, will be exhibited by low-status members as a means of improving their status within the group.

This hypothesis could be tested empirically by comparing the reactions of low-status members toward the outgroup when in the presence of ingroup members high in status, and when high-status members of their ingroup are not present. Since the primary concern of Stage 2 in this experiment was the end products of intergroup friction, we did not make this empirical test relating to the behavior of ingroup members. As stated in Chapter 2, it was necessary to limit such devices in the present study so that excessive intervention by experimenters would not complicate the interaction processes within groups and between groups. The test situations and more precise methods of measurement used during Stage 2 were all devoted to tapping the end products of intergroup friction.

Observational data bearing on this hypothesis cannot be conclusive without an empirical test such as that suggested above. The data available are not contradictory of the hypothesis *as modified*. One consistent finding supports it, namely, that in those instances in which low-status members *initiated* aggressive acts directed toward the outgroup, group action followed *when the suggestion* was *approved or taken over entirely by high-status members, particularly the leader.* Conversely, there were instances of suggested aggressive action toward the outgroup initiated by low-status members (and even upper-status members) that was *not* carried out because the leader did not assent to it. The number of raids suggested by various group members far exceeded the number actually carried out. In every case, the leader decided on the major details of the raid. Mills set the time for both of the

Rattler raids, and Mason (who was the moving force in making the suggestion and in its execution) managed the Eagles' morning raid on the Rattler cabin, even though Cutler (low status) led the way to the cabin after the decision was reached.

Verification of Observational Findings Through Laboratory-Type Tasks

In this stage of negative intergroup relations, Hypothesis 1 (Stage 2) is crucial:

> In the course of competition and frustrating relations between two groups, unfavorable stereotypes will come into use in relation to the outgroup and its members and will be standardized in time, placing the outgroup át a certain social distance (proportional to the degree of negative relations between groups).

This hypothesis goes to the core of issues concerning the formation and standardization, prevailing in actual social life, of prejudice and of social distance scales in relation to outgroups.

The main events between groups in this stage were manifested through rivalry and actual conflict. Our emphasis in formulation of the crucial hypothesis was on *end products* in the form of standardized norms relating to the outgroup, rather than on specific events revealing conflict, fights, and rivalry. If negative functional relations between groups are more than momentary affairs and give rise repeatedly to fights and hurling of derogatory terms, the end products will be standardized generalizations concerning the outgroup that are expressed in the form of unfavorable stereotypes. These standardizations constitute the basis of the institution of group prejudice or social distance. Once standardized, such institutions, crystallized in negative stereotypes, outlast the actual state of negative relations, henceforth predisposing ingroup members to categorize outgroup members in the light of unfavorable generalizations, even at times when the acts of outgroup members are not unfavorable. Therefore, our emphasis in formulating hypotheses concerning negative relations between groups has been on negative generalizations concerning the outgroup—that is, standardized stereotypes—rather than on a syllabus of behavioral items revealing hostility, aggression, and other expressions of intergroup conflict.

As the account of interaction during Stage 2 (Chapter 5) indicates, there were many specific examples of conflict (in some of which members of the two experimental groups had to be separated), much name calling of the outgroup, much use of derogatory terms and ridicule. Briefly, one end result of competition and rivalry and of situations in which one group was frustrating to the other was a desire manifested by both groups to have nothing further to do with each other. With the assumption that generalizations concerning the outgroup and attitudes toward it would outlast the state of actual conflict that engendered them, the two groups were brought within hearing distance of each other after a full day of exclusively ingroup association. The result was repetition of the name calling, derogation, and other manifestations of attitudes revealed during the period of intergroup conflict itself. This point was the critical time to tap these end products of intergroup conflict through more precise laboratory methods to check further the validity of the observations. We took this action on the following day, two days after the end of the tournament and the climactic raid by the Rattlers. The two experimental units undertaken at that time are reported on the pages that follow.

Stereotype Ratings

At the end of Stage 2, we obtained judgmental ratings of stereotypes actually used by the subjects in relation to the outgroup. This unit was carried out to provide a further test of Hypothesis 1 (Stage 2), namely, that unfavorable stereotypes regarding the outgroup and its members will arise from competitive and frustrating relations between the two groups and will become standardized in time.

The procedures for this unit were repeated at the end of Stage 3. A comparison of the data obtained at the end of Stage 2 with those obtained at the end of Stage 3 provides a crucial test of the prediction that cooperative efforts in situations embodying superordinate goals will have a cumulative effect in reducing intergroup tensions (Hypothesis 1b, Stage 3). Chapter 7 presents this comparison with the summary of Stage 3.

The judgments in this experimental unit were obtained to supplement data from observers' reports and to provide a more clear-cut check of Hypothesis 1 (Stage 2). No new hypotheses were tested separately by this experimental unit. Throughout the entire study, results obtained by as many methods as feasible were brought together to test a particular hypothesis. In this particular instance, judgments of ingroup and outgroup members were used as further evidence for conceptual products (stereotypes) of intergroup interaction under conditions of competitive rivalry. The hypothesis is to be evaluated in terms of all relevant evidence obtained, including observational and sociometric data summarized in the last chapter and in this chapter, and judgmental data presented here.

In reviewing the problem of prejudice, Sherif (1948) emphasized that prejudice and stereotypes held toward outgroups are products of past or present relationships between the groups in question:

> The favorable or unfavorable properties or "traits" attributed to "they" groups, and inevitably to their individual members in a rather absolutistic way, are determined by the nature of positive or negative relations between the groups in question. If the interests, direction, and goals of the intergroup relations are integrated or in harmony, the features attributed to "they" groups are favorable. If the activities and views clash while the interacting groups pursue their peculiar interests and goals, the features attributed are negative (357).

The intergroup relations of such small groups as gangs show this situation strikingly. In the process of group formation, the group tends to appropriate certain areas, objects, places, and so on, as their "own." Encroachment or invasion of these private domains by an outgroup results in clashes that tend to be accompanied by attribution of unfavorable characteristics to the "intruders." If the relationship of conflict endures for any length of time, derogatory terms for the outgroup become standardized and mirror the nature of the underlying attitudes of prejudice or social distance.

When stereotypes become standardized with an ingroup, they often persist beyond the functional relationships between groups of which they are a product. Existing stereotypes may then be manipulated by powerful members of the ingroup or, at times, by other interest groups, and extended to groups with whom there has been little or no contact. However, the present experiment on intergroup relationships is concerned with studying stereotypes from scratch, that is, tracing their formation from the time of first contact between groups in conditions of rivalry through a period of intergroup conflict. Therefore, those studies that reveal differential response to contact with outgroups under varying conditions of interactions were especially persistent in formulating our hypotheses.

A survey of historical studies in various countries reveals that social distance scales do reflect the nature of intergroup relationships in which they evolve and that over a period of time they are responsive to altered conditions of intergroup interaction.[1] For example, MacCrone's (1937) intensive historical study tracing intergroup relations and social distance attitudes in South Africa during a period of over 200 years shows "radical alteration" of attitudes of original European settlers. Originally, the settlers placed natives in the "heathen" category, which offered at least the possibility of salvation. As a consequence of active efforts to utilize native labor, reactions of native groups to these efforts, importation of more docile groups as slaves, and many actual intergroup conflicts, as well as developments external to the area itself (e.g., expansion of imperialism, industrial developments, etc.), contemporary emphasis on "the white man and his civilization" in contrast to "inferior" native groups began to emerge in the early nineteenth century.

Klineberg's summary (1950) of changing stereotypes of the Chinese by Americans on the West Coast at different periods in American history is particularly illuminating. When there was a great demand for Chinese labor, and thus, conditions of interdependence between Chinese and white settlers, favorable verbal pictures of Chinese were common in journals and newspapers. However, around the 1860s, when other groups began to compete strongly with Chinese for their positions, descriptions of the Chinese began to undergo a radical shift in the negative direction. Whereas they had been described earlier as "thrifty," "sober," "inoffensive," and "most worthy" adopted citizens, the stereotype now became negative. The Chinese who had earlier been seen as possessing "adaptability beyond praise" were newly pictured as "a distinct people" who were "unassimilable," "debased," "servile," and so on.

Experimental evidence supporting the view that stereotypes arise as products of functional relationships between ingroups was provided by Sherif's 1949 experiment on intergroup relations (Sherif 1951; Sherif and Sherif 1953). The design of the last two phases of that study was the same as that of Stages 1 and 2 of the present experiment (see Chapter 2). The hypothesis tested in the final phase of

1. Representative historical studies of social distance scales in formation are presented in M. Sherif and C. W. Sherif, *Groups in Harmony and Tension* (New York: Harper, 1953), Chapter 5.

the 1949 experiment was essentially the same as our main hypothesis for Stage 2. In the course of interaction in intergroup situations of competition and frustration, highly derogatory labels were used in relation to the outgroup. In time, such terms as "pig," "bums," and "cheaters" were standardized for reference to members of the outgroup.

Using such leads from the 1949 intergroup experiment, Avigdor (1951) carried out her doctoral study at New York University on the specific problem of "The spontaneous development of stereotypes as a result of a specific type of group interaction." By subtly controlling conditions, Avigdor was able first to create a relationship of cooperation between small groups and later to turn this relationship into one of unfriendliness between certain of the interacting groups.

Groups of ten-year-old girls ("friendship clubs") were paired by Avigdor (who became an adult leader of the groups for the purpose of the experiment) in both cooperative and competing activities. The cooperative situation was one in which a compelling common goal existed for each of the paired groups, that of earning enough money to purchase highly desired club jackets. Attainment of this goal required that two groups work together to put on a play. At the height of the cooperative activities, each group rated the other cooperating group on 32 characteristics, half favorable and half unfavorable, on a 5-point rating scale.

The conflict situation developed when two of the cooperating groups were more successful in preparing their play than the other groups. Intergroup conflict reached such an intensity that when one group, which was lagging behind, was brought to a final rehearsal of the play being prepared by two more successful groups, the visitors became objectionable and were forcibly expelled. At this point, ratings on the 32 characteristics were obtained from members of the expelled group in relation to the two other groups, and from members of those two cooperating groups in relation to the group thrown out.

Among Avigdor's conclusions were that the ratings made after the cooperative interaction were generalized in the favorable direction—"that is, development of favorable stereotypes"—while the ratings obtained after interaction involving conflict generalized in the unfavorable direction—"that is, development of an unfavorable stereotype" (65).

In one aspect of an experimental study of negative and positive relations between small groups existing in everyday life, Harvey (1954) obtained results in line with those reported above. He found that when the interacting groups were positively related, preponderantly favorable adjectives were attributed to the outgroup and its members. But when the relationship between groups was negative, derogatory adjectives were used in relation to members of the outgroup.

Before presenting results of stereotype ratings obtained in the present experiment, it should be stressed that negative relations between groups with accompanying patterns of social distance and negative stereotypes do not imply that a similar pattern of relationships prevails among members of the ingroup. Evidence from the present intergroup study, as well as from the 1949 study and sociological field work, indicates that conflict with an outgroup tends to result in increased ingroup solidarity with consequent favorable verbal pictures of ingroup members. (This significant point was elaborated in relation to Hypothesis 2, Stage 2.)

Procedure

At the end of Stage 2, the two experimental groups, Eagles and Rattlers, were asked to make ratings of their own and each other's group. It was explained to the subjects that they were being asked to do so to help the administration find out what they thought of their new acquaintances and how they were enjoying camp.

The stereotype scale contained critical characteristics as well as uncritical or favorable ones, and a 5-point rating scale for each of the terms. The 5 points or categories were the same as those used by Avigdor: "All of the (Rattlers or Eagles) are . . . ," "Most of the ____ are . . . ," "Some of the ____ are . . . ," "A few of the ____ are . . . ," and "None of the ____ are . . .". The subject made his rating on each characteristic by writing that particular term in the one of five incompleted categories that, in his opinion, was the most appropriate description of the group being rated, ingroup or outgroup.

The characteristics on which ingroup and outgroup were rated were not postulated merely on a priori grounds. They were terms that the subjects themselves had used during Stage 2. Thus there was some assurance of the appropriateness of the characteristic chosen. Although more terms were presented on the scale, six were chosen as critical. It was thought that these six characteristics were sufficiently standardized in both groups to provide a clear-cut distinction between ingroup and outgroup ratings. The critical characteristics included three favorable terms (brave, tough, friendly) and three unfavorable ones (sneaky, smart alecs, stinkers).

Results

The frequency of ratings was determined for the six characteristics within each of the five categories. The categories were then numbered from 1 to 5, 1 being the most unfavorable and 5 the most favorable category. Thus a response of "All of the ____ are (unfavorable term)" would go into category 1, while a response of "All of the ____ are (favorable term)" would be tabulated in category 5. The results are presented in terms of ratings in the six characteristics combined.

Table 6.3 presents the ratings of outgroup members by each group at the end of Stage 2. These results confirm observational data indicating that members of both groups tended to rate the outgroup unfavorably following the stage of intergroup competition and friction. Of the ratings made by the Rattlers, 53.0 percent were negative and 24.9 percent were favorable. The Eagles' unfavorable picture of the outgroup is even more accentuated. Their ratings of the Rattlers were 76.9 percent unfavorable and only 15.4 percent favorable.

Table 6.4 presents a composite picture of how the Rattlers and Eagles rated their own groups (ingroups) at the end of Stage 2. From these results it can be seen that at the end of Stage 2, in which condi-

TABLE 6.3

Stereotype ratings of the outgroup on six characteristics (combined) by members of Rattler and Eagle groups (end of Stage 2)

Category	Rattlers' ratings of Eagles		Eagles' ratings of Rattlers	
	N	%	N	%
1 [a]	14	21.2	19	36.5
2	21	31.8	21	40.4
3	8	12.1	4	7.7
4	13	19.9	5	9.6
5 [b]	10	15.0	3	5.8

[a] Most unfavorable category.
[b] Most favorable category.

TABLE 6.4

*Stereotype ratings of the ingroup on six characteristics (combined)
by members of Rattler and Eagle groups (end of Stage 2)*

	Rattlers' ratings of Rattlers		Eagles' ratings of Eagles	
Category	N	%	N	%
1 [a]	0	0	0	0
2	0	0	2	3.8
3	0	0	1	1.9
4	9	13.7	8	14.7
5 [b]	57	86.3	43	79.6

[a] Most unfavorable category.
[b] Most favorable category.

tions gave rise to intergroup friction, members of both the Rattler and Eagle groups were rated favorably by other members of their respective ingroup. While the tendency was to rate outgroup members unfavorably at this stage (Table 6.3), there was an even more pronounced tendency to rate ingroup members favorably (100 percent favorable ratings of ingroup by Rattlers and 94.3 percent favorable ratings by Eagles).

Figure 6.3 presents the main findings in graphic form. Ratings of the outgroup by both Eagles and Rattlers are significant in the unfavorable direction; ratings of the ingroup by both groups are significant in the favorable direction. And, as noted above, ratings of ingroup and outgroup differ significantly in direction.

Thus, competition and rivalry between the groups led to attribution of unfavorable characteristics to the outgroup and was accompanied by a marked tendency to see ingroup members in a highly favorable light. This finding is relevant to the prediction of intense ingroup solidarity under conditions of intergroup competition, rivalry, and hostility (Hypothesis 2, Stage 2). It constitutes further evidence that intergroup relations do not necessarily follow the same pattern as ingroup relations, particularly when the relationship between the interacting groups is one of rivalry and antagonism.

Observational and sociometric data, and evidence in this unit, support Hypothesis 1 (Stage 2). During the course of competition and frustrating relations between the experimentally formed groups, unfavorable labels were assigned to the outgroup and its members and

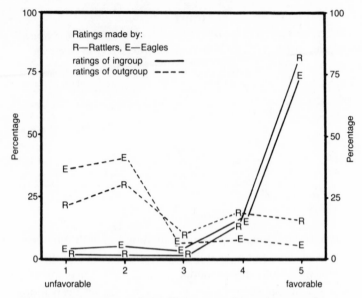

Figure 6.3 Stereotype ratings of ingroup and outgroup members on six characteristics (combined) (end of Stage 2)

were used and shared to varying extents by members of the ingroup. Social distances crystallized in these standardized derogations were great enough that for a time, members of each group expressed a strong desire not to associate in any way with the outgroup or its members (see Chapter 5).

Performance Estimates

A second experimental unit was introduced at the end of Stage 2 to obtain further evidence of the products of prolonged negative interaction between the two experimentally formed ingroups. In this experiment, direct numerical judgments were obtained in such a way that they might reflect the character and intensity of intergroup relations after a period of competition, rivalry, and friction between the two groups. Members of both experimental groups judged items presumably achieved by members of their own ingroup and by members of the rival outgroup while the groups were performing a task for which the winning group would be rewarded.

As already discussed, it was proposed that negative intergroup relations would in time produce derogatory conceptions (stereotypes) of the outgroup accompanied by intensified ingroup solidarity and a highly positive picture of the ingroup. It was further proposed that the deprecatory picture of the outgroup and the flattering picture of the ingroup would be internalized by individual members as negative attitudes toward the outgroup and positive attitudes toward the ingroup, and that these attitudes would be revealed not just in stereotype ratings, as described in the preceding section, but also in judgments of the performance by members of the ingroup and outgroup on a relevant task. The task chosen for the latter purpose was a bean toss contest; judgments of the number of beans presumably collected by each individual were made after the contest.

Specifically it was predicted (Hypothesis 1a, Stage 2) that as a consequence of intergroup competition, rivalry, and hostility:

Ingroup members will tend to overestimate the number of items purportedly attained by ingroup members and to underestimate the number of items attributed to outgroup members.

The data from this experimental unit are to be evaluated in conjunction with observational findings showing, as a consequence of intergroup rivalry and conflict, increased glorification of the ingroup and its members and deprecation of the outgroup.[2] The judgmental indices obtained should reflect this state of affairs reported by observers and are intended to supplement their findings, not to replace them.

The plan to obtain experimental measures of attitudes formed toward the groups by the end of Stage 2 represents an extension to the level of intergroup relations of a basic psychological principle underlying the conception of this entire study, namely, that all psychological activity is determined by the frame of reference within which it occurs (see Chapter 2). The frame of reference consists of the totality of functionally related factors, external and internal, that operate interdependently to determine the psychological reaction at any given time. The *relative* weights of the external and internal factors in determining psychological activity are not necessarily the same in different

2. It had been planned to repeat this experimental unit and the stereotype ratings at the end of Stage 3, to secure further evidence of the differential effects of intergroup cooperation toward superordinate goals. However, to avoid possible cluttering of the ongoing trend that evolved in Stage 3, this unit was not repeated.

instances. The relative weights of these factors vary with the degree of stimulus structure and the nature and intensity of internal states at the time. When stimulus conditions are compelling in structure, the effects of internal (e.g., motivational) factors in patterning perception and behavior are not readily apparent; but under conditions of minimum stimulus structure, of ambiguity or flux, internal factors operating at the time may be clearly reflected in the subsequent behavior. Therefore, in attempts to study motivational factors through their influence on the patterning of perceptual and judgmental responses, stimulus conditions should be both appropriate and sufficiently unstructured that the nature of the motivational factors can be revealed through the resulting behavior.

Since the presentation of the foregoing formulation (Sherif 1935), a number of studies have investigated various motivational factors through their influence on such processes as perceiving and judging. The distinctive feature of the present experiment is that judgments are used as indices of the *relationship between experimentally produced ingroups.*

In Sherif's 1949 intergroup relations experiment, ingroups and negative relationships between them were produced through controlling conditions of interactions in essentially the same way as in this 1954 experiment. It was observed that as a consequence of the negative relationship between groups, ingroup members extolled and maximized the peformance of ingroup members, while deprecating and belittling the performance of members of the unfriendly outgroup. This observation called attention to the feasibility of obtaining precise experimental indices of intergroup relations through their differential effects on the perceptions and judgments of individual members. These judgments and perceptions will reflect the influence of membership and participation in the ongoing activities of the group.

This being the case, the effects of the group situation, and the changes brought about in attitudes toward the in-group and the out-group and their respective members, can be studied in terms of precise laboratory experiments, such as the currently accumulating judgment and perception studies. This will constitute a significant advance in method over observation of actual behavioral events alone. The actual behavioral events are more difficult to observe with precision and present baffling problems in their ordering along definite dimensions. If the psychological significance can be epitomized and measured in terms of representative judgmental and perceptual situations, we shall be achieving a methodological gain close to the laboratory level (Sherif 1951, 422).

This proposed method of studying group relations through judgmental indices was applied to a study of status relations within *groups that already existed in everyday life* (Harvey 1953). It was found that judgments of future performance of group members provided an index of their relative status positions within the group. Owing to the differential expectations that had become standardized for each status position, performance of high-ranking members tended to be overestimated, while that of lower-ranking members was estimated as significantly lower, even to the point of underestimation of actual performance.

The same methodological approach was applied in Sherif, Harvey, and White's 1953 experiment to the study of status relations in experimentally produced groups. Going a step further, that study tapped the differential expectations for members occupying positions in a status structure that was itself experimentally produced.[3] Members of the experimental groups judged the performance of ingroup members on the task of throwing hardballs at a target board designed so that there was little indication of actual performance. The status positions that had evolved during the period of group interaction were reliably revealed in the subject's judgments of other members' performance, made immediately following each throw. The performance of higher-ranking members was judged significantly higher than that of lower-ranking members.

More recently this technique was extended to the study of negative and positive relationships between small groups existing in everyday life. Harvey (1954) showed that the relationship prevailing between interacting groups is revealed in the judgments of group members under appropriate stimulus conditions. The performance actually achieved by each subject—the number of city names written under conditions of distraction—were projected on a screen too briefly for actual count, and the number was judged by both ingroup and outgroup members. When intergroup relations were negative, the tendency was to judge the performance of ingroup members at a significantly higher level than that of outgroup members.

We reiterate that the present experimental unit is concerned with obtaining judgmental indices of the relationships between two groups

3. The plans for the 1953 study called for using the same methods to tap attitudes toward ingroup and outgroup after a period of intergroup friction. However, this unit was not undertaken until this 1954 study.

*that were experimentally produced and that came into conflict as a con-
sequence of experimentally introduced conditions of competition and
frustration.*

Procedure

Members of the two groups (Eagles and Rattlers) participated in a
bean toss contest under strongly competitive conditions. They then
made judgments of the number of beans collected by each ingroup
and outgroup member, as the beans purportedly collected by the particular individual were projected on a screen by an opaque projector.

The contest was held after the tournament and various raids of
Stage 2 (see Chapter 5). Social distance between the groups was sufficiently great that neither wanted to be in a situation with the other.
They entered into this contest when told that the staff members of
their respective groups had made a wager on the outcome and were
offering a $5 reward to the winning group. Before the contest, the
leader of the Eagle group predicted darkly, "It will turn into a gang
fight." In spite of this initial resistance, both groups participated in the
contest with considerable zeal once it was under way.

The beans were spread in equal density in two marked-off areas of
similar size. The Rattlers picked up beans from one area, while the
Eagles gathered beans from the adjoining area (see Figure 6.4). Separate areas were used to prevent pushing and shoving of outgroup
members. The time allowed for picking up beans was 1 minute. Pretests with comparable subjects before the experiment showed that
1 minute permitted the collection of 25−40 beans. To prevent the
subjects from exceeding this range and to limit possibilities of their
counting the beans collected, each was given a small brown paper
sack, the open end of which was gathered around a hollow rubber
tube with a half-inch opening. Subjects were instructed to pick up
only one bean at a time and put it in the sack through the half-inch
opening. Thus, speed of performance was at a premium. They were
instructed not to count the beans, that this would be done later, and
were told that everyone would judge the performance of everyone
else. The judgmental aspect of the task, which was actually the crucial one for this unit, was presented as a regular part of the bean toss
contest.

Figure 6.4 Bean toss experiment on judgments of ingroup and outgroup performance (end of Stage 2)

The two groups performing the task

The experimental setup

After the beans had been collected, the subjects went to an experimental room (large recreation hall) where the beans collected of each member of both groups were purportedly projected by an opaque projector and judged by both ingroup and outgroup members. Actually the *same number* of beans (35) was projected every time as the performance by every individual in the two groups. The number chosen had been found in pretests prior to the experiment to be the optimum number for the brief exposure time used (5 seconds). It was necessary that the number of items projected should be too great to count in 5 seconds, but at the same time should be few enough that the subjects would feel that if they had tried just a little harder, they could have finished the count. If the actual number could have been accurately established by the subjects, obviously there would have been no indication of motivational factors in their judgments.

The experimenter made it appear that he was putting in new beans to be projected each time, but the same ones were retained for every projection. The experimenter moved the location of some of the beans each time only slightly. Therefore, the form of the projection (circular) remained essentially the same, but the pattern was slightly different from projection to projection.

A coin toss determined that the performance of members of the Eagle group should be projected and judged first. Before the purported performance of each boy was projected, the experimenter called his name and the boy stood up so that both ingroup and outgroup members would know exactly whose performance was being judged. The subjects wrote their judgments on small pads of paper. Each boy wrote down the name called out. When the biggest of the Rattlers was called off, "Red Brown," one of the Eagles (Wilson, a lieutenant) said, "I'm just going to put Red Bum on mine."

Results

To test the hypothesis, it was necessary to ascertain the extent to which the performance of each ingroup and outgroup member was over- or underestimated and to compare these mean differences. Since the same number of items (35) was projected as the performance of each subject, this constant was subtracted from each judgment of performance. Means of these differences were then computed for judgments of performance by ingroup members and by outgroup

TABLE 6.5

*Comparison of mean discrepancies between judgments of
performance and number of items projected (35):
ingroup and outgroup members*

| Group judging | Group being judged | | Mean differences | t | p |
	Rattlers	*Eagles*			
Rattlers	3.404	− .293	3.697	3.452 < .01
Eagles	4.556	11.802	7.246	4.069 < .01

members. The differences between the means were subjected to the *t*-test, using the formula for correlated means. Results of this analysis are given in Table 6.5.

From the table it can be inferred that the performance of ingroup members was judged significantly higher than that of members of the outgroup. The Rattlers' mean discrepancy for judgments of performance by ingroup members was 3.404 and that by members of the outgroup (Eagles) was − .293. Thus while members of the Rattler group overestimated the performance of ingroup members, they tended to underestimate the performance of negatively related outgroup members. (When the beans supposedly collected by the leader of the Rattlers were projected, a member of his group whistled appreciatively.)

Members of the Eagle group greatly overestimated the performance of ingroup members (mean discrepancy of 11.802) and overestimated the performance of outgroup members significantly *less*, although not to the point of underestimation reached by the Rattlers in their judgments of the Eagles' performance. (Perhaps the Eagles' recent victory in the tournament over great odds had something to do with this difference.)

For both groups, the performance of ingroup members was judged significantly higher than that of outgroup members. For two reasons, the results cannot be explained in terms of differences in actual performance: since speed was the crucial factor and each bean had to be inserted through a small opening in the bag, individuals did not have an opportunity to observe each other's performance; and the number of items projected as the performance of each individual in both groups was identical (35).

These results are concordant with observational findings concerning the valuation of ingroup members and deprecation of members of the outgroup, and with sociometric findings that revealed a preponderance of ingroup choices. Therefore, it can be concluded that the results reflect the solidarity within groups and the negative attitudes toward outgroups at the end of Stage 2. Data from this unit also support the hypothesis that, as a consequence of intergroup competition and conflict, ingroup members will tend to overestimate the performance of members of their own group and to deprecate the performance by members of a rival outgroup.

The findings indicate that conceptions of the ingroup and outgroup can be tapped experimentally through judgments obtained from individual members of the functionally related groups. Their larger significance bears on the individual-group relationship. They point again to the fallacy of dichotomies between the individual and the group. Here, the relationship between groups, a phenomenon at the group level, has consequences not only for the formation of values or social norms within the group, but for the perception and judgments of individual members as well.

End Products of Intergroup Friction

As a consequence of repeated interaction between the two experimentally formed groups in competitive and reciprocally frustrating situations, and of the cumulative intergroup friction thus engendered, the members of each ingroup formed negative attitudes toward the outgroup. These negative attitudes toward the outgroup, crystallized in unfavorable stereotypes, were manifested by name calling, derogation of the outgroup, and the explicit desire to avoid association with the outgroup (see the observational data summarized in Chapter 5). To check these observations and to ascertain that they indicated more than merely momentary reactions in intergroup conflict situations, an entire day was devoted to ingroup activities following the close of actual competition and conflict between the groups. On the next day following, attitudes toward ingroup and outgroup were tapped through sociometric choices, stereotype ratings of the ingroup and outgroup, and judgments of performance by ingroup and outgroup members in a competitive task (bean toss contest). Analysis of these results confirms, in a more precise way, the observational findings.

The methodological importance of this correspondence between observational and judgmental data is twofold. First, it provides a check on the validity of the conclusions reached. Second, it indicates the possibilities of using judgments of ingroups and outgroups as indices of the state of affairs prevailing on the level of group relationships.

The methodology we have described stems from the approach, stated in Chapters 1 and 2, to the study of the complex processes of interaction in intra- and intergroup relations. On the one hand, this methodology made it feasible to set up the flow of interaction processes in a lifelike, natural way; on the other hand, validity and precision could be ensured through obtaining data by observation (looking from without), by sociometric techniques (looking from within) and by the introduction of precise laboratory-type experiments at choice points. In our opinion, only through the use of such a combination of methods, applied to the flow of interaction processes without chopping them into disjointed pieces, can we hope to attain generalizations with some bearing on the persistent group problems of actual life situations. If we follow such an approach in testing hypotheses, we are less likely to be troubled with the problems of validity that have plagued so many studies in this area.

From a theoretical point of view, the results of these experimental units, carried out after actual intergroup conflict had ceased, indicate that events occurring between groups have consequences at both a group level (norms relating to the outgroup) and at a psychological level (formation of negative attitudes toward the outgroup), and that these consequences outlast the intergroup events themselves.

The crucial question remaining is whether or not changes in the character of relationships between groups, wrought through altering the conditions in which the groups interact from those conducive to friction to those of interdependence, will result in a reduction of friction between the groups and in changes in negative attitudes and stereotypes standardized in relation to the outgroup. This question was the point of departure for Stage 3 of this experiment, to which the next chapter is devoted.

7

Intergroup Relations: Reducing Friction

At this stage of the experiment, we could undertake the main objective of our study, namely the reduction of intergroup friction. There were now two distinct groups in an unmistakable state of friction with one another. The groups exhibited, in word and deed, repeated hostility toward one another; they standardized unflattering attitudes and stereotypes toward one another.

The derogatory attitudes toward one another were not the consequence of preexisting feelings or attitudes that the subjects had when they came to the experimental site. They were not the consequence of ethnic, religious, educational, or other background differentiation among the subjects. Nor were they the result of any extraordinary personal frustration in the particular life histories of the subjects, or of marked differentiation in physical, intellectual, or other psychological abilities or characteristics of the subjects. Possible effects of such differences were carefully ruled out in the laborious procedures used in subject selection (see Chapter 3).

The state of friction was produced systematically by introducing conditions of rivalry and frustration perceived by the subjects as stemming from the other group. By the end of Stage 2, as we have seen, the intergroup friction was crystallized in some unfavorable stereotypes and in the repeatedly expressed desire to have nothing more to do with the other group. To be sure, the words and deeds of hostility, the unflattering stereotypes toward the outgroup, and the self-righteousness of the ingroup were not expressed with the same determination, the same vehemence, the same degree of feeling by any two group members. But, whatever the differentiating degree or intensity in the unique personal manifestation of hostility, the general trend of a negative attitude toward the outgroup was a property common to all group members. The intergroup hostility prevailed despite the occurrence of occasional interpersonal rivalry, bickering, and friction in the relations within each group. Two boys who at a given moment engaged in some interpersonal exchange of unfavorable reactions toward one another would join hands a few minutes later in a concerted, common front in carrying out the developing intergroup trend in relation to the outgroup. It should also be remembered that the ingroup identification and solidarity in ingroup and intergroup relations did not stem from preexisting interpersonal ties. The boys were not even personally acquainted with one another prior to the study. The two ingroups themselves were experimentally produced from scratch in the manner reported in Chapter 4.

Approach to Reducing Friction

It would have been a relatively easy task to bring about positive relations or harmony between groups right after the formation of the two ingroups. We deliberately postponed this positive step in intergroup relations until after the unpleasant task of producing a state of friction, because the vital issue of intergroup relations in the present-day world is the reduction of existing intergroup friction.

The general character of the alternative chosen in our attempt to reduce friction was stated in Chapter 2. Our choice represented a rejection of several other alternatives. The alternative of appeal to a "common enemy," which was effectively used in our 1949 study because of expediency at the time, was not used. The unification of groups against a common enemy necessarily implies widening the area of conflict.

We also rejected the alternative of reducing tension by disintegrating the groups as units through devices that make individual "shining" and rivalry supreme without concern for the other fellow. By following such an approach, we would have destroyed the property of intergroup relations that makes its study so crucial, namely, the relations between group units.

Likewise, the alternative that exclusively emphasizes the role of leaders in charge misses the mark, because the effectiveness of leaders, even though weighty, is not unlimited. Leaders are not immune to influences coming from the rank and file, once a group trend gets rolling, even though initially the leaders might have been largely responsible for starting the trend.

With such considerations in mind, we chose the alternative of introducing common, superordinate goals of sufficient appeal value. But before doing so, we studied the possible effect of mere intergroup *contact* as *equals,* because there are adherents of this approach in both academic and practitioner circles.

At this point a word of clarification concerning the concept of *contact* will be helpful. The word *contact* has flexible denotations that allow it to become a blanket term. It could be used to refer to any kind of perceptible interpersonal or intergroup interaction. In customary usage in intergroup relations, though, the word *contact* refers to having individuals from different social, ethnic, or national backgrounds come together on some specific occasion, such as a tea party, lecture, dinner, or dancing party. We are using the term in this customary sense and reserving the concept of *interaction* for broader generic reference.

We report the intergroup contact situations and their results in the next section. The common superordinate goal situations and their products are presented in the third section.

Contacts Introduced to Reduce Friction

Nature of Contact Situations

The first part of Stage 3 was devoted to a series of contact situations varying in duration from about 15 minutes to an hour or so. The situations were of differing character, such as participating together in a psychological experiment with the opportunity to interact before and after the experiment, attending a movie together, or having meals together in the same mess hall with the utmost freedom to choose seats and interact with anyone in any way desired.

Essentially the same general procedure was followed in each of the contact situations. The two groups were taken to the place of contact (for example, the recreation hall or mess hall), both groups arriving at the same time or one shortly after the other, and then they were left to their own devices. Once the groups were in the contact situation, the staff walked away from the immediate contact range and pretended to be engaged in some activity, such as sitting under a tree in conversation. In no contact situations did the Eagle and Rattler staff members associate with one another while the contact situations were being initiated and carried out.

First Contact

The first contact situation was during the second part of the bean toss experiment, in which the subjects were to estimate individually the projected number of beans supposedly picked up by each of the subjects in both groups. (See the end of Chapter 6 for a description of this experiment.) Each group was strongly opposed to taking part in the bean toss experiment because it involved association with the other group. Even the offered prize of $5 for the winners was not very effective at first in reducing the resistance of the groups.

Later in the day, during a Rattler cookout at Lake Carlton, the public picnic ground near the camp, it was announced to them that they had won the bean toss contest and they were given the prize, a $5 bill. They were told they could spend it any way they liked. The group unanimously assented to the first suggestion offered—that they spend their $5 for the repair of one of their two boats, which they had been unable to use for several days because of a leak.

The Eagles, especially, were dead set against participating in any activity having anything whatsoever to do with the Rattlers. In an early morning swim that day, the Eagles had discovered their flag in the water, burned the previous evening by the Rattlers. Upon making this discovery, they denounced the Rattlers as "dirty bums" and accused them of having put ice in the water (because it appeared to one of them as colder than usual) and of throwing rocks in their creek (because one of them stubbed his toes a number of times during the swim).

Shortly after the beans were collected in the first part of the experiment, both groups were instructed to come to the recreation hall to estimate the number of beans each "picked up." Two sets of four rows of benches were arranged for subjects during the experiment, only a narrow aisle of about 1 yard separating the two sets of benches (see Figure 6.4). When both groups arrived in front of the building, they were told to wait there for a short time until the apparatus was fixed. During the wait there was some bantering back and forth between the groups about who had won the tournament. During this waiting period the staff kept away from the groups. When the staff gave the signal to enter (addressed to no particular group), the Rattlers went in the building first. One of the Eagles remarked, "Ladies first." Until the last days of Stage 3, when the Rattlers went in first on such occasions, the Eagles made this "Ladies first" remark. The Rattlers took the front seats, leaving the back seats for the Eagles and thus producing seating arrangements strictly along group lines.

There were jeering, catcalls, and insulting remarks as the proceedings permitted. During the event, Mason (E) warned Simpson (R) to stay out of the Eagles' swimming hole. When the beans that were supposed to be Mills's (R leader) were projected, Everett (R) said "Whew!" and several other Rattlers whistled, presumably in respect. It will be remembered that the number of beans projected for all subjects was exactly the same (35). Toward the end of the event, a Rattler noticed that the pencils were "Eagle" brand, and dropped his, saying in a loud voice that he did not want to touch anything that had anything to do with the Eagles. Most of the other Rattlers followed suit. When the affair was over and the groups parted, they yelled insults at each other; outstanding among them were Eagles calling Rattlers "dirty bums" and Rattlers calling Eagles "sissies" and "babies."

Second Contact

The second contact situation took place about half an hour later before the first stereotype rating session. Neither group appeared to be pleased with the prospect of participating in this task in the company of the other group. The Rattlers felt positively insulted at being asked to do so. The same procedure of a short wait for both groups in front of the building was followed. When they were asked to come in, with no indication of which group was to enter first, the Rattlers again entered first, eliciting the "Ladies first" remark from the Eagles. The response to this remark was derisive. The tables for this event were arranged in a V shape, something that had not been done before. The aim was that position habits would not determine that the groups sit separately, in their accustomed eating positions. The seating arrangement was still strictly along group lines. Again there were no signs of intermingling, but there were complaints about the Eagle pencils, and derogatory remarks were hurled, especially by Rattlers.

The rest of the day was spent in ingroup activities. The Rattlers had their lunch at Lake Carlton. The picnic area was full of outside people. The Rattlers' dealings were almost entirely within their ingroup. The Eagles had lunch at the usual camp mess hall. The Eagle participant observer intentionally sat down at the Rattlers' table to see what would happen. Only Bryan came to sit beside him. Wilson shouted to him to get up because he would get all dirty sitting at that table. Bryan got up and brushed his clothes off.

Third Contact

The third contact situation was before supper, in front of the mess hall. Both groups waited in close proximity, the pretext for the wait being that the food was not yet ready. The staff again withdrew from the scene. While the groups waited, an argument arose as to which was the best, and invectives were exchanged. When a neutral party gave the signal that the food was ready, the Rattlers started in first, accompanied by the Eagles' now standardized remark, "Ladies first." The Rattlers were in the mess hall quite a while, but the Eagles were not making a move to go in as they usually did. Seeing this, the Eagle participant observer told them to go in when they wanted to. The Eagles waited until the Rattlers had all gotten food on their trays. After the Eagles entered the mess hall, the exchange of unflattering words between the two groups became louder and louder. The Rattlers lived up to their "tough" self-image and became somewhat vulgar.

Staff stayed outside, talking until supper was halfway through. The row inside increased. Both sides were throwing papers and leftovers at each other. This lasted until the Eagles finished eating and left the hall (at their observer's instructions), followed by yells and jeers.

Fourth Contact

The fourth contact situation was centered around the showing of two 15-minute films, both devoted to maritime topics. The procedure of a joint wait in front of the building (while the projector was being "fixed) and free choice of seats was again followed. The Eagles passed the Rattler cabin on the way and were yelled at by Rattlers. The staff moved away. There was again the exchange of hostile remarks; again the same "Ladies first" remark. During the movie there was practically no exchange between groups. But there was some exchange during the change of films. The seating arrangement was strikingly along group lines. When the event ended, around 9:30 P.M., the staff walked out without telling the boys to leave or anything else. The boys arose and went out, intermingling. But at the door they completely split—each group in the direction of its respective cabin.

Fifth Contact

The fifth contact situation was planned as breakfast the following morning. The positions of the tables in the mess hall had been completely changed, so that any habitual fixations on a particular table would be broken. The two tables, which had been placed across the mess hall, now ran longitudinally; and the staff table was moved to the opposite end of the hall—away from the boys. (At no meal during any of the three stages did any of the staff members sit at any of the subjects' tables in the mess hall.) When both groups arrived in front of the hall, the counselors and other authority figures withdrew on a pretext. During a short wait, an argument arose as to which group had the most firecrackers. Again a person who had no authority in the eyes of the subjects announced that breakfast was ready. The same "Ladies first" ritual followed.

One of the low-status Rattlers (Allen) happened to be the first one in front of the Rattler line. He picked up his food first and carried his tray to the table by the south wall of the mess hall. (The south side of the mess hall was in the general direction of the Eagle area.) Seeing one Rattler at that table (the choice of which had no basis in previous experience), all the rest of the Rattlers sat at that table. This, of course, determined that the Eagles choose the table by the north wall of the mess hall. During the meal there was razzing and yelling, but it was not as intense as during supper on the previous night, and two different Rattler and Eagle pairs made attempts to kick each other.

Sixth Contact

The sixth contact situation was planned in relation to shooting firecrackers. (It was the Fourth of July.) In line with the decision not to appeal to values from the larger setting in achieving reduction of intergroup friction, and in line with the subjects' preference, each group held separate ceremonies appropriate to the national holiday. However, the shooting of firecrackers was planned as a special contact situation. On the previous day, the Eagles went to town as a group with their staff and bought firecrackers. A similar supply of firecrackers was bought for the Rattlers. Both groups were taken in close succession to a place by the wayside outside of the State Park area to shoot their firecrackers. (Shooting firecrackers is prohibited within the park area, and the camp is within its bounds.) Wilson of the Eagles said that he didn't want to get out of the truck if they had to shoot their firecrackers with the Rattlers. The subjects were told that they could shoot their firecrackers with anyone they wanted to. Both groups started shooting them at about the same time. At no time was there intermingling of the two groups (see Figure 7.1). At one particular time, Simpson (R) and Clark (E) were closest to one another. Simpson accused Clark of shooting a rock up in the air and hitting him on the head.

Seventh Contact

The seventh contact situation began when both groups arrived at the mess hall for lunch at the same time, as planned. All staff members withdrew from the immediate area of contact. From that distance, conversation within or between groups could not be heard. Each group stayed on the side of the mess hall entrance nearest its own cabin. There was no crossing over between groups.

At the announcement "food is ready," both groups moved in. This time the Eagles rushed in first to form the line to pick up trays and food. The Rattlers followed them. McGraw (E), who was the first person through the line, sat at the same table that the Eagles had used in the morning after the new table arrangement.

After the boys had been eating for a while, someone threw something, and the fight was on. It consisted of throwing rolls, napkins rolled into a ball, mashed potatoes, and so forth, accompanied by yelling the standardized unflattering words at each other. The throwing continued for about 8 to 10 minutes, then the cook announced that cake and ice cream were ready. Some members of each group

Figure 7.1 Intergroup relations: (above) effects of intergroup contact without superordinate goals; (below) intergroup interaction after the introduction of superordinate goals

The two groups shooting fireworks. Rattlers in foreground; Eagles in background

Mess hall after one of the "garbage fights" between the groups eating together

Members of both groups climb up to see if the water tank is empty

Members of both groups cluster around and take turns trying to clear the faucet

went after their dessert, but most of them continued throwing things a while longer. As soon as each boy had gobbled his dessert, he resumed throwing. As the Eagles were leaving they shouted at the Rattlers *that they would resume the fight at supper,* and the Rattlers responded to this challenge with counterchallenges.

Summary of Contacts

After describing the events summarized above, the Eagle participant observer added the following comment to his report written that day: "It was apparent by this time that mere contact between the groups without the introduction of superordinate goals was going to be insufficient to reduce the negative relationships between the groups. The Rattler participant observer wrote in much stronger terms in his daily report his opinion concerning the inadequacy of mere contact situations in reducing the intergroup friction and name calling.

The intergroup events accompanying and following the series of contact situations summarized above confirm Hypothesis 1 (Stage 3):

> It is predicted that the contact phase in itself will not produce marked decrease in the existing state of tension between groups.

Accordingly, it was decided to start introducing interaction situations involving common superordinate goals, instead of situations involving mere contact. In spite of the fact that the activity engaged in during contacts (such as eating and shooting firecrackers) was gratifying or pleasing for each individual member within the ingroup bounds, the mere fact of contact had no positive effect toward reducing existing hostility.

Intergroup Interaction Involving Superordinate Goals

Thus, contacts that did not involve superordinate goals in the sense defined at the outset (Chapter 2), were far from effective in reducing intergroup friction. If anything, such contacts served as occasions for further irritations and for expressing unflattering attitudes of group against group.

At this point we turned to procedures suitable for testing the main hypothesis (Hypothesis 2, Stage 3) concerning the reduction of inter-group conflict:

> When groups in a state of friction are brought into contact under conditions embodying superordinate goals, the attainment of which is compelling but which cannot be achieved by the efforts of one group alone, the groups will tend to cooperate toward the common goal.

The present section summarizes the stimulus conditions introduced that were conducive to the emergence of superordinate goals, and the reactions of the subjects obtained by various measurement techniques. Thus this section includes, first, a brief account of stimulus conditions introduced for the arousal of superordinate goals and observational data relevant to the hypothesis stated above. Second, we describe sociometric choices of group members revealing their attitudes toward ingroup and outgroup members and we compare these choices with those obtained at the end of Stage 2. Third, we report judgment indices of attitudes toward the respective ingroups and outgroups in the form of stereotype ratings and their comparison with the stereotype ratings obtained at the end of Stage 2.

Superordinate Goals and Related Interaction Episodes

The Drinking Water Problem

The first superordinate goal introduced pertained to drinking water at a time when both groups faced the prospect of thirst and became progressively thirstier with the successive steps of activities directed toward solution of the problem. In general outline, the plan consisted of having members of both groups perceive common deprivation, which could be alleviated (so it appeared to them) by the cooperation of members of both groups. Thus a situation of functional interdependence involving a common goal was produced.

First, a word is necessary concerning the preparation of stimulus conditions. All of the drinking water in the camp, which is distributed to various parts of the camp (kitchen, latrines, drinking fountains located near cabins, and other convenient spots), comes from a reservoir on the mountain north of the camp. It is pumped up to a large water tank higher on the mountain (about 1 1/4 miles from camp—see Figure 3.2) and stored there in sufficient supply for a certain period. A valve at one end of the tank controls the flow of water and can be cut off to prevent the passage of water to the main pipe which, as it reaches the camp grounds, runs into various smaller pipes to the various outlets.

Several hours before the execution of the plan, the valve on the tank was closed, leaving only the water already in the main pipe to supply the camp for the time being. After turning off the valve, staff placed two large boulders over it, which had to be removed before the valve could be turned on again. In addition, the faucet at the end of the tank opposite the valve was stuffed with pieces of sacking so that no water came from the faucet when it was turned on. The latter device was planned to require a solution of the problem if the boys were to get water, and getting a drink when members of both groups were thirsty would itself have very high common appeal value.

Right after the water was cut off at the tank, the boys were informed by their respective participant observers that there might be a water shortage in the whole camp, as there seemed to be some trouble with the water system, but that the trouble was being investigated. They advised members of each group to fill their canteens in case the water shortage became worse. The boys were told that in the past, on occasion, vandals had tinkered with the water system, causing difficulties. This warning was given so that the boys would not blame their thirst on the camp staff. After this introduction, all of the remaining water was drained out through faucets that were out of sight of the subjects. (Of course, for any emergency, sufficient water was stored in the small tank in the kitchen for both cooking and drinking. But the subjects did not know it.)

The execution of the plan was postponed until 4 P.M. so that there would be little if any water left in the subjects' canteens. Before actual efforts began toward getting the water to run again, the topic of the water shortage became a common topic of concern in both groups.

To summarize the experimentally planned activities, all members of both groups were present at the announcement that the water system had completely failed, depriving the entire camp of drinking water. To make the situation real to the subjects, this announcement took place at the spot where the end of the main water pipe from the tank was visible and where a number of faucets in a row could be turned on. Thus subjects could see for themselves that there was not a drop of water coming through.

After this demonstration the subjects were informed that there was something wrong with the water system and that the trouble could not be located. They were told that the difficulty might be a leak in the pipe between camp and the reservoir; it might be at the pump by the reservoir; or it might be at the tank. Thus, the first step was to find the cause so that necessary steps could be taken to remedy the difficulty. The announcement went on to say that the help of about 25 people was needed.

Upon hearing the announcement, members of both groups volunteered to help. The area between the camp and the reservoir, it was announced, was to be divided into four segments to be inspected by four different search details. One staff member would accompany each detail. It was announced that five boys were needed for the area around the reservoir. This detail would go farthest, and it would be accompanied by an Eagle staff member. The volunteers that stepped forward for this detail were all Eagles. The detail for the segment adjacent to the reservoir area, up to the tank, was to be accompanied by a Rattler staff member. Volunteers for that detail were all Rattlers. The same alternation was followed for the remaining two segments, with an Eagle staff member and Rattler staff member accompanying the two details, respectively. Without any exception, each detail consisted of volunteers from the same group as the accompanying staff member. (A detail of two boys and a staff member was to stay by the faucets in camp for an hour and then go to report at the tank area.) The details at the end segments were to move toward the tank area, reporting, on the way, to the adjacent detail if they found any difficulty. All groups would congregate at the tank to investigate it if nothing was found along the way. Thus, the division of the area into segments and alternation of adjacent segments between Rattlers and Eagles produced a situation of interdependence in a coordinated activity.

In a little over an hour, all the details from both sides congregated at the tank, of course having found nothing wrong on the way. Thus the tank was the only alternative left for locating the trouble.

The first object to attract the attention of everyone in both groups was the faucet at the north end of the tank, since most of them were thirsty. Some of the Rattlers still had a little water in their canteens, but the Eagles did not even have their canteens with them. The appeal of water was great and urgent, especially for the Eagles. (Both groups had come to this faucet for drinking water during their campouts at the reservoir during Stage 1.) Of course, no water came out of the faucet. The next problem was immediate and compelling: to secure drinking water then and there. That no water came out of the faucet led to a discussion within and between groups as to whether there was any water in the tank. During this discussion, boys pounded on the sides of the tank. Then some Rattlers discovered a ladder about 30 feet from the tank (where it had been moved in the morning when the faucet was stopped up and the valve turned off). There was rejoicing over this discovery. Immediately some of the Rattlers brought the ladder to the side of the tank and climbed to the top, followed by the Eagles. The boys took turns taking off the lid to inspect the inside of the tank (see Figure 7.1). There were several exclamations that the tank was three-fourths full.

The discovery of a practically full tank turned the attention of both groups to the faucet again. In investigating the outlet, Mills (R leader) found the sack stuffed in the faucet. Almost all the boys gathered around the faucet to try to clear it. Suggestions from members of both groups concerning effective ways to do it were thrown in from all sides, simultaneously with actual efforts at the work itself. Craig (E), especially, gave continual advice to whoever was trying to get the material out, no matter which group that boy belonged to.

In actually extracting the sack, the boys used various improvised tools (knives) belonging to different individuals. Mills worked for a time; Clark (E) was one of the first to work, making suggestions at the same time. First one and then another boy tried to get the sacking out: Simpson (R), Clark (E), Mills (R), McGraw (E), Brown (R), Mason (E), Allen (R), Swift (R) all taking turns. The work on the faucet lasted over 45 minutes and during the first 30 minutes was the focus of interest for most members of both groups. During this first period, there were continually from 15 to 19 boys standing in a tight bunch watching the work. A few drops of water aroused enthusiasm, but completion of the task was not in view. Interest started lagging toward the end. At this point Everett (R) suggested that the Eagle participant observer (calling him by his first name) was a big guy, and how about letting him try it. (This same Everett had been very vociferous in denouncing this same Eagle staff member when he had come near the Rattler cabin on some occasion.) Everett's suggestion was taken up by other boys, and the staff took over, eventually completing the job with the use of wrenches.

When the water finally came through, the boys rejoiced in common. The Rattlers did not object to having the Eagles get ahead of them when they all got a drink, since the Eagles did not have canteens with them and were thirstier. No protests or "Ladies first"-type remarks were made.

When the first enthusiasm for the work on clearing the faucet had died down, individuals increasingly drifted away from the faucet. Among these boys there was a noticeable increase of mingling across group lines in such activities as catching lizards and making wooden whistles. This good-natured mingling in several spontaneous activities took place within the framework of the common deprivation and of the interdependence that arose as a consequence of the immediate concern of everyone. This problem situation was the first striking instance in which we observed friendly interaction among members of the two groups on a general scale. For example, during the work, Everett (R) offered the use of his knife. Craig (E) told him that if it worked he would shake hands with him for supplying the tool that did the job.

After the Eagle staff member took over work on the faucet, staff called attention to the fact that there should be a valve leading to the main water pipe, which might be the source of the water shortage at camp. Some of the Rattlers went to that side of the tank and removed the boulders, then turned on the valve. Subsequently there were contradictory claims as to who discovered the valve.

It cannot be said that the negative attitudes toward the outgroups, the standardized unfavorable stereotypes, were disappearing as a consequence of the introduction of this single superordinate goal of high appeal value, even though there was cooperation and friendly mingling at the time of the activities related to it. The carry-over effects of the negative intergroup attitudes were observed at supper that very evening, and on subsequent occasions as well.

At supper time the procedure was followed again of having both groups wait for a short time before the meal while the staff members withdrew from the contact area. When the announcement was made for the groups to enter, the Eagles went in first, and this time the Rattlers expressed the insinuation "Ladies first." During the meal, members of both groups started throwing leftovers, bottle caps, and paper. Thus did they live up to the public promise they had made to each other when leaving the mess hall after lunch that they would resume the "garbage fight," as the Eagles called it. At this supper, throwing of objects started in a rather good-natured way but, in time, took on serious proportions and had to be stopped.

On the way to breakfast the following morning, the Rattlers saw the Eagles coming and made several derisive comments. Barton (R) remarked that the Eagles had gone in the mess hall first the last time. When they got close to the front of the mess hall, Simpson (high-status R) said "Howdy," and was answered by several Eagles. The same procedure was followed of having both groups wait for a time while staff members kept away. The Eagles entered first again. While in line, the Rattlers started singing the Caisson Song and were joined by several Eagles. As the boys started putting food on their trays, the cook (who had no special authority in their eyes) asked for their attention. She told them that throwing things at each other during meals made such a mess and cleaning up was taking so much time that she would not be able to cook such good meals if it did not stop. This appeal was effective. During breakfast there was some horseplay and intermingling between groups. Someone started to throw something, and McGraw (E) said, "Remember, you guys, no throwing." The groups parted peacefully after the meal.

In spite of the cessation of "garbage fights" there was tangible evidence of negative intergroup attitudes when the Rattlers were told before lunch that there was a possibility of going to a nice lake 60 miles away for an overnight campout. The Rattlers showed general enthusiasm until Mills (R leader) asked, "Are those damn Eagles going?" Another Rattler added, "I'm not going if *they* go."

Similarly, when the Eagles were told of the possibility of getting a movie to show, Craig said, "Do we have to do it with the Rattlers?" Later he said, "We want to do some things by ourselves." On the other hand, other Eagles indicated that they had no serious objection if the Rattlers were in on the movie too.

The Problem of Securing a Movie

The next superordinate goal to be introduced was a feature-length movie that had been a favorite for boys of this age level. Two films had been chosen, after consulting experts on films, and brought to camp along with other stimulus materials. The plan was to ascertain the appeal value of the film for the boys and then to make securing it (supposedly from the neighboring town) dependent on both groups contributing a sum of money that would appear rather prohibitive for one group to contribute alone.

In the afternoon, the boys were called together and the staff suggested the possibility of securing either *Treasure Island* or *Kidnapped.* Both groups yelled approval of these films. After some discussion, one Rattler said, "Everyone that wants *Treasure Island* raise their hands." The majority of members in both groups gave enthusiastic approval to *Treasure Island,* even though a few dissensions were expressed.

Then the staff announced that securing the film would cost $15 and the camp could not pay the whole sum. Members of both groups began to make all kinds of suggestions. Mills (R leader) jumped out between the two groups and suggested $5 each from the camp, Rattlers, and Eagles. Myers (E) said the camp should pay $5, the Rattlers $10, and the Eagles nothing. Harrison (R) suggested that the Eagles pay $15 and the camp and Rattlers nothing. Simpson (R) suggested that the Eagles pay $5 and the Rattlers $2. Then Myers (E) proposed that each group pay $3.50. Mills (R) took this suggestion from Myers (E) and called for a vote. He counted votes in both groups. The proposal was strongly supported. Afterward, both groups heatedly discussed who would do the figuring for each group to find out how much each member would have to pay. While the groups were figuring this out, a great deal of horseplay and intermixing took place between them.

At last, each group came up with its solution. The Rattlers figured that each of the 11 Rattlers would have to contribute 31¢; each of the 9 Eagles would have to contribute 39¢ toward securing the common goal. The Rattlers asked their staff members to contribute so that their total would come to $3.50. McGraw and Myers (E's) told the Eagle staff members that they would have to pay also, and gave the reason that the staff would get to see the movie too. Both staff members agreed to do so. Martin read the list of contributions from the Rattlers, and McGraw those of the Eagles.

It is worth noting that in individual terms, this scheme of contribution was not equitable. But it was an equitable solution between the two groups. The cooperation needed to secure the movie was cooperation *between groups,* and it was perceived as such by individual members. Therefore, the solution was seen as an equitable one by individual members of both groups.

At supper there were no objections to eating together. Some scuffling and play at sticking chewing gum around occurred between members of the two groups, but it involved fewer boys on both sides than were usually involved in such encounters. It looked like a fist fight might develop between Simpson (R) and Mason (E), but their tempers cooled off.

After supper, *Treasure Island* was shown in the mess hall. Five rows of benches were placed in the hall with an aisle in between. Both groups were waiting to enter and were told to come in. There was some confusion momentarily as to where to sit. When the milling about stopped, the seating arrangement was pretty much along group lines, with a few exceptions. The boys were absorbed in the film, and there was very little conversation.

Additional Superordinate Goals

In line with the main hypotheses of this stage, it was planned to have a series of situations embodying superordinate goals. However, a serious concern arose for further planning of superordinate goals. It became evident that in a camp situation like this one, isolated from a city or town and from outside influences, the facilities for daily activities were by this time acquiring decidedly routine aspects. Since the subjects had come to know the facilities afforded by the camp and in the general surroundings, it became increasingly difficult to introduce superordinate goals that would arouse high motivational appeal but were also inherent in the situations. Therefore, an attempt was made during the next day to secure additional transportation facilities to take both groups to Cedar Lake, which is 60 miles southeast of the camp and in many respects affords complete detachment from the ac-customed camp facilities.

Of course, this procedure does not imply that under all circum-stances and for all groups one has to search for an isolated place to find situations embodying superordinate goals for functionally related groups. If there are goals of sufficient strength for both groups in question, or serious issues in which both groups are involved with high concern, superordinate goals can be introduced even within some neighborhood of a metropolis. But in a camp situation that was by now familiar and with subjects of the age level in question, the alternatives for superordinate goals were limited in number. The immediate possibilities at the camp were fairly static, since no outside influences intervened.

Failure to secure transportation thwarted the plan to go to Cedar Lake on the day following the showing of *Treasure Island*. Therefore, instead of introducing superordinate goals in an improvised way with items that might appear artificial to the subjects, we let the day be marked by a return to ingroup areas and activities.

While waiting in line for breakfast on the day following the movie, the two groups, after discussion, reached an agreement that the Rattlers would go into breakfast first, and at lunch the Eagles would be first. (Such alternation had been discussed the previous day, but no agreement had been reached.) Thus the notion of "taking turns" was introduced by the boys on the *intergroup level* to regulate matters of mutual concern, rather than each group rushing to be first.

The Rattler group went to their hideout to look after their boat, tent, and other equipment there and to take them back to their cabin. One of the activities they engaged in had important carry-over effects and significant implications in the course of intergroup interaction on the following day, when the joint overnight campout actually did materialize. Before lunch, the Rattlers again started chopping on a big, dead pine tree which they had been trying to chop down in leisure moments for two days. When the trunk was chopped through, the tree still did not fall. The standing tree constituted both a challenge and a hazard (since it might crash down at some inopportune moment). The boys discussed how to get it down. One suggested that they had beaten the Eagles at tug-of-war, so let's have a tug-of-war against the tree. The tug rope was tied to the tree, and they all pulled the tree down—to everyone's great satisfaction. Thus, a means once used in conflict with the outgroup was now employed to defeat a stubborn and hazardous tree.

In the meantime, the staff was planning the overnight campout at Cedar Lake, both its introduction to the groups and its execution. Both groups were asked to name their preferred activities for the remaining three days of camp, with the promise that as many as possible would be carried out. The two groups discussed the selection of activities separately. Camping out was on the list of preferred activities prepared by both groups. During the two previous days, the staff had been dropping descriptions of the Cedar Lake site, 14 miles south of

Heavener, Oklahoma. Objectively, the site is an attractive spot—a clear-water lake surrounded by wooded hills; picnic facilities on high flat ground with tall shady trees; a freshwater pump, centrally located. This site's greatest advantage was that there were practically no people visiting there. It looked as though it were an abandoned island. This isolation, as well as other characteristics of the site, was carefully checked beforehand on two trips to the site by different staff members.

The "buildup" of the Cedar Lake site to the subjects became almost superfluous. While the Eagle participant observer was trying to describe it, the boys had decided they wanted to go there before he even finished. One of the attractions for them was riding there in a truck. When it was mentioned that Cedar Lake was only about 30 miles from Arkansas, the immediate response was, "Maybe we could go to Arkansas." This desire spread among the members of both groups. However, Mason (E) asked in a displeased way if the Rattlers would be in on everything the Eagles wanted to do.

It will be recalled that the Rattlers had also raised some objections on the previous day to going to Cedar Lake with the Eagles. Staff members in both groups assured the members that they could have their own trucks for the trip to Cedar Lake.

Campout at Cedar Lake

The staff spent most of the night before the departure for Cedar Lake on final preparations. A separate truck was parked near each cabin, and equipment for each group was placed near their respective trucks. A special point was made by staff to mix up the tent accessories (poles, stakes, hammers) in a way that would make it impossible for either group to erect their tent without exchanging parts with the other group. Food for lunch was chosen in bulk form, so that the problem of dividing it between groups and then of slicing it into individual portions would arise.

Both groups were most enthusiastic about the trip, and ate breakfast at 6 A.M. in short order. Especially in the case of the Rattlers, enthusiasm was so great that their insistence on an early start grew to nuisance proportions for the staff. They had voluntarily loaded and packed the truck before breakfast, the truck being floored with mattresses, with bedrolls around the sides to lean on. The trucks pulled out around seven o'clock, the Rattlers' shortly after the Eagles'. Except for intervals of rest, the boys sang their preferred songs during most of the trip.

On arrival at Cedar Lake, each group was taken first to a level place over the concrete dock by the lake. The swimming place was about one-fifth of a mile from the main camping area and separated from it by a little valley and trees so that it was not visible. When the Rattlers arrived, the Eagles were already in the water. The Rattlers went in the water also. There was about a half-hour overlap when both groups were in the water together. There was some intermingling between groups, but most conversation was directed to fellow group members.

While both groups were swimming, the trucks moved to the main camp area. The gear, tents, and so on, were dumped in two piles about 50 to 60 yards apart, the water pump being approximately halfway between the Eagle pile and the Rattler pile. Beside each pile of belongings there were separate picnic tables and fireplaces in case the Eagles and Rattlers chose to have their meals separately. Only one truck was left at this main camp area, and this was the older looking of the two. The tug-of-war rope was thrown on the ground about 20 feet from the truck, which was parked at a central point. The newer truck and a station wagon were removed and hidden behind trees on side paths away from the main camping area. The food was left in the station wagon; however, eating utensils (paper plates, cups, flatware) and jars of pickles and mustard were stacked on a table centrally located and near the lake.

After the swimming session, each group's counselor took his group to its respective tent location and picnic table. The boys were getting hungry after the early breakfast, trip, and swim. Members of both groups went to inspect the centrally located table piled with utensils and accessories. This situation set the stage for the introduction of a superordinate goal.

Tug-of-War Against the Truck

The staff member who drove the truck announced, so that everyone could hear, that he would go down the road a piece to get the food. Both groups (about 15 yards apart now) watched with interest as the driver got into the truck. The driver feigned great effort, the truck made all sorts of noises, but it just would not start (as planned). The boys became more and more interested. Several Rattlers suggested, "Let's push it," but they abandoned the idea because the truck was parked facing uphill. The tug-of-war rope was in plain sight of both groups. Mills (R) said, "Let's get 'our' tug-of-war rope and have a tug-of-war against the truck." Someone said, "Yeah, we can't push it." Swift (R) said, "20 of us can." Several boys agreed loudly with this, Mills adding, "20 of us can pull it for sure." The idea of having a tug-of-war against the truck was repeated by several boys in both groups. Mills (R) ran over to get the rope and started to tie it to the front bumper of the truck. An Eagle said it would be too long, and suggested pulling it halfway through the bumper, thus making two pulling ropes (see Figure 7.2). Clark (E) fed it through the bumper while Mills (R) stretched it out. Harrison (R) suggested that the Eagles pull one rope and the Rattlers the other. Barton (R) said, "It doesn't make any difference."

The lineup pulling on the two ends of the rope was Eagles on one side and Rattlers on the other, with the exception that Swift (big R) joined the Eagle side as anchor man and Craig (E) was next to Brown (R), the anchorman on the Rattler side.

The first pull did not "start" the truck, and it was allowed to roll back down the hill for another pull. (The truck was, of course, in running order, but the performance was completely convincing.) On the second pull, the members of both groups were thoroughly intermixed on both ropes. Some members of both groups began chanting "Heave, heave" in rhythm, something the Eagles had started during the tug-of-wars in Stage 2. Finally, the truck started, and the boys all jumped and cheered. Allen (R) shouted, "We won the tug-of-war against the truck!" Bryan (E) repeated, "Yeah! We won the tug-of-war against the truck." This cry was echoed with satisfaction by others from both groups.

Much intermingling of groups, friendly talk, and backslapping immediately followed this success. Four boys went to the pump and pumped water for each other: Mills (R), Hill (R), Craig (E), and Bryan (E). Thus the successful, interdependent efforts of both groups in pulling the truck, which was to get their food, had an immediate effect similar to that of superordinate goals introduced on previous days at the camp—intermingling of members of the two groups and friendly interaction between them.

Figure 7.2 Intergroup relations: cooperating to start the truck

First efforts to start the truck: some boys from both groups try to push it

Successful effort to start the truck: both groups have tug-of-war against the vehicle

Figure 7.3 Intergroup relations: meal preparation and trip to Arkansas

Meals on the overnight campout show intergroup mingling in preparation and serving

Members from both groups asked to be photographed on attaining the
Arkansas state line

Meal Preparation

The driver went in the truck to get the food. While waiting for it to
arrive, the participant observer of each group brought up the problem
of whether his group wanted to alternate preparing meals with the
other group or prepare them separately for themselves. In the Rattler
group, Mills (leader) suggested that the Rattlers prepare one meal that
day and the Eagles the other. This was discussed at some length and
agreed upon by the Rattlers. There were no derisive comments about
the Eagles during this discussion and no objections made to eating
with them, although prior to the trip several Rattlers had objected to
the idea of coming to the same place as the Eagles.

The discussion on this topic in the Eagle group took a different
turn. At the outset, Craig and McGraw objected to an alternating arrangement in preparing meals, saying they wanted to cook for themselves. Low-status Eagles (Clark, Cutler, and Lane) were in favor of
alternating with the Rattlers. After some discussion, the decision was
crystallized by Mason (E leader), who stated his opposition to alternating food preparation, and other high-status members supported
his position, one after another.

These discussions and the decisions reached are particularly enlightening in view of what actually took place immediately thereafter. The lunch materials had been selected so that if the groups decided to eat separately, they would have to divide the ingredients before doing so. For example, the main item was an 8-pound can of uncut luncheon meat. These situational factors, including the location of the food, took the upper hand in determining how the meal would be prepared. Here, curtailment of the effort involved in division of the supplies became dominant.

When the truck arrived with the food, both groups rushed from their respective camp areas and started carrying the food to the centrally located picnic table. At the table, they gathered around discussing across group lines whether they would alternate in meal preparation, the Rattlers favoring it and the Eagles opposing it. But in the midst of this discussion, food preparation *together* actually began. McGraw, the customary meat cutter in the Eagle group, began cutting the meat. He received much advice from everyone, and Mills (R) stood at his elbow for a time and helped him. In the meantime, Simpson (R) and Craig (E) poured Kool Aid into a bucket, Harrison (R) went for water to mix it, and Myers (E) poured in what he thought was sugar. Unfortunately, it turned out to be salt; but Myers was not berated by either Eagles or Rattlers for his mistake, even though the only immediately available Kool Aid was ruined. Harrison (R) pointed out that it wasn't really Myers's fault, since the salt was in a sugar sack. Low-status members of both sides became particularly active in preparing and distributing food. At one point, Mason (E leader) and Simpson (R) were talking, and Simpson said, "You never thought we'd be eating together?" The reply was laughter (see Figure 7.3).

The first Eagles through the line went to a centrally located picnic shed nearby and sat down at the tables. The first five or six Rattlers went to tables near their own camp area. Allen (R) asked a staff member where he should sit, and was told to sit any place he wanted. He then went to the shed and sat down with the Eagles. Neither at this time nor later was he criticized for his action. After eating, Mills (R) and Barton (R) also drifed over to the Eagle table for a short time. Shortly, both groups went to their respective camp areas for a rest period.

After separate rests, the two groups were taken to swim, one shortly after the other. This time the Rattlers were in first, but got out of the water on seeing a water moccasin darting about. When the Eagles arrived, the Rattlers told them in excited tones of a snake moving around in the vicinity, describing it in detail. For about 15 minutes, all of the boys stood together at the pier and discussed this common threat coming from nature. Then they swam together at another spot for a short period, both groups mixing together in the water.

Tent Pitching

At about four o'clock in the afternoon, after the swim, another superordinate goal was introduced. It will be remembered that in packing the tents, the accessories were mixed so that for either group to erect a tent, some exchange of parts would be necessary. Now, when each group prepared to erect their tent for the night, each noticed right away that they did not have all the complete and necessary accessories. The staff member who was regarded by the boys as the camp authority was standing between the two camp areas. The two groups started toward him carrying extra parts and arrived in front of him at about the same time. Members of the two groups began telling *each other* what extra parts they had and what they needed. After exchanging very few words, the trading of necessary items was accomplished in a matter-of-fact way between the two groups—the perceptual situation was that compelling.

When the Rattlers started to erect their tent, they found they had neglected to get a stake-driving mallet in the trade. They used rocks instead, with staff assistance, finishing the job by themselves. They were aware throughout of the Eagles' progress in tent pitching and felt quite satisfied when their own tent was up first, since the Eagles had won two out of three tent-pitching contests in Stage 2. Someone commented that they had won this time even using rocks; and another Rattler suggested that maybe they should have used rocks for driving stakes in the contest. The Eagles were also aware of the Rattlers' progress; but since they were having a hard time putting their tent up on uneven ground, they did not try to compete with the Rattlers.

The Truck Stalls Again

Before supper, the truck going to get food stalled again, as planned. This time discussion was practically unnecessary. The pattern for co-operation was established. The first effort, initiated by Rattlers, was again to push the truck. When the truck rolled into a hanging tree limb, Mills (R) got the tug-of-war rope again. The rope was pulled through the bumper, and two bunches of boys lined up to pull. How-ever, these two lines on each side were not the Eagle and Rattler groups. Members of both groups were thoroughly mixed together in the pulling, which was accompanied by concerted rhythmic chants of "Heave, heave."

They got the truck going, and again there was pride in the joint ac-complishment. Thus the same tool that had first served in a competi-tive situation during group conflict, and that was later used by one group in their efforts to fell a tree, now became the standard means for interdependent efforts by both groups toward a common, super-ordinate goal (starting the truck, which brought food for all).

This sequence probably points to the fact that the nature of inter-group relations—for good or evil—does not necessarily stem from the existence of tools and techniques: the same tools and techniques can serve harmony and integration as well as deadly competition and conflict.

As soon as the boys saw the truck returning with food, they rushed to the table where food was served at noon. This time the main dish was steak meat in a big chunk, and the necessary division of labor was more elaborate. However, the cooperative pattern was now estab-lished and there was no appreciable discussion of it. As soon as the truck was unloaded, in which the boys helped, both groups began to work at preparing supper. There was much intermingling—Rattlers and Eagles working side by side, taking suggestions from each other and reaching decisions about what to do together. For example, McGraw (E) told three Rattlers, "Come on, boys, and put that Kool Aid in there," and they did. Simpson (R), Hill (R), and McGraw (E) all tried their hand in the initial stage of cutting steaks off the big chunk of meat. McGraw (E), Simpson (R), and Wilson (E) declared that they were going to cook.

After these boys declared their intention to cut meat and cook, staff members stepped in to give effective assistance in cutting the meat and broiling the steaks. Other Eagles and Rattlers worked together in setting out utensils and other food. After the preliminary preparations, those boys who were not helping rushed to pick up paper plates and to form a line by the fire, in which no one gave a moment's thought of preserving arrangements in terms of group lines.

All of the boys ate under the shed where the Eagles had eaten lunch. Eagles and Rattlers were interspersed up and down the table on both sides. Considerable changing and shifting back and forth in the seating arrangements occurred throughout the meal.

After supper a good-natured water fight started at the edge of the lake, but the throwing and splashing was not along group lines. The leading parties on one side were Simpson (R), Mason (E), and Swift (R), while those leading the other side were Mills (R) and Brown (R). The boys engaged in this play until they were soaking wet, then dried out by the fire. Rain clouds came up over the hill with a strong wind. The boys retired for the night to their respective group areas.

The Trip to the Border

The following morning (day 6, Stage 3), the Rattlers awoke first and started talking about the trip to Arkansas, exchanging notes on the states they had visited. The Rattlers' attention was concentrated on the Eagle camp. Martin (R) asked if the Eagles were going to Arkansas too. When the counselor answered affirmatively, there was no objection or comment. Simpson, Newman, Harrison, and Allen (all R's) went to the Eagle camp to see the lizards Mason (E) had caught and some frogs that Cutler (E) and Clark (E) had collected. The Rattlers were anxious to start on the trip to Arkansas before breakfast, and they kept getting in and out of their truck, which they had loaded before breakfast. A short time later both groups were asked to come to a central location for an announcement.

It was announced that as they well knew from experiences of the previous day, the older truck was not in good shape for the trip to Arkansas and back to the camp. (The truck referred to happened to be the Eagle truck. Of course, as noted, it was in running condition. But it had been demonstrated on the previous day to be liable to break down, and this buildup of a poor reputation for the truck was also appropriate for the introduction of the problem situation now being described.) It was added that in view of the condition of the truck, it might be preferable to give up the idea of going to Arkansas, since there was only one truck. Both groups voiced general disappointment, especially the Eagles.

McGraw (E) suggested that the Rattlers go to Arkansas first, and then that the Eagles would go in the Rattler truck when they returned. But Craig (E) objected that the Eagles didn't want to wait around all morning; and when Mason (former E leader, by now displaced, as will be discussed later in the chapter) started chanting "Let's go home, Let's go home . . ." (meaning back to the camp), Craig joined him.

At one point, Clark (E) said, "We could all go together," but Simpson (R) said, "No"—that the Rattlers would go to Arkansas and the Eagles could go back to the camp. This discussion illustrates well the state of flux that prevailed at this time in intergroup affairs. At times, as at supper the previous evening, the group lines seemed to disappear; at others, the group demarcations would reappear. Whether or not group lines would be followed was coming to depend more and more on factors in the immediate situation (*situational factors*).

In this instance, the problem at hand was discussed for a short time. Then Mills (R leader) proposed that they all go in the Rattler truck: "We can move some of the mattresses into the other truck, and then we can all get in our truck." Allen (low-status R) repeated this suggestion and several Eagles expressed approval. Simpson (R) agreed that it would be possible but added, "Let's don't."

Mills (R) now moved out of his group and paced up and down between the groups, explaining his ideas to both of them. When staff asked what they were going to do, there was a general hubbub, which was resolved when Mills (R) and Clark (E) said, "Let's go!" and headed for the Rattler truck. All the other boys, both Rattlers and Eagles, ran after them, piled in the truck, and yelled out to staff, "Hurry up! Let's go!" This is another striking instance of action taking precedence over verbal discussion, although the latter played an important part even in this decision.

While both groups were in the Rattler truck waiting to pull out, the Rattlers asked the Eagles to tell them who got homesick and went home from their group. Then, as the truck started out on the trip, notes and memories were exchanged concerning the raids that had aroused so much indignation during Stage 2. Now there was mirth over some of the episodes, and some bragging over who did what. Shortly, Clark (E) began to whistle the "Star Spangled Banner" and was joined by several boys. Boys from both groups joined, and shortly everyone was singing. Without any discussion, the members of both groups now continued singing for about half an hour, alternating a song that had become associated with the Eagles with one that the Rattlers had adopted. No one suggested that the songs of the two groups be alternated, but in fact they were. The arrangement of "taking turns" at an intergroup level was being extended from one activity to others.

The truck stopped in Heavener, Oklahoma, to allow the boys to have cool drinks. They streamed out of the truck into a drugstore; and the seating arrangements at the tables, which seated four or five boys each, reflected little of the group demarcations.

A few miles out of Heavener but before the Arkansas state line the road turned from a hard-surfaced highway to a dirt road. Conversation died down during this dusty portion of the trip. When the truck finally arrived at the prearranged lunch stop, the boys felt they had "been through" something together: the fine dust was deposited over everything and everyone.

Lunch was eaten in a private dining room at a restaurant, amid much laughter and boisterous conversation. Members from both groups were thoroughly intermixed at the four tables. After second servings, a paper and pencil were placed on each table, and the boys were told to list the flavors of ice cream they wanted. Then they were told to combine the lists at a side table. Myers (E) and Martin (R) both volunteered to do the combining. Myers was closest to the table, and therefore was able to get the pencil and paper first. But boys from both groups intervened, insisting that Myers and Martin work up the combined lists together, which they did.

After lunch most of the boys wrote postcards to send home as evidence that they had been in Arkansas. Then the trip continued back to the Arkansas line, which had been crossed in the morning, but not noted because there was no marker and the road was so dusty.

At a Coke stop near Fort Smith, Craig (E) and Allen (R) suggested that when the camp was over everyone should return to Oklahoma City together on the same bus. This idea was approved by most boys in both groups, although some said nothing and Harrison (R) muttered, "Let's go back like we came." Mills (R leader) said nothing until it was evident that the majority supported the idea; then he backed it too.

When the truck arrived at the state line between Arkansas and Oklahoma, the boys got out of the truck and most of them posed to have their pictures taken. Many of them stood straddling the state line so they could tell their family and friends that they had been in two states at the same time (see Figure 7.3).

During the entire trip from Cedar Lake into Arkansas and back across the line into Oklahoma, there were very few signs of group demarcations or identifications. However, when the truck arrived at camp and the Eagles were dropped off at their cabin, the Rattlers started yelling "Goodbye, Eagles," and the Eagles reciprocated.

The Last Evening in Camp

To check the influence of situational factors at this rather fluid state of intergroup relations, the staff rearranged the camp dining room while the two groups were at their cabins cleaning up from the trip. Four tables smaller than the usual mess hall tables were brought from various parts of the camp. They were square and could conveniently seat eight people, two to a side. This change was made so that the habitual spacing and size of tables in the mess hall situation would be entirely different. The influence of situational factors has been noted. It was thought that if the mess hall situation were different than it had been previously, the present state of the relationship between the two groups would be revealed more clearly through a new seating arrangement.

The wisdom of this plan was confirmed even outside of the mess hall. There, the two groups formed two lines, just as they had done prior to the Cedar Lake campout, even though they had been mixing up at meals as well as in other situations during the past 24 hours. The groups began discussing who would go in first, the trip away from camp having upset their "taking turns" arrangement. There was discussion on both sides as to whose "turn" it was. When Simpson (R) finally said, "O.K., let them go ahead," the Eagles entered the mess hall first without further objections by the Rattlers.

Once inside, the two groups went separately through the line to get their food, but there was friendly conversation between members. The reactions to the new table arrangement were as anticipated. Even though the groups had lined up separately in habitual fashion to get food, the seating at the newly arranged tables cut across the ingroup demarcations. The two tables in the middle were occupied by Eagles and Rattlers, sitting together. The few Rattlers left over occupied one or the other of the two end tables.

During the meal several boys commented that everyone was going back to Oklahoma City on the same bus. Almost all the boys seemed to be planning on it, although one voice was heard to say, "No, we're not." There was even some talk about what they would do on the bus.

After supper the boys were asked what they wanted to do on their last night at camp. There were several suggestions, including a Rattler's that they all go to the Stone Corral. The Rattlers backed this idea strongly, since the Stone Corral was the site of their campfires and was considered "theirs." Wilson (E) wanted to go to Robbers Cave, and most of the Eagles backed this idea. But the Rattlers replied that the Stone Corral was a part of Robbers Cave, and they couldn't build a fire at the cave itself. The discussion ended when Mills (R) announced they would all meet in 5 minutes to go to the Stone Corral. The Eagles said they would meet at the mess hall, but Mills (R) kept insisting that they should meet at the Rattlers' cabin because it was closer to the Stone Corral. The groups parted with that understanding.

When the Eagles arrived at the Rattler cabin, both groups went together to the Stone Corral. Simpson (R) took his ukulele with him and began to play as soon as they arrived. Everyone began singing the favorite songs of both groups, then it started to rain. The boys scattered to find cover. Some of them continued singing until the rain stopped and the campfire could be built. While waiting for the fire, a Rattler suggested that the two groups entertain each other by putting on the skits they had done for the tournament. Two or three boys thought this was a good idea, but nothing came of it until after both groups joined in roasting marshmallows.

Then Mills (R leader) started organizing the "Dragnet" skit he had put on with several other Rattlers before his own group earlier in camp. Myers and Craig, both Eagles, were asked to help the Rattlers put the skit on. Some of the Eagles called to Myers (E), and he answered that he would be in the Eagle skit too.

After the Rattler skit, Mills (R) announced that the Eagles were next. There was some discussion on what to do, then Wilson and

Figure 7.4 Intergroup relations: the end of Stage 3

Joint campfire at the Stone Corral: the groups take turns entertaining each other

Getting ready to return home: *All together*

Myers put on an act for the Eagles. The Rattlers next started trying to persuade Brown to do his Donald Duck imitation. This performance was received with great enthusiasm. Then Allen (R) said, "Now it's the Eagles' turn," and the Eagles did a "spitball act."

At this point the Eagles wanted the Rattlers to be next on the evening's program; but the Rattlers replied that since the Eagles had won the singing during the tournament, they should sing for them now. After some discussion, Myers (E) announced that Simpson (R) would sing a song, which he did. Then the Eagles took their turn, singing "Zem Bones" (actually "Dem Bones").

Following this request performance by the Eagles, Mills (R) announced that the Rattlers would do a skit called "Murder in the Haunted House." The evening ended with both groups singing some of their favorite songs together (see Figure 7.4).

Up to the time of this joint campfire at the Stone Corral, the observations had revealed increasing reduction of intergroup friction, and increasingly friendly relations between the groups, as a consequence of interdependent activities embodying superordinate goals that were experimentally introduced. The Eagle observer noted that derogatory references to the outgroups had decreased gradually, until there were none.

However, the evening campfire strikingly demonstrated the cumulative effectiveness of situations requiring interdependent activities toward common superordinate goals. Procedures for cooperative give-and-take between the groups had been developed. The entire program was arranged and presented by the two groups themselves, to entertain each other. The notion of "taking turns," which had started as a way of regulating activities in which a conflict of interest was involved (going in to meals), had been extended to joint singing of the two groups' favorite songs on previous occasions. Now the "taking turns" idea was spontaneously used to regulate group participation in entertaining one another, as groups and as individuals. Thus the friendly relations between groups established through functional interdependence in situations involving experimentally introduced goals, were carried over (transferred) to spontaneous intergroup cooperation in a situation in which no superordinate goal was formally introduced.

During the following day, which was the last day of camp, no planned stimulus conditions were introduced. It was designated as *follow-up day.* Observations were restricted to striking instances of the interaction patterns and carry-over effects of the experimentally introduced conditions. At breakfast and lunch, the seating arrangements were again mixed up insofar as group membership was concerned. The morning was devoted to preparations for leaving camp and to securing sociometric choices and stereotype ratings to check on observational findings. The results of these units are reported in the following parts of this chapter.

The Trip Home

The majority of subjects had agreed by the last day that it would be good to return to Oklahoma City all together on one bus. When they asked if this might be possible and received an affirmative answer from the staff, some of them actually cheered. When the bus pulled out, the seating arrangement did not follow group lines. Many boys looked back at the camp, and Wilson (E) cried because camp was over.

Just before the bus pulled into the town where a refreshment stop was planned, a Rattler inquired if they still had the $5 reward they had won in the bean toss contest. This inquiry was repeated by others when the boys were at the refreshment stand, and Mills (R leader) suggested that their $5 be spent on malts for all the boys in both groups. Several Rattlers nearby agreed; the others approved the idea when asked. This meant that malted milks for all 20 boys would be paid for exactly with the $5 contributed by the Rattlers, but that each boy would have to pay for sandwiches and other treats himself.

Several Rattlers were questioned by observers while they were eating, and they were all fully aware that this sum would have paid for everything the Rattlers wanted if it had not been shared with the Eagles. Nevertheless, they were glad they had shared it. A few boys were short of money for other refreshments and other boys (several from the outgroup) paid for them.

Nearing Oklahoma City, the boys at the front of the bus (mostly high-status members from both groups) began to sing "Oklahoma." Several boys seated near the back rushed up to join them. Everyone in both groups took part, all sitting or standing as close together as possible in the front end of the bus. The gaiety lasted during the last half-hour of the trip; no one went back to the rear. A few boys exchanged addresses, and many told their closest companions that they would meet again.

At the bus station, good-byes blended with the excitement of meeting parents.

Summary of Observations in Stage 3

The above observations reported by participant observers and independent observations by other staff members confirm our hypotheses:

Hypothesis 2 (Stage 3)

When groups in a state of friction are brought into contact under conditions embodying superordinate goals, the attainment of which is compelling but which cannot be achieved by the efforts of one group alone, the groups will tend to cooperate toward the common goal.

Hypothesis 2a (Stage 3)

Intergroup cooperation necessitated by a series of situations embodying superordinate goals will have a cumulative effect in the direction of reducing existing tensions between groups.

The following parts of this chapter report on how the validity of these conclusions based on observational findings was tested in terms of sociometric choices and also in terms of laboratory-type judgmental indices.

Verification of Observations

Reduced intergroup friction and increasingly cooperative relations during the closing days of Stage 3 were dramatically evident to those who had witnessed the hectic days of intergroup conflict in Stage 2 and the early contact situations without superordinate goals early in Stage 3. The intermingling among members of the previously antagonistic groups at meals, at campfires, and at play; their joint efforts at tasks and entertainment during the campout and on the return to camp; their preference to return home together—all of these and other observational data indicated unmistakable shifts in attitudes toward the outgroup. If these observed alterations in behavior in fact indicated changed attitudes toward the outgroup, they would be revealed as well through more precise methods for assessing the attitudes of individual members.

Accordingly, at the end of Stage 3, attitudes toward ingroup and outgroup were tapped, as a further check on observational data, through sociometric choices of ingroup and outgroup members, and through ratings of ingroup and outgroup in terms of the stereotypes actually used during the period of intergroup friction.

The results of both measurements could be evaluated in relation to the observational findings of Stage 3 and the results obtained by these same methods at the end of Stage 2, when ingroup solidarity and glorification and outgroup avoidance and derogation were at their height.

In line with the chief methodological concern of this experiment, findings throughout were checked by as many different methods as it was feasible to introduce without destroying the dominant trend of the ongoing interaction processes. We sought to achieve a combination of methods that are frequently (although erroneously) viewed as antithetical: observation of the natural flow of interaction processes in lifelike situations and more precise measurement, through laboratory-type methods, of the effects of interaction on the perception and judgment of individual members.

The interaction situations were lifelike because they embodied valued goals and appeared to subjects as spontaneous and natural, even though they were controlled and systematically altered by experimenters. The techniques used for verification of observational data were laboratory-type because they were introduced with little of the artificiality of the laboratory, but with no loss in precision. When necessary, we sacrificed precision rather than clutter or unduly interrupt the interaction process. We did so with the conviction that the flow, events, and effects of interaction within and between groups are the basic data, which cannot be easily restored if trifled with. Sociometric choices were not obtained at the end of Stage 1, but only at the close of Stages 2 and 3, on the grounds that three repetitions within such a short time might very well arouse the subjects' suspicion. Similarly, the experimental unit tapping attitudes toward ingroup and outgroup members through judgments of their performance, which was executed at the end of Stage 2, was not repeated in Stage 3 because of the serious concern that its repetition would clutter the main flow of the interaction process at that time.

The results of the two techniques employed at the end of Stage 3 to check the validity of observational findings are summarized in the following two sections.

Verification of Shifts in Attitudes: Sociometric Choices

At the end of Stage 3, sociometric choices were obtained by participant observers through *informal* interviews with individual members of their groups. Sociometric scores were again computed for each group member on the basis of total weighted choices on four criteria (see Chapter 6). Since the most general criterion permitted outgroup choices as well as ingroup choices, total scores were computed separately for ingroup and outgroup choices and also by combining ingroup and outgroup choices (the latter had been insignificant at the end of Stage 2). The ranks within each group were the same by either

TABLE 7.1

*Comparison of ranks in sociometric scores and status ratings
by participant observers of Rattler and Eagle groups
(end of Stage 3)*

	rho	t	p
Rattlers	.853	4.903	<.001
Eagles	.836	4.038	<.003

TABLE 7.2

Rank by sociometric score, Rattlers and Eagles

Rattlers	Eagles
Mills	Wilson
Newman	Mason
Simpson	
	Myers
Martin	Bryan
Brown	
	Craig
Harrison	Clark
Everett	Cutler
Hill	McGraw
Swift	Lane
Barton	
Allen	

method of computing total sociometric scores (viz., including outgroup choices or not including them).

Table 7.1 compares the ranks of members of each group in terms of
sociometric scores with the status ratings by each group's participant
observer. The rank order correlations for status ranking by the two
methods are high and significant for both groups.

For purposes of comparison with data at the end of Stage 2, Table 7.2
lists the members of the Rattler and Eagle groups in terms of rank of
sociometric score at the end of Stage 3. The list of boys in each group
is divided in terms of score values. Those boys in the top level of the
list received scores above 50; those in the second section 40–50; in
the third section 20–30; and in the bottom section below 20 (see the
sociograms in Figures 6.1 and 6.2).

In line with the hypothesis stated in general form in Stage 2, it was
predicted that shifts in ingroup relationships might occur concomitant

with changes of consequence in relations between groups (Hypothesis 3, Stage 2). The most significant of these (according to sociometric indices) is Mason's slip from the leadership position in the Eagles. As elaborated in Chapter 6, Mason came to the leadership position in the Eagle group in the early days of intergroup competition and rivalry in the tournament. He was intensely involved with the group effort to win and was identified with its victory. It was Mason who took the lead in attempting retaliation on the Rattlers for their last raid. Perhaps this partially explains why Mason resisted the trend in his group toward increased intermingling with the Rattlers near the end of Stage 3. While he became quite friendly with individual Rattlers, he made it known that he preferred that the Eagles do things together and without the Rattlers. Although his status in the Eagle group remained high, he was followed less and less in his separatist preferences.

Ingroup and Outgroup Choices

The data obtained from the most general criterion on the sociometric questionnaire, and through an item on the questionnaire tapping rejections (dislike), provide clear-cut verification of changed attitudes toward the outgroup as a consequence of intergroup relationships in a series of situations embodying superordinate goals.

Table 7.3 gives the choices of ingroup and outgroup members by Rattlers and Eagles at the end of Stage 3. As indicated in the table, friendship choices were still predominantly for ingroup members. However when the choices of outgroup members at the end of Stage 3 are compared with those at the end of Stage 2, a substantial and significant increase is found for both groups. This comparison is made in graphic form in Figure 7.5.

TABLE 7.3
Friendship choices of ingroup and outgroup members
by Rattlers and Eagles (end of Stage 3)

	Rattlers		Eagles	
	f	%	*f*	%
Ingroup choices	63	63.6	41	76.8
Outgroup choices	36	36.4	15	23.2

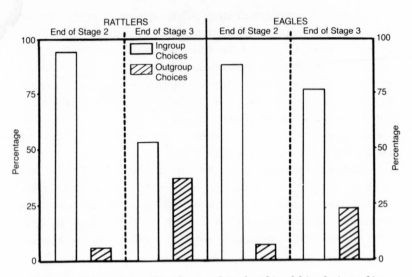

Figure 7.5 Comparison of Rattlers' and Eagles' friendship choices of ingroup and outgroup members at the ends of Stage 2 and Stage 3

At the end of Stage 2, only 6.4 percent of the Rattlers' choices were for Eagles, but by the end of Stage 3, 36.4 percent were. In the Eagle group, the proportion of choices for the Rattlers shifted from 7.5 percent at the end of Stage 2 to 23.3 percent at the end of Stage 3.

Concomitant with the increased tendency to choose outgroup members as friends, there was a decreased tendency to reject members of the outgroup as persons most disliked. In the Rattler group, 75 percent of the rejections at the end of Stage 2 were Eagles; however, by the end of Stage 3, only 15 percent were. Similarly, in the Eagle group, 95 percent of their rejections at the end of Stage 2 were Rattlers, but the proportion decreased to 47.1 percent at the end of Stage 3.

Table 7.4 compares the changes toward increased choice of outgroup members from Stage 2 to the end of Stage 3 and the changes toward decreased rejection of outgroup members for both groups. In the Rattler group, the increase in outgroup choices from the end of Stage 2 to the end of Stage 3 is significant at less than .001 level (McNemar test). The decrease in rejection of outgroup members from Stage 2 to the end of Stage 3 is significant at less than the .01 level. The observational data revealed some divergence among members of

TABLE 7.4

*Comparison of differences in friendship choices
and in rejections of outgroup members
(ends of Stage 2 and Stage 3)*

Difference Between	Rattlers		Eagles	
	chi-square	*p*	*chi-square*	*p*
Outgroup choices,				
Stage 2 and Stage 3	21.950	<.001	4.050	<.05
Outgroup rejections,				
Stage 2 and Stage 3	7.251	<.01	3.703	ca. .05

the Eagle group in attitudes toward the outgroup. As might be expected, the differences between outgroup choices at the end of Stage 2 and at the end of Stage 3 were slightly less than for Rattlers and significant at lower levels.

These data obtained through sociometric techniques therefore constitute clear-cut verification of observational findings that when the two hostile outgroups interacted repeatedly in situations embodying goals superordinate to both, the prevailing tendency in both groups was to intermingle with the other and to have increasingly friendly associations with outgroup members and friendly attitudes toward them.

Verification of Effects on Attitudes: Stereotype Ratings

As a result of the series of situations in Stage 3, the two groups engaged in a greater variety of activities together and with increasing freedom. The observations during Stage 3 revealed a sharp decrease in the standardized name calling and derogation of the outgroup that had become so familiar during the closing days of Stage 2 and the contact situations early in Stage 3. In addition, there was less blatant glorification of the ingroup and bragging about its accomplishments than during the days of rivalry in Stage 2. These observational data were believed to imply changes, in a more favorable direction, in attitudes toward the outgroup; weakening of negative stereotypes of the outgroup; and shifts in the conception of the ingroup as well.

The validity of these observational findings was checked at the end of Stage 3 through stereotype ratings by both groups of their ingroup and the outgroup. The stereotypes used were the ones that had been standardized in Stage 2. It is significant that when it was announced that the ratings were to be made again, several boys remarked that they were glad, because they had changed their minds since the last ratings.

At the end of Stage 3, the procedures used for tapping stereotypes at the end of Stage 2 (see Chapter 6) were repeated. The second ratings were obtained in order to compare them with those obtained before the series of superordinate goals was introduced in Stage 3. The comparison reveals the effects of the interdependence created and of the subsequent cooperation between groups. The data to be presented here, therefore, constitute additional evidence for the verification of Hypothesis 2a (Stage 3)—that cooperation between groups necessitated by superordinate goals will cumulatively reduce intergroup tension. Observational and sociometric data relevant to this hypothesis were summarized earlier in this chapter.

Table 7.5 shows the ratings of outgroup members made by the Rattlers and Eagles at the end of Stage 2 and at the end of Stage 3. A comparison of these data shows a marked shift in the nature of characteristics attributed to the outgroup. At the end of the friction stage, ratings of outgroup members tended to be unfavorable, but by the end of the integration stage, ratings of outgroup members were preponderantly favorable in both groups. At the end of Stage 2, 53.0

TABLE 7.5

Stereotype ratings of the outgroup on six characteristics
by members of Rattler and Eagle groups
(ends of Stage 2 and Stage 3)

Category	Rattlers' ratings of Eagles		Eagles' ratings of Rattlers	
	Stage 2 (%)	Stage 3 (%)	Stage 2 (%)	Stage 3 (%)
1[a]	21.2	1.5	36.5	5.6
2	31.8	3.0	40.4	17.0
3	12.1	9.2	7.7	9.4
4	19.9	28.7	9.6	35.9
5[b]	15.0	57.6	5.8	32.1
Chi-square diff.	44.67		34.51	
p	<.001		<.001	

[a] Most unfavorable.
[b] Most favorable.

TABLE 7.6

*Stereotype ratings of ingroup members on six
characteristics by Rattler and Eagle groups
(ends of Stage 2 and Stage 3)*

| | Rattlers' ratings of Rattlers | | Eagles' ratings of Eagles | |
| | Stage 2 (%) | Stage 3 (%) | Stage 2 (%) | Stage 3 (%) |
Category				
1 [a]	0	0	0	0
2	0	0	3.8	9.2
3	0	4.5	1.9	3.8
4	13.7	18.2	14.7	33.3
5 [b]	86.3	77.3	79.6	53.7
Chi-square diff.	3.546		7.501	
p	>.30		.10−.11	

[a] Most unfavorable.
[b] Most favorable.

percent of the ratings made by Rattlers of the Eagles had been unfavorable; but at the end of Stage 3 only 4.5 percent of these ratings
were unfavorable and 86.3 percent were favorable. Most ratings of the
Rattlers by the Eagles (76.9 percent) were unfavorable at the end of
the friction stage; but by the end of Stage 3 the proportion of unfavorable ratings was reduced to 22.6, and the favorable ratings of Rattlers
increased to 68.0 percent. The Eagles' ratings of the Rattlers did not
change as much in the favorable direction as did the Rattlers' ratings
of the Eagles. However, these shifts in the positive direction from
Stage 2 to Stage 3 were significant for both groups.

Table 7.6 presents ratings made of members of the ingroup at the
end of Stage 2 and of Stage 3. These results suggest that changes in
the functional relations between groups tend to produce changes
in the conceptions of the ingroup. The ratings of ingroup members
after cooperation with the outgroup were not as favorable as the
highly positive ratings of the ingroup made after the intense intergroup rivalry of Stage 2, although the trend is not statistically significant. At the end of Stage 3, ingroups were still rated favorably by their
own members.

For the Rattler group, the difference in proportions of ratings in the
most favorable category at the end of Stage 2 and the end of Stage 3
was 9 percent, and the proportion of ratings in the middle category

increased by 4.5 percent. In the Eagle group, the proportion of ratings in the most favorable category after the cooperative activities with the outgroup was 25.9 percent less than at the end of Stage 2.

The trend toward rating the ingroup less favorably was more pronounced in the Eagle group. This finding is in line with observational data indicating that the Eagle group revealed shifts in status structure during the Stage 3 interaction in cooperative activities with the Rattlers. Briefly, most of the Eagles were drawn into the compelling interdependence between groups in Stage 3, and all participated in cooperative intergroup activities. A few Eagles, including the leader during Stage 2, entered into these activities and became friendly with individual members of the Rattler group but were more tenacious than others in preferring ingroup association to contacts with the whole Rattler group. As noted earlier, this state of affairs, in turn, reduced the effectiveness of the Eagle leader, who had achieved his greatest eminence during intergroup rivalry.

Figures 7.6 and 7.7 present a graphic summary of the Eagles' and Rattlers' stereotype ratings of ingroup and outgroup on the six characteristics (combined) following Stage 2 and Stage 3. At the end of Stage 3, ratings of ingroup and outgroup members did not differ significantly ($p > .10$).

Thus, three statements can summarize circumstances at the end of Stage 3. Favorable characteristics tended to be attributed to the outgroup, in contrast to the predominantly unfavorable picture of the outgroup at the end of the friction stage. Ratings of both the ingroup and the outgroup were favorable and did not differ significantly. The relative frequency of favorable ratings made in relation to ingroup members was slightly less than at the end of Stage 2, particularly in the case of the Eagle group, which was undergoing some shifts in ingroup structure.

Competition and rivalry between groups in Stage 2 was accompanied by attribution of unfavorable characteristics to the outgroup and favorable characteristics to the ingroup (Chapter 6). This generalization takes on added significance when viewed in terms of the backgrounds, personal and sociocultural, of the two groups of boys. All were normal, well-adjusted boys who enjoyed high and secure status positions both at home and in school. None were problem children who had suffered unusual frustrations and privations. The results indicating the formation of negative stereotypes of the outgroup

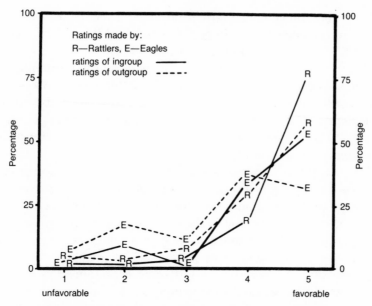

Figure 7.6 Stereotype ratings of ingroup and outgroup members on six characteristics (combined) (end of Stage 3)

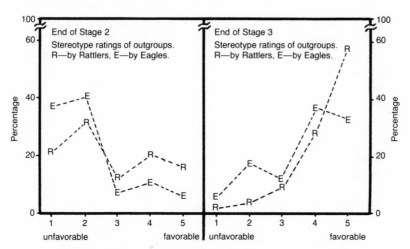

Figure 7.7 Comparison of stereotype ratings of outgroups at ends of Stage 2 and Stage 3

during competitive intergroup relationships cannot be attributed to unusual psychological conditions brought by the boys to the experimental situation. The enthusiastic participation in intergroup competition reflects, of course, the strong emphasis on competition in the larger sociocultural setting. However, the rise of intergroup hostility and attribution of derogatory labels to the outgroup was a development opposite in direction to another important value from the larger setting, namely "good sportsmanship" on the part of the participants in competitive activities.

The observance of norms of social distance between the groups and the maintenance of a derogatory picture of the outgroup did not decrease until the two groups had interacted in a series of situations embodying superordinate goals. The subsequent cooperation between the groups was accompanied in time by a marked change, in the favorable direction, in the conception of the outgroup.

These results may be taken as further evidence supporting our hypothesis that cooperation between groups as a consequence of interaction in situations embodying superordinate goals has a cumulative effect in the direction of reducing existing intergroup tensions (Hypothesis 2a, Stage 3).

The data obtained by tapping judgments concerning the character of one's ingroup and of the outgroup, under conditions of competition and rivalry, and then conditions leading to cooperative intergroup activity, are congruent with observational findings concerning behavior in relation to the ingroup and outgroup. Together these data and observations are presented as a contribution to the study of the formation and change of values or *social norms*. Specifically, they confirm the hypotheses concerning conditions conducive to the formation of unfavorable attitudes toward functionally related outgroups and conditions conducive to their change to attitudes of cooperation and friendship between groups.

8

Summary and Conclusions

The Approach of This Study

In this book we have presented an experiment on intergroup relations. The theoretical approach to the problem, the definitions of groups and relations between them, the hypotheses, the selection of subjects, the study design in successive stages, the methods and techniques, and the conclusions to be drawn are closely related. This chapter is a summary statement of these interrelated parts.

The word *group* in the phrase *intergroup relations* is not a superfluous label. If our claim is to study relations between two or more groups or to investigate intergroup attitudes, we have to bring into the picture the properties of the groups and the consequences of membership for the individuals in question. Otherwise, whatever we may be studying, we are not, properly speaking, studying intergroup problems.

Accordingly, our first concern was an adequate conception of the key word *group* and clarification of the implications of an individual's membership in groups. A definition of the concept improvised just for the sake of research convenience does not take us very far if we are interested in the validity of our conclusions. We have to spell out the actual properties of groups, which brought them to the foreground in the study of serious human problems.

The task of defining groups and intergroup relations can be carried out only through an *interdisciplinary approach*. Problems pertaining to groups and their relations are not studied by psychologists alone. They are studied on various levels of analysis by people in different social sciences. In the extensive literature on relations within and between small groups, we found crucial leads for a realistic conception of groups and their relations, as discussed in Chapter 1.

Abstracting the recurrent properties of actual groups, we attained a definition applicable to small groups of any description. A *group* is a social unit that consists of a number of individuals who, at a given time, stand in more or less definite interdependent status and role relationships with one another, and that explicitly or implicitly possesses a set of norms or values regulating the behavior of the individual members, at least in matters of consequence to the group.

Intergroup relations refers to relations between groups thus defined. Intergroup attitudes (such as prejudice) and intergroup behavior (such as discriminatory practice) refer to the attitudes and the behavior manifested by members of groups collectively or individually. The characteristic of an intergroup attitude or an intergroup behavior is that it is related to the individual's membership in a group. Research must make explicit the relationship between a given attitude and facts pertaining to the individual's role relative to the groups in question.

Unrepresentative intergroup attitudes and behavior are, to be sure, important psychological facts. But attitude and behavior unrepresentative of a group do not constitute the focal problem of intergroup relations, nor are they the cases that make the study of intergroup relations crucial in human affairs. The central problem of intergroup relations is not primarily the problem of *deviate behavior.*

In shaping the reciprocal attitudes of members of two groups toward one another, the limiting determinant is the nature of functional relations between the groups. The groups in question may be competing to attain some goal or some vital prize, so that the success of one group necessarily means the failure of the other. One group may have claims on another group in the way of managing, controlling, or exploiting them, in the way of taking over their actual or assumed rights or possessions. On the other hand, groups may have complementary goals, such that each may attain its goal without hindering the achievement of the other and even aiding this achievement.

Although the nature of relations between groups is the limiting condition, various other factors have to be brought into the picture for an adequate accounting of the resulting intergroup trends and intergroup products (such as norms for positive or negative treatment of the other group, stereotypes of one's own group and the other group, etc.). Among these factors are the kind of leadership, the degree of solidarity, and the kind of norms prevailing within each group. Reciprocal intergroup appraisals of the groups' relative strengths and resources and the intellectual level attained in assessing the groups' worth and rights in relation to others need special mention among these factors. The frustrations, deprivations, and gratifications in the life histories of the individual members also have to be considered.

Theories of intergroup relations that posit single factors (such as the kind of leadership, national character, or individual frustrations) as sovereign determinants of intergroup conflict or harmony have, at best, explained only selectively chosen cases. Of course, leadership counts in shaping intergroup behavior, the prevailing norms of social distance count, so do the structure and practices within the groups, and so do the personal frustrations of individual members. But none of these singly determines the trend of intergroup behavior at a given time. They all contribute to the structuring of intergroup behavior, but with different relative weights at different times. Intergroup behavior at a given time can be explained only in terms of the entire frame of reference in which all these various factors function interdependently. This approach, here stated briefly, constituted the starting point of our experiments on intergroup relations. The approach was elaborated fully in our previous work, *Groups in Harmony and Tension.*

The relative weights of various factors contributing to intergroup trends and practices are not fixed quantities. Their relative importance varies according to the particular set of conditions prevailing at the time. For example, in more or less closed, homogeneous, or highly organized groups, and in times of stability, the prevailing social distance scale and established practices toward the outgroup that have been standardized in the past for group members will have greater weight in determining the intergroup behavior of individual members. But when groups are in greater functional interdependence with each other, and during periods of transition and flux, other factors contribute more heavily. In these latter cases, there is a greater discrepancy between expressed attitude and intergroup behavior in different situations, attributable to situational factors, as insistently noted by some leading investigators in this area of research. Alliances and combinations among groups that seem strange bedfellows are not infrequent in our modern world of flux and tension.

Because of their influence in social psychology, two other approaches to intergroup behavior deserve explicit mention. A brief discussion of them will help clarify the conception of the experiment reported in this book.

One of these approaches advances frustration suffered in the life history of the individual as the main causal factor and constructs a whole explanatory edifice for intergroup aggression on this basis. Certainly aggression is *one* of the possible consequences of frustration experienced by the individual. But, for individual frustration to appreciably affect the course of intergroup trends and be conducive to standardization of negative attitudes toward an outgroup, the frustration has to be shared by other group members and perceived *as an issue* in group interaction. Whether interaction focuses on matters within a group or between groups, group trends and attitudes of members are not crystallized from thin air. The problem of intergroup behavior, we repeat, is not primarily the problem of the behavior of one or a few deviate individuals. The realistic contribution of frustration as a factor can be studied only within the framework of ingroup and intergroup relations.

The other important approach to intergroup relations concentrates primarily on processes within the groups in question. It assumes that measures introduced to increase cooperativeness and harmony *within* the groups will be conducive to cooperativeness and harmony in intergroup relations. This assumption amounts to extrapolating the properties of ingroup relations to intergroup relations, as if ingroup norms and practices were easily transferable commodities. Probably, when friendly relations already prevail between groups, cooperative and harmonious ingroup relations do contribute to solutions of joint problems among groups. However, numerous cases show that ingroup cooperativeness and harmony may contribute effectively to intergroup competitiveness and conflict when interaction between groups is negative and incompatible.

The important generalization to be drawn is that the properties of intergroup relations cannot be extrapolated either from individual experiences and behavior or from the properties of interaction within groups. The limiting factor bounding intergroup attitudes and behavior is the nature of relations between groups. Demonstration of these generalizations was one of the primary objectives of our experiment.

The Experiment

The Design in Successive Stages

Experimental Formation of Groups

To deal with the essential characteristics of intergroup relations, one prerequisite was the production of two distinct groups, each with a definite hierarchical structure and a set of norms. The formation of groups whose natural histories could thus be ascertained has a decided advantage for experimental control and exclusion of other influences. Accordingly, Stage 1 of the experiment was devoted to the formation of two autonomous groups under specified conditions. A major precaution during this initial stage was that group formation proceed independently in each group, without contacts between them. This separation was necessary to ensure that the specified conditions introduced, and not intergroup relations, were the determining factors in group formation. Independent formation of distinct groups permitted conclusions to be drawn later from observations on the effects of intergroup encounters and engagements upon the group structure.

The distinctive features of our study are Stages 2 and 3, pertaining to intergroup relations. The main objective of the study was to find effective measures for reducing friction between groups and to discover realistic steps toward harmonious relations between them. If we had attempted to get two groups to cooperate without first bringing about a state of friction between them, there would have been no serious problem to be solved. The great task that social scientists, practitioners, and policy makers face today is the reduction of prevailing intergroup frictions.

Intergroup Conflict

After formation of definite ingroups, we introduced a period of intergroup relations as Stage 2 of the experiment. During this stage, the two experimentally formed groups came into contact under competitive conditions, so that the victory of one group meant loss for the other. This series of encounters was conducive to successive frustrations whose causes were perceived as coming from the other group.

We introduced the stage of reducing intergroup friction only after an unmistakable state of friction between the two groups was manifested in hostile acts and derogatory stereotypes.

Reduction of Intergroup Hostility

Various measures could have been tried in this experimental attempt toward the reduction of intergroup friction. One possible measure would have been the introduction of a "common enemy." Exposed to a common enemy, groups may join hands to do away with the common threat. We rejected this measure because it implies intergroup conflict on a larger scale.

Another possible approach would have been dissemination of specific information designed to correct prevailing group stereotypes. This measure was not seriously considered because of the large body of research showing that discrete information, unrelated to a group's central concerns, is relatively ineffective in changing attitudes. Stereotypes crystallized during the eventful course of competition and conflict with the outgroup are usually more real in the experience of the group members than bits of information handed down to them.

The alternative of channeling competition for highly valued rewards and prizes along individualized directions may be effective in reducing intergroup friction by breaking down group action to individual action. This measure may be practicable for small groups and is attempted at times by supervisors in classroom and recreational situations. However, frictions and conflicts of significant consequence in life, and the problem of their resolution, exist in terms of group demarcations and alignments.

The initial phase of Stage 3 tested the effects of intergroup contact involving close physical proximity in activities that were satisfying in themselves, such as eating meals or seeing a movie. This initial phase was introduced with the objective of clarifying the blanket term *contact* as applied to intergroup relations.

The alternative chosen as the most effective measure for reducing intergroup friction was the introduction of a series of *superordinate goals*, in line with the hypothesis stated prior to the experiment. Superordinate goals are goals of high appeal value for both groups, which cannot be ignored by the groups in question, but whose attainment is beyond the resources and efforts of one group alone.

Research Methods

To bring about the formation of attitude and behavior and their subsequent change in directions predicted by the hypotheses, this experiment used neither lecture method nor discussion method. Instead, the procedure was to place the members of respective groups in demanding problem situations, the specifications of which met the criteria established for the experimental stage in question. The problem situations concerned activities, objects, or materials that we knew, on the basis of the expressed preferences of the individuals or the state of their organisms, were highly appealing to them at the time. Facing a problem situation that is immediate, that must be attended to, that embodies a goal that cannot be ignored group members do initiate discussion, do plan, do make decisions, and do carry through the plans by word and deed until the objective is achieved. In this process, the discussion becomes *their* discussion, the plan becomes *their* plan, the decision becomes *their* decision, the action becomes *their* action. In this process, discussion has its place, planning has its place, action has its place, and when occasion arises, lecture has its place too. The sequence of these related activities need not be the same in all cases. In many instances, we observed two or three of them carried on simultaneously.

Thus, problem situations introduced in Stage 1 embodied goals of immediate appeal value to all members within a group, and attaining the goals required group members' concerted activity or coordinated division of labor. The problem situations of Stage 2 offered goals whose attainment by one group necessarily meant failure for the other group. Intergroup conflict was generated in the course of such engagements. The main part of Stage 3 consisted of introducing a series of situations conducive to superordinate goals requiring joint action by both groups toward common ends. In every stage, changes in attitudes and action were not attempted through a single problem situation, but through the cumulative effect of a series of varied activities which, during each stage, had the distinctive characteristics summarized here.

All problem situations were introduced in a naturalistic setting and were in harmony with activities usually carried out in such a setting. The individuals participating in the study were not aware that each step was especially designed to study a particular phase of group relations. Once the problem situation was introduced under specified conditions and at a specified time, the initiative, discussion, and planning were theirs, of course within bounds ensuring their health, security and well-being.

Every effort was exerted to make the activities and the flow of interaction in these activities appear natural to the subjects. Yet these activities and the interaction in them were *experimental*: problem situations were chosen for each stage according to specified criteria (see Chapter 2) and were introduced under specified conditions (including the place, terrain, time, arrangement of facilities, stimulus materials available, etc.). The choice of an isolated site made it possible to restrict interaction situations and the individuals involved in them to those appropriate during each experimental stage.

Techniques of data collection were also determined by the theoretical approach and methodological considerations briefly stated above. The subjects were not aware that behavioral trends reflecting favorable or unfavorable, friendly or hostile intergroup attitudes were being studied. Knowing that one is under constant observation cannot help but become a factor in structuring experience and behavior, particularly when the observation is related to one's status concerns, one's acceptance or rejection by others, one's good or bad intentions toward others.

To the subjects, the participant observers appeared to be personnel of a usual camp situation. They were introduced as senior counselors. In this capacity they were continually close to their respective groups. True to their announced roles, the participant observers jotted down relevant observations out of the subjects' sight, and then expanded their notes later each day.

When the technique of observation is adapted to the flow of interaction, there is danger of being selective in the choice of events recorded. The effective remedy against possible selectivity is using a *combination of methods* to check the findings obtained with one method against those obtained by other methods.

The events that revealed stabilization and shifts in status and crystallization of negative and then positive intergroup attitudes were recurrent and so striking that one could not help but observe them. However, in testing our main hypotheses, we supplemented the observational method with sociometric and laboratory-type methods.

One distinctive feature of this study was its introduction, at choice points, of laboratory-type techniques to assess emerging attitudes through indirect, yet precise indices. Such laboratory-type assessment of attitudes is based on the finding that under relevant conditions, simple judgments or perceptions reflect major concerns, attitudes, and other motives.

The reliability of observation and observer ratings was checked by comparing those of the participant observer with independent observations by others made in crucial test situations. One such test situation illustrates the technique. When the status hierarchy in one group became stabilized toward the end of Stage 1, a problem situation was introduced that, like other problem situations of this stage, required initiative and coordination of the membership. A staff member who was not with the group regularly and who had not rated the status positions from day to day observed the group interaction in this situation. On this basis he made independent ratings of the status hierarchy, which were significantly correlated with those of the participant observer of that group.

Main Conclusions

Individual Characteristics and Intergroup Behavior

This experiment's rigorous criteria and painstaking procedures for selecting subjects ruled out differences in socioeconomic, ethnic, religious, or family backgrounds as bases for explaining hostile or friendly intergroup attitudes. Similarly, the criteria for subject selection ensured against explanations on the basis of unusual individual frustrations, failures, maladjustment, or instability.

The subjects came from families who were established residents of the same city. They were stable families composed of natural parents and siblings. No subjects came from broken homes. Their religious affiliations were similar. They were from the middle socioeconomic class. They were of the same chronological and educational level. They had all made satisfactory progress academically; none had failed in school. In school and neighborhood, their social adjustment was above average. None presented a behavior problem in home, neighborhood, or school. In short, the subjects were normal, healthy, socially well-adjusted boys who came from families with the same or closely similar socioeconomic, ethnic, and religious backgrounds.

Since none of the individuals studied was personally acquainted with others prior to the experiment, preexisting positive or negative interpersonal relations did not enter into the rise of ingroup or intergroup attitudes.

The conclusion that rules out individual characteristics as the basis for explaining the intergroup trends and attitudes in this experiment should not be construed to mean that the relative contributions of individuals within their own groups and in intergroup relationships are unimportant. Individuals do contribute differentially both in shaping and carrying on the trend of group relationships. This experiment does indicate, however, that intergroup attitudes are not merely products of severe individual frustrations or background differences brought to the situation.

Formation of Group Organization and Norms

When the individuals interacted in a series of situations toward goals with common appeal value, whose attainment required interdependent activity, definite group structures arose. These groups developed stable, but by no means immutable *status hierarchies* and *group norms* regulating the experience and behavior of individual members.

More concretely, a pattern of leader-follower relations evolved within each group as members faced compelling problem situations and attained goals through coordinated action. As group structure was stabilized, the group was unmistakably delineated as an ingroup. Certain places and objects important in group activities were incorporated as "ours." Ways of doing things, of meeting problems, of behaving under certain conditions were standardized, permitting variation only within limits. Beyond the limits of the group norms, behavior was subject to group sanctions, which ranged from ridicule, through ignoring the offender and his behavior, to threats, and occasionally to physical chastisement.

Ingroup Cooperativeness: Not Directly Transferable

When two groups met in competitive and reciprocally frustrating engagements, ingroup solidarity and cooperativeness increased. Toward the end of intergroup friction (Stage 2), ingroup solidarity became so strong that when they were taken to a public beach crowded with outsiders and affording various distractions, our groups stuck almost exclusively to activities within their respective ingroups. Psychologically, other people did not count as far as they were concerned. In the presence of so many people and distractions, this intense concentration of interests and activities within the group atmosphere would have been impossible before the groups had attained such a high degree of solidarity.

This heightened ingroup solidarity and cooperativeness were observed at the very time when intergroup hostility was at its peak, during the period when the groups asserted emphatically that they would not have anything more to do with each other. This can only mean that the nature of intergroup relations cannot be extrapolated from the nature of ingroup relations. Ingroup solidarity, ingroup cooperativeness, and democratic procedures need not necessarily be transferred to the outgroup and its members. Intergroup relations cannot be improved simply by developing cooperative and friendly attitudes and habits within groups.

Effect of Consequential Intergroup Relations on Ingroup Relations

Special note should be made of a related finding, namely, that consequential intergroup relations have an impact on the ingroup organization.

When it became evident that during the eventful course of intergroup competition, certain members of one group, including the leader, were not living up to the responsibilities expected of them by other members, leadership changed hands. Those individuals who distinguished themselves by giving a good account of their group rose in the status hierarchy. Internal shifts in status were observed again during the cooperative intergroup activities of Stage 3. Functional relations of consequence between groups tend to bring about changes in the pattern of ingroup relations.

The Limiting Condition for Intergroup Attitude and Behavior

We have seen that this experiment's subject-selection criteria ruled out explaining the direction of intergroup behavior on the basis of differences in the subjects' backgrounds or on the basis of their individual frustrations, instabilities, and the like. In the preceding sections, we have seen evidence that ingroup properties were affected by consequential intergroup relations. Thus the intergroup hostility and its reduction cannot be explained merely by the nature of relationships within the groups.

Our findings indicate that the limiting condition determining friendly or hostile attitudes between groups is the nature of functional relations between them, as defined by analysis of their goals. When the groups competed for goals that could be attained by only one group, to the dismay and disappointment of the other, hostile deeds and unflattering labels developed in relation to the outgroup. In time, derogatory stereotypes and negative attitudes toward the outgroup crystallized. These conclusions are based on observations made independently by observers of both groups and other staff members. Sociometric indices pointed to the overwhelming preponderance of ingroup members as friendship choices. Experimental assessment of intergroup attitudes showed unmistakable attribution of derogatory stereotypes to the villainous outgroup and of favorable qualities to the ingroup. Laboratory-type judgments of performance showed the tendency to overestimate the performance attributed to fellow group members and to minimize the performance of members of the outgroup.

What Kind of Contact Between Groups Is Effective?

The novel step in this experiment was Stage 3, in which intergroup friction was reduced. We have already stated why we discarded certain procedures in this stage, such as introducing a "common enemy" or disseminating information. To clarify the term *contact*, we tried the method of bringing the groups into close proximity in a series of activities. Most of these contact situations involved activities that were satisfying in themselves, such as eating good food in the same room, attending a movie together, or engaging in an exciting activity like shooting fireworks. But none of them created a state of interdependence between the groups. Such contact situations did not prove effective in reducing friction. Instead, contact situations not conducive to interdependence were used by our groups for overt acts of hostility and further exchanges of unflattering invectives.

Thus we can assert the ineffectiveness of contacts during which hostile groups engaged, while in close physical contiguity, in activities that were themselves satisfying to each individual. This ineffectiveness has obvious implications for psychological theorizing.

The Introduction of Superordinate Goals

During the final stage of the experiment, the prevailing friction between groups was reduced. Reduction of the conflict and hostility was observed in reciprocally cooperative and helpful intergroup actions, in friendly exchanges of tools, in developing standard procedures for alternating responsibilities, and in meeting problems. The change in behavior and patterns of interaction between the groups was striking to all observers. The reliability of these observations is established by sociometric indices that showed increases of friendship choices from the erstwhile antagonists and also in the sharp decrease of unfavorable stereotypes toward the outgroup. Favorable conceptions of the outgroup developed, so that ratings of the ingroup and outgroup no longer formed a set of contrasted polarities.

The end result was obtained through the introduction of a series of superordinate goals, which had compelling appeal value for both groups, but which could not be achieved by the efforts and resources of one group alone. When a state of interdependence between groups was thus produced, the groups realistically faced common problems. They took them up as common problems, jointly moving toward their solution, proceeding to plan and to execute the plans they had jointly envisaged.

In this experiment, the setting and circumstances for the introduction of superordinate goals were elaborately prepared by the experimenters. But beyond setting the scene, we left the methods followed, the discussion necessary for the solution, the plans to be made and executed to the groups themselves. Faced with superordinate goals, the groups carried on discussion when necessary, listened to the advice and suggestions of members of both groups who were resource-ful, made decisions, and even combined discussion, decision, and deeds simultaneously when the goal was attained more effectively that way.

Cumulative Effects of Superordinate Goals

If the hostile attitudes generated during intergroup friction had any stability, it could not be expected that one or two situations embody-ing superordinate goals would wipe them out. Indeed, intergroup antagonisms did not disappear in one stroke. At first, cooperative interaction involving both groups developed in specific situations in response to common problems and goals, only to be followed by a renewal of sharply drawn group lines and intergroup friction after the challenge had been met. Patterns and procedures for intergroup coop-eration were laid down at first on a small scale in specific activities. Only during interaction in a series of situations involving super-ordinate goals did intergroup friction begin to disappear, and only then did the procedures for intergroup reciprocity, which developed in specific situations, extend spontaneously to widening areas of activity.

The sequential events of Stage 3 (Chapter 7) made it abundantly evident that the series of activities conducive to superordinate goals provided opportunities for members of the two groups to work out and develop procedures for cooperation in various spheres of action. Once a cooperative pattern was effective in a specific activity, it was extended by members of both groups to related actions. In the face of successful functioning of such procedures, the occasional dissident member who preferred the old days of intergroup strife or self-imposed separation found it more difficult to make his voice count in his own group.

Some procedures successful in intergroup interaction had previ-ously been used by the groups in meeting problems within their own groups. But transferring these procedures to intergroup interaction involved a significant step: the tacit recognition that the procedures now involved groups of individuals and not merely so many individ-ual members within a group. Each individual within his group had been expected and encouraged by others to contribute to group efforts to the best of his abilities. Now, each group expected the other to contribute its share to meeting intergroup problems. While previously, solutions were experienced as equitable or not relative to the individual's expectations and contributions within his group, now justice was also evaluated relative to equitable participation and opportunity for the groups as well.

Tools Serving Intergroup Conflict or Cooperation

In planning and working toward superordinate goals, the groups at times used jointly the tools and techniques that had been used by one or both groups separately in the service of hostility during the intergroup conflict. Tools and techniques can be put to the service of harmony and integration as well as of deadly competition and conflict. Tools, in themselves, do not forestall cooperation among individuals using them. It is the individuals as group members who put the tools to use in their opposition to other groups.

Even the proprietary pride dictating that a place, a technique, or a tool is "ours" takes on a different significance when the trend in intergroup relations is cooperation toward superordinate goals. Use of the technique or the tool in intergroup activities now implies a contribution toward a goal common to both groups—a contribution in which members of the "owning" group may take personal pride, and which the other group, equally enjoying its benefits, can reciprocate through its own contributions on that or future occasions.

Altering the Significance of Other Influences

Contacts between groups in the course of action toward superordinate goals are effective. They are used for developing plans, for making decisions, and for pleasant personal exchanges. *Information* about the outgroup becomes a matter of interest to group members and is actually sought in the course of interactions between members of the two groups. *Leaders* find that the trend toward intergroup cooperation in activities involving superordinate goals widens the spheres in which they may take positive steps toward working out procedures for joint endeavors and planning future contacts. Mingling with members of the other group and sharing in activities with them is no longer perceived by ingroup members as "betrayal" or "treason." Similarly, ingroup members no longer see the outgroup member who engages in activities with them as a strange and threatening figure in "our midst." On the contrary, intermingling of persons from different groups becomes a joint opportunity to work toward goals shared by both groups.

These harmonious results are products of interaction toward goals superordinate to all groups—goals that genuinely appeal to all and that, if they are to be attained, require equitable participation and contributions from all groups in interdependent activities.

References

Introduction

Adorno, T. W., E. Frenkel-Brunswik, D. J. Levinson, and R. N. Sanford. *The Authoritarian Personality.* New York: Harper, 1950.

Brewer, M. B. "Determinants of Social Distance Among East African Tribal Groups." *Journal of Personality and Social Psychology* 10 (1968): 279–289.

———. "In-Group Bias in the Minimal Intergroup Situation: A Cognitive-Motivational Analysis." *Psychological Bulletin* 86 (2) (1979): 307–324.

———, and D. T. Campbell. *Ethnocentrism and Intergroup Attitudes: East African Evidence.* New York: Halsted Press, 1976.

———, and N. Miller. "Beyond the Contact Hypothesis: Theoretical Perspectives on Desegregation." In *Groups in Contact,* edited by N. Miller and M. B. Brewer, Chapter 13. Orlando, Florida: Academic Press, 1984.

Campbell, D. T. "Social Attitudes and Other Acquired Behavioral Dispositions." In *Psychology: A Study of a Science,* edited by S. Koch, vol. 6, *Investigations of Man as Socius.* New York: McGraw-Hill, 1963.

———. "Ethnocentric and Other Altruistic Motives." In *Nebraska Symposium on Motivation: 1965,* edited by D. LeVine, 283–311. Lincoln, Nebraska: University of Nebraska Press, 1965.

———. "Stereotypes and Perception of Group Differences." *American Psychologist* 22 (1967): 812–829.

———. "A Phenomenology of the Other One: Corrigible, Hypothetical and Critical." *Human Action: Conceptual and Empirical Issues,* edited by T. Mischel. New York: Academic Press, 1969.

———, W. A. Hunt, and N. A. Lewis. "The Relative Susceptibility of Two Rating Scales to Disturbances Resulting from Shifts in Stimulus Context." *Journal of Applied Psychology* 42 (1958): 213–217.

———, and R. A. LeVine. "A Proposal for Cooperative Cross-Cultural Research on Ethnocentrism." *Journal of Conflict Resolution* 5 (1961): 82–108.

———. "Ethnocentrism and Intergroup Relations." In *Theories of Cognitive Consistency: A Sourcebook,* edited by R. P. Abelson, E. Aronson, W. J. McGuire, T. M. Newcomb, M. J. Rosenberg, and P. H. Tannenbaum, 551–564. Chicago: Rand-McNally, 1968.

———. "Field Manual Anthropology." In *A Handbook of Method in Cultural Anthropology,* edited by R. Naroll and R. Cohen, Chapter 20. Garden City, New York: Natural History Press, 1970.

———, and W. A. Hunt. "Context Effects with Judgmental Language That Is Absolute, Extensive, and Extra-experimentally Anchored." *Journal of Experimental Psychology* 55 (1958): 220–228.

Dollard, J. "Hostility and Fear in Social Life." *Social Forces* 17 (1938): 15–25.
———, L. W. Doob, N. E. Miller, O. H. Mowrer, and R. R. Sears. *Frustration and Aggression.* New Haven: Yale University Press, 1939.
Frenkel-Brunswik, E., D. F. Levinson, and R. N. Sanford. "The Antidemocratic Personality." In *Readings in Social Psychology,* edited by T. M. Newcomb, E. L. Hartley, et al., 531–541. New York: Henry Holt, 1947.
Geertz, C. "Thick Description: Toward an Interpretive Theory of Culture." Pages 3–30 in *The Interpretation of Cultures.* New York: Basic Books, 1973.
Harvey, O. J., and D. T. Campbell. "Judgments of Weight as Affected by Adaptation Range, Adaptation Duration, Magnitude of Unlabeled Anchor, and Judgmental Language." *Journal of Experimental Psychology* 65 (1963): 12–21.
Helson, H. "Adaptation-Level as Frame of Reference for Prediction of Psychophysical Data." *American Journal of Psychology* 60 (1947): 1–29.
———. *Adaptation-Level Theory: An Experimental and Systematic Approach to Behavior.* New York: Harper, 1964.
Herskovits, M. J. *Man and His Works.* New York: Knopf, 1948.
Hicks, J. M., and D. T. Campbell. "Zero-Point Scaling as Affected by Social Object, Scaling Method, and Context." *Journal of Personality and Social Psychology* 2 (1965): 793–808.
Jacobs, R. C., and D. T. Campbell. "The Perpetuation of an Arbitrary Tradition Through Several Generations of a Laboratory Microculture." *Journal of Abnormal and Social Psychology* 62 (1961): 649–658.
Krantz, D. L., and D. T. Campbell. "Separating Perceptual and Linguistic Effects of Context Shifts upon Absolute Judgments." *Journal of Experimental Psychology* 62 (1961): 35–42.
LeVine, R. A. "Anthropology and the Study of Conflict: An Introduction." *Journal of Conflict Resolution* 5 (1961): 3–15.
———. "Socialization, Social Structure, and Intersocietal Images." In *International Behavior: A Social Psychological Analysis,* edited by H. Kelman. New York: Holt, Rinehart, 1965.
———. "Outsiders' Judgments: An Ethnographic Approach to Group Differnces in Personality." *Southwestern Journal of Anthropology* 22 (1966): 101–116.
———, D. T. Campbell, with M. B. Brewer. *Ethnocentrism: Theories of Conflict, Ethnic Attitudes, and Group Behavior.* New York: Wiley, 1972.
MacCrone, I. D. *Race Attitudes in South Africa.* London: Oxford University Press. Reprint 1957, 1965, Witwatersrand University Press.
Murphy, G. Editor's introduction to M. Sherif, *An Outline of Social Psychology.* New York: Harper, 1948, ix–xii.
———, and L. B. Murphy. *Experimental Social Psychology: An Interpretation of Research upon the Socialization of the Individual.* New York: Harper, 1931.
———, and T. M. Newcomb. *Experimental Social Psychology: An Interpretation of Research upon the Socialization of the Individual.* New York: Harper, 1937.
Paller, B. T., and D. T. Campbell. "Maxwell and van Fraassen on Observability, Reality, and Justification." In *Science, Mind and Psychology: Essays on Grover Maxwell's World View,* edited by M. L. Maxwell and C. W. Savage. Dordrecht: D. Reidel, 1987.
Segall, M. H., D. T. Campbell, and M. J. Herskovits. *The Influence of Culture on Visual Perception.* Indianapolis: Bobbs-Merrill, 1966.

Sherif, M. *The Psychology of Social Norms.* New York: Harper, 1936.

———. *An Outline of Social Psychology.* New York: Harper, 1948.

———. "A Preliminary Experimental Study of Inter-Group Relations." In *Social Psychology at the Crossroads,* edited by J. H. Rohrer and M. Sherif, 388–424. New York: Harper, 1951.

———. *In Common Predicament: Social Psychology of Intergroup Conflict and Cooperation.* New York: Houghton Mifflin, 1966.

———, and H. Cantril. *The Psychology of Ego-Involvements.* New York: Wiley, 1947.

———, and C. I. Hovland, *Social Judgment.* New Haven: Yale University Press, 1961.

———, and C. W. Sherif. *Groups in Harmony and Tension.* New York: Harper, 1953.

———. *An Outline of Social Psychology,* rev. ed. New York: Harper, 1956.

———. *Interdisciplinary Relationships in the Social Science.* Chicago: Aldine, 1969.

1. Integrating Field Work and Laboratory in Small Group Research

Arensberg, C. H. "Behavior and Organization: Industrial Studies." In *Social Psychology at the Crossroads,* edited by J. Rohrer and M. Sherif, New York: Harper, 1951.

Avigdor, R. "The Development of Stereotypes as a Result of Group Interaction." Ph.D. diss., New York University, 1952. Summarized in M. and C. W. Sherif, *Groups in Harmony and Tension.* New York: Harper, 1953, 290–294.

Blake, R. R., and J. W. Brehm. "The Use of Tape Recording To Simulate a Group Atmosphere." *Journal of Abnormal and Social Psychology* 49 (1954): 311–313.

Bovard, E. W. Jr. "Social Norms and the Individual." *Journal of Abnormal and Social Psychology* 43 (1948): 62–69.

Faris, Robert E. L. "Development of the Small Group Research Movement." In *Group Relations at the Crossroads,* edited by M. Sherif and M. O. Wilson, Chapter 7. New York: Harper, 1953.

Harvey, O. J. "An Experimental Approach to the Study of Status Relations in Informal Groups." *American Sociological Review* 18 (1953): 357–367.

———. "An Experimental Investigation of Negative and Positive Relationships Between Small Informal Groups Through Judgmental Indices." Ph.D. diss., University of Oklahoma, 1954. A condensed report appears in *Sociometry* 19 (1956): 201–209.

———, and M. Sherif. "Level of Aspiration as a Case of Judgmental Activity in which Ego-Involvements Operate as Factors." *Sociometry* 14 (1951): 121–147.

Hoffman, E. L., D. V. Swander, S. H. Baron, and J. H. Rohrer. "Generalization and Exposure Time as Related to Autokinetic Movement." *Journal of Experimental Psychology* 46 (1953): 171–177.

Malinowski, B. *Argonauts of the Western Pacific.* London: Routledge, 1922, 83.

Murphy, Gardner. *In the Minds of Men.* New York: Basic Books, 1953, 114–115.

Piaget, J. *The Moral Judgment of the Child.* London: Kegan, Paul, 1932.

Rohrer, J. H., S. H. Baron, E. L. Hoffman, and D. V. Swander. "The Stability of Autokinetic Judgments." *Journal of Abnormal and Social Psychology* 49 (1954): 595–597.

Schachter, S. "Deviation, Rejection, and Communication." *Journal of Abnormal and Social Psychology* 46 (1951): 190–207.

Sherif, M. *The Psychology of Social Norms,* New York: Harper, 1936.

———. "An Experimental Approach to the Study of Attitudes." *Sociometry* 1 (1937): 90–98.

———. *An Outline of Social Psychology,* New York: Harper, 1948.

———. "Socio-Cultural Influences in Small Group Research." *Sociology and Social Research* 39 (1954): 1–10.

———, and C. W. Sherif. *Groups in Harmony and Tension,* New York: Harper, 1953, Chapters 9 and 10.

———, B. J. White, and O. J. Harvey. "Status in Experimentally Produced Groups." *American Journal of Sociology* 60 (1955): 370–379.

Thrasher, James D. "Interpersonal Relations and Gradations of Stimulus Structure as Factors in Judgmental Variation: An Experimental Approach." *Sociometry* 17 (1954): 228–241.

Walter, Norman. "A Study of the Effects of Conflicting Suggestions upon Judgment of the Autokinetic Situation." Ph.D. diss., University of Oklahoma, 1952. A condensed report appears in *Sociometry* 18 (1955): 138–146.

Whyte, W. F. "Small Groups and Large Organizations." In *Social Psychology at the Crossroads,* edited by J. H. Rohrer and M. Sherif, Chapter 12. New York: Harper, 1951.

5. Intergroup Relations: Production of Negative Attitudes Toward the Outgroup

Mann, H. B., and D. R. Whitney. "A Test of Whether One of Two Random Variables Is Stochastically Larger than the Other." *Annals of Mathematical Statistics* 18 (1947): 50–60.

6. Intergroup Relations: Assessment of Ingroup Functioning and Negative Attitudes Toward the Outgroup

Avigdor, R. "The Development of Stereotypes as a Result of Group Interaction." On file in the Library, New York University, 1951.

Harvey, O. J. "An Experimental Approach to the Study of Status Relations in Informal Groups." *American Sociological Review* 18 (1953): 357–367.

———. "An Experimental Investigation of Negative and Positive Relationships Between Small Informal Groups Through Judgmental Indices." Ph.D. diss., University of Oklahoma, 1954.

Klineberg, O. *Tensions Affecting International Understanding.* New York: Social Science Research Council, Bull. 62 (1950): 114–115.

MacCrone, I. D. *Race Attitudes in South Africa.* London: Oxford University Press, 1937.

Sherif, M. "A Study of Some Social Factors in Perception." *Archives of Psychology* 187 (1935).

———. *An Outline of Social Psychology.* New York: Harper, 1948.

————. "Experimental Study of Intergroup Relations." In *Social Psychology at the Crossroads,* edited by J. H. Rohrer and M. Sherif, Chapter 17. New York: Harper, 1951.

————, and Sherif, C. W. *Groups in Harmony and Tension.* New York: Harper, 1953, especially Chapter 8.

————, B. J. White, and O. J. Harvey. "Status in Experimentally Produced Groups." *American Journal Sociology* 60·(1955): 370–379.

Index

About the Authors

Muzafer Sherif was professor emeritus of sociology at Penn State from 1961 until his retirement in 1975. O. J. Harvey is professor of psychology at the University of Colorado where he has taught since 1958. B. Jack White was professor of psychology at the University of Utah until his retirement in 1987. William R. Hood was a social psychologist at the University of Oklahoma Medical School from 1960 until his death in 1966. Carolyn W. Sherif was professor of psychology at Penn State from 1970 until her death in 1985.

Donald T. Campbell is University Professor of Social Relations, Psychology, and Education at Lehigh University. He is the author of numerous articles and books including, with R. A. LeVine, *Ethnocentrism: Theories of Conflict, Ethnic Attitudes and Group Behavior.*

About the Book

The Robbers Cave Experiment was composed in Meridien by G & S Typesetters, of Austin, Texas. It was printed on 55-pound Sebago paper and bound by Halliday Lithograph, of West Hanover, Massachusetts. It was designed by Kachergis Book Design, of Pittsboro, North Carolina.

Wesleyan University Press, 1988

Fundamental Statistics for Behavioral Sciences
Robt. B. McCall   + Study Guide